Daniel Paterson

A New and Accurate Description of all the Direct and Principle Cross

in England and Wales

Daniel Paterson

A New and Accurate Description of all the Direct and Principle Cross in England and Wales

ISBN/EAN: 9783744693509

Printed in Europe, USA, Canada, Australia, Japan

Cover: Foto ©ninafisch / pixelio.de

More available books at **www.hansebooks.com**

PREFACE.

THE Utility of an accurate Defcription of the Roads is fo obvious to every Perfon who travels as not to require any Demonftration; and as the Preference which the following Work claims, before any other of the Kind hitherto publifhed, will be evident on the leaft Comparifon, we fhall decline enlarging on that Head, and only mention what is neceffary by Way of Explanation.

By the Plan adopted in executing this Work, it contains all the new Roads down to the prefent Time, with the Alterations and Improvements made in the old; and exhibits, at firft View, the Diftance of each City, Town, or remarkable Village, from London, with a particular Account of the Roads leading to it, meafured from the different Standards in London, according to the Mile-Stones on each Road, and arranged in the following Order, *viz.*

1. The Kent Roads, meafured from *London Bridge.*
2. The Croydon, Ryegate, and Epfom, Roads, from *Weftminfter Bridge.*
3. The Kingfton Road, from the *Stones End in the Borough.*
4. The Brentford Road, from *Hyde-Park Corner.*
5. The Uxbridge and Edgeware Roads, from *Tyburn Turnpike.*
6. The Barnet Road, from the Spot where *Hicks's Hall* lately ftood, in *St. John's Street*, near *Smithfield.*
7. The Ware Road, from *Shoreditch Church.*
8. The Effex Road, from *Whitechapel Church.*

The

The Meafurements, which are taken in Miles, Halves and Quarters of Miles, are arranged in two Columns, the firſt giving the Diſtance from one City, Town, or Village, to the next; the ſecond, the Number of Miles from the Commencement of the Road. And (for the farther Amuſement of the Traveller) at the End of each Road is given a brief Account of whatever is worthy of Obſervation; ſuch as Parks, Seats, Caſtles, Ruins, &c.

To find the Road from London to any City, Town, or remarkable Village, in England or Wales, look for the Name of the Place in *the Index to the Roads from London*, and the Figure oppoſite to it refers to the Page in which is that Part of the Road containing the Place looked for; thus, from London to Durham, the Index directs you to Page 168, where you find Durham with its Diſtance from London, &c. though the Deſcription of the Road in which it is ſituated (being that from London to Edinburgh) begins in Page 165, and ends in Page 168.

In deſcribing the leſs Roads branching out from the greater, the laſt remarkable Place on the great Road, or the Spot where the leſs turns off, is firſt given, with a Reference to the Place in which you will find the Road ſo far as to that Place; and afterwards the Branch is continued: as, for Inſtance, to find the Road from London to Chertſey, in Surry, the Index refers you to Page 50, where you find it in the following Form, *viz.*

To Hounſlow, p. 31.			9¾
Feltham		3½	13¼
Littleton		3¾	17
Chertſey,	Surry	3	20

By which it appears you are referred to Page 31 for this Road, as far as Hounſlow, (the laſt remarkable Place on the great Road,) thence the Remainder of the Road to Chertſey is given after the above Form in Page 50, as
directed

directed by the Index. In like Manner, for the Roads from London to Aſkrig, the Index directs to Page 176, whence you are referred to Page 167 for one Road as far as Boroughbridge, and (in Page 176) to Page 159 for another as far as Settle, the Continuation of each Road being given in Page 176. Theſe References are made uſe of in order to prevent the numberleſs Repetitions, which otherwiſe would unavoidaly occur in a Work of this Kind.

In looking for the Croſs Roads, Recourſe muſt likewiſe be had to *their* Index, which is ſo plain as to require no farther Explanation than what is there mentioned.

Having thus, to the beſt of our Abilities, ſupplied the Traveller with a full and accurate Deſcription of a much greater Collection of Roads than was ever before attempted ; yet, as the different Routs which Travellers may have Occaſion to take are almoſt infinite, and conſequently not compriſable in a Volume of this Size, we have, in order to complete our Plan, compiled, and publiſhed ſeparately, a *Second Part* to this Work, entitled, A TRAVELLING DICTIONARY: or *Alphabetical Tables of the Diſtances of all the Cities, Borough, Market, and Sea-Port Towns, in Great-Britain, from each other*, &c. By theſe Tables, the Traveller will find the Compaſs he muſt make to viſit any Place or Places which he may be deſirous of taking in the Courſe of his Journey; and will likewiſe be enabled, at ſetting out, to form an Eſtimate of his Time and Expence, by aſcertaining the Number of Miles he muſt travel, with the greateſt Exactneſs, ſhould the Tour he propoſes to make be ever ſo much about, or irregular. Thoſe who have experienced how varying, and often contradictory, have been the beſt Accounts they could procure of the Diſtances of Places on their Journey, and how vexatious in their Conſequences, will readily acknowledge the Utility of a Work of this Kind.

The

viii

PREFACE.

The *Travelling Dictionary* being printed on the same Size as the *Description of the Roads*, the two bound together make a complete Travelling Companion.

The Roads of Scotland are also printed of the same Size, and may be had bound up with the above, or separate, Price 6d.

The Distances from the *Obelisk*, in *Fleet-street* to the Standards in London, from which the different Roads are measured.

From the Obelisk in Fleet-street.

	Miles.	Furlongs.
To the Surry Side of London Bridge	1	1
To the Surry Side of Westminster Bridge by Charing-Cross	1	7
To ditto, by St. George's Fields	1	6
To Stones End in the Borough	1	3
To Hyde-Park Corner	2	2
To Tyburn Turnpike	2	4
To Tottenham-Court	1	7
To Holborn-Bars	0	4
To Hicks's Hall	0	4½
To Shoreditch Church	1	7
To Whitechapel Church	1	5

⁎ *The Editor returns his sincere Thanks for the various Communications he has received. To such Gentlemen as may favour him with Additions, Corrections, or Improvements, for a future Edition, he will be the more obliged if they will point out the* Number of the Page *where such Alteration should take Place. Many kind Correspondents have done this; but, some having omitted taking this Precaution, it has caused some Trouble and Time to introduce their Remarks properly. They are also requested to note the* Distances *from Place to Place, without which, the pointing out of any new Roads is almost useless. All Communications transmitted to the Editor, at* T. N. Longman's, Pater-noster Row, *will be carefully attended to, and duly inserted.*

I

GENERAL INDEX.

When the *Travelling Dictionary* is bound up with this,

Then the Diftances between any two Places (London not being one cf them) follow the Index to the Gentlemens' Seats; and, at the End of them, are the Diftances of the feveral Towns and Bridges upon the River Thames, from London Bridge, and from each other, by Water.

INDEX

TO THE

ROADS FROM LONDON,

To all the CITIES, TOWNS, and remarkable VILLAGES,

IN

ENGLAND AND WALES.

☞ The First Column contains the Name of the Place; the Second, the County it lies in; the Third, its Market Days; and the Fourth, the Page in which the Road is to be found.

A.							
Abbotsbury	Dorset	Th.	52	Amersham	Bucks	Tue.	107
Aberavon	Glam.	——	88	Ampthill	Bedf.	Th.	132
Aberconway	Caern.	Fr.	122	Ancaster	Lincoln.	——	189
Aberford	Yorksh.	We.	167	Andover	Hants	Sat.	31
Aberfraw	Angl.	——	103	Appleby	Westm.	Mo.	172
Abergavenny	Monm.	Tue.	83	Appledore	Kent	——	14
Abergeley	Denbys.	——	122	Arundel	Suffex	W.S	22
Aberystwith	Card.	Mo.	99	Ashbourn	Derbys.	Sat.	145
Abingdon	Berks	M.F	76	Ashburton	Devon.	TuS	37
Acton	Midd.	——	81	Ashby de la			
Albourn	Wilts	Tue.	79	Zouch	Leicest.	Sat.	134
Alconbury	Hunt.	——	166	Ashford	Kent	Sat.	6
Aldborough	Yorksh.	——	179	Atkrig	Yorksh.	Th.	176
Aldborough	Suffolk.	Sat.	216	Atherston	Warw.	Tue	133
Alford	Linc.	Tue.	191	Attleborough	Norfolk	Th.	205
Alfreton	Derbys.	Mo.	155	Auckland	Durh.	Th.	181
Almondbury	Yorksh.	——	158	Aulcester	Warw.	Tue.	111
Alnwic	N.umb.	Sat.	173	Axbridge	Somers.	Th.	75
Alresford	Hants	Th.	44	Axminster	Devon.	Sat.	32
Alston Moor	Cumb.	Sat.	144	Aylesbury	Bucks	Sat.	107
Alton	Hants	Sat.	44	Aylesford	Kent	——	8
Altringham	Chesh.	Tue.	132	Aylesham	Norfolk	Sat.	205
Amberley	Suffex	——	24	Aynho	N.ham.	——	107
Ambleside	Westm.	We.	143	B			
Ambresbury	Wilts	Fr.	56	Baddow	Essex	——	248

Place	County	Day	Page
Boroughbridge	Yorksh.	Sat.	157
Boscastle	Cornw.	Th.	55
Bossiney	Cornw.	—	55
Boston	Linc.	W.S	192
Bosworth	Leic.	—	151
Botesdale	Suffolk	Th.	221
Bourn	Linc.	Sat.	186
Bournbridge	Camb.	—	198
Bow	Devon.	Th.	55
Bow	Midd.	—	196
Bowes	Yorksh.	—	172
Brackley	N. ampt	We.	108
Bracknell	Berks	—	51
Bradfield	Essex	Th.	216
Bradford	Wilts	Mo.	70
Bradley (Maiden)	Wilts	—	62
Bradwell	Essex	—	218
Braintree	Essex	We	211
Brampton	Cumb.	Tue.	144
Brandon	Suffolk	—	198
Brecon	Brec.	W.F	83
Brent	Devon.	Sat.	38
Brentford	Midd.	Tue.	31
Brentwood	Essex	Th.	206
Brewood	Staff.	Tue.	132
Bridgend	Glam.	Sat.	91
Bridgenorth	Salop	Sat.	211
Bridgewater	Somers.	ThS	59
Bridport	Dorset	Sat.	32
Brighthelmston	Sussex	Th.	16
Bristol	Somers.	WFS	71
Broadway	Gloc.	—	99
Bromley	Kent	Th.	10
Bromley	Staff.	Tue.	134
Bromyard	Heref.	Tue.	99
Broomsgrove	Worc.	Tue.	111
Brough	Westm.	Tue.	172
Bruton	Somers.	Th.	56
Backenham	Norfolk	Sat.	214
Buckingham	Bucks	Sat.	107
Bugden	Hunt.	—	166
Builth	Brec.	M.S	102
Bungay	Suffolk	T.S	215
Bunny	Nott.	—	152
Buntingford	Herts	Mo.	193
Burbage	Wilts	—	73
Burford	Oxf.	Sat.	82
Burgh	Linc.	—	197
Burnham	Norfolk	M.S	204
Burnham	Essex	—	218
Burnley	Lancas.	Mo.	152
Burton	Linc.	Mo.	188
Burton	Westm.	Tue.	137
Burton	Staff.	Th.	133
Bury	Lancas.	Th.	152
Bury St. Edm.	Suffolk	W.S	211
Buxton	Derbysh.	—	143

C

Place	County	Day	Page
Caermartken	Caerm.	W.S	83
Caernarvon	Caern.	Sat.	103
Caerleon	Monm.	Th.	91
Caerphilly	Glam.	Th.	91
Caerwis	Flintsh.	Tue.	122
Caistoor	Linc.	Sat.	189
Calne	Wilts.	Tue.	64
Cambridge	Camb.	W.S	196
Camelford	Cornw.	Fri.	55
Campden	Gloc.	We.	101
Cannoc	Staff.	—	134
Canterbury	Kent	W.S	2
Cardiff	Glam.	W.S	88
Cardigan	Card.	TuS	92
Carlisle	Cumb.	Sat.	137
Cartmel	Lanc.	Mo.	141
Castle Carey	Somers.	Tue.	56
Castlecomb	Wilts	—	72

b

Castle Bromwich	Warw.	Tue.	127	Chipping-Norton	Oxf.	We.	100
Castle Rising	Norfolk	——	190	Chislehurst	Kent	——	9
Catsworth	Hunt.	——	178	Chorley	Lanc.	Sat.	146
Catteric	Yorksh.	——	172	Christchurch	Hants	Mo.	48
Cawood	Yorksh.	——	179	Chudleigh	Devon.	Sat.	37
Cawston	Norfolk	Mo.	204	Cirencester	Gloc.	M. F	77
Caxton	Camb.	Tue.	193	Clare	Suffolk	Mo.	214
Cerne	Dorset	We.	52	Claydon	Suffolk	——	215
Chalfront	Bucks	Mo.	107	Cleobury	Salop	We.	109
Chapel in Frith	Derbysh.	Sat.	156	Cley	Norfolk	Mo.	204
				Cliff	N. amp	Tue.	164
Chapel House	Oxf.	——	99	Clithero	Lanc.	Sat.	152
Chard	Somers.	Mo.	54	Clown	Derbys.	——	158
Charing	Kent	——	9	Cobham	Surry	——	25
Charlebury	Oxf.	——	93	Cockermouth	Cumb.	Mo.	143
Chatham	Kent	——	1	Coggershall	Essex	Sat.	214
Chatteris	Camb.	——	195	Coldstream	Berw.	——	168
Cheadle	Staff.	Sat.	134	Colchester	Essex	W. S	206
Chegford	Devon.	——	40	Colnbrook	Bucks	We.	63
Chellington	Bedf.	——	164	Coleshill	Warw.	——	120
Chelmsford	Essex	Fri.	206	Coleshill	Berks	——	79
Cheltenham	Gloc.	Th.	93	Colford	Gloc.	Tue.	83
Chepstow	Monm.	Sat.	90	Colne	Lanc.	We.	152
Chertsey	Surry	We.	50	Colney	Herts	——	119
Chesham	Bucks	We	108	Coltsworth	Linc.	——	166
Cheshunt	Herts	——	193	Colyford	Devon.	——	53
Chester	Chesh.	W S	121	Comb Martin	Devon.	——	63
Chester le Street	Durh.	——	168	Congleton	Chesh.	Sat.	134
				Conway	Caern.	——	125
Chesterfield	Derbys.	Sat	153	Corfe Castle	Dorset	Th.	52
Chesterford	Essex	——	198	Cornhill	N. umb.	——	168
Chewton	Somers.	——	75	Corsham	Wilts	——	70
Chichester	Suffex	W. S	26	Coventry	Warw.	Fri.	120
Chidiock	Dors.	——	32	Cowbridge	Glam.	Tue.	88
Chiddingford	Surry	——	29	Cowes	Hants	——	30
Chigwell	Essex	——	200	Cranbourn	Dorset	We.	49
Chimleigh	Devon.	We.	56	Cranbrook	Kent	Sat.	8
Chippenham	Wilts	Sat.	64	Cranford Br.	Midd.	——	63
Chippenham	Camb.	——	202	Crawley	Suffex	——	18

5

Odiham	Hants	Sat.	51	Piercebridge	Durh.	——	183
Offam	Kent	——	9	Plymouth	Devon.	MTh	38
Okingham	Berks	Tue.	51	Plympton	Devon.	Sat.	38
Ollerton	Nott.	——	180	Pocklington	Yorksh.	Sat.	179
Olney	Bucks	Mo.	162	Polesworth	Staff.	——	149
Ongar	Essex	Sat.	200	Pontefract	Yorksh.	Sat.	179
Orford	Suffolk	Mo.	216	Pontypool	Monm.	Sat.	91
Ormskirk	Lancas.	Tue.	140	Poole	Dors.	Mo.	44
Orton	Westm.	We.	142	Popham Lane	Hants	——	32
Ofmondston	Norfolk	——	215	Porloc	Somers.	Th.	63
Ofweftry	Salop	We.	125	Portfmouth	Hants	ThS	26
Otley	Yorksh.	Fri.	163	Potton	Bedf.	Sat.	177
Ottery	Devon	Tue.	52	Poulton	Lancas.	Mo.	140
Oundle	N.amp.	Sat.	164	Prescot	Lancas.	Tue.	140
Overton	Salop	——	112	Presteign	Radn.	Sat.	99
Overton	Hants	——	31	Prefton	Lancas.	WFS	136
Oxford	Oxf.	W.S	76	Prittlewell	Essex	——	220
				Probus	Cornw.	——	42
P.				Puckeridge	Herts	——	193
Paddington	Midd.	——	114	Pulhely	Caern.	We.	107
Padftow	Cornw.	Sat.	55	Putney	Surry		25
Pancras	Midd.	——	118				
Painfwic	Gloc.	Tue.	81	**Q.**			
Parkgate	Chefh.	——	128	Quat	Salop	——	111
Patrington	Yorksh.	Sat.	188	Queenboro'.	Kent	MTh	4
Pembridge	Heref.	Tue.	95	Queenhope	Flintsh.	——	112
Pembroke	Pemb.	Sat.	92	Quarndon	Leic.	——	145
Penkridge	Staff.	Tue.	132				
Penrice	Glam.	Th.	91	**R.**			
Penrith	Cumb.	Tue.	137	Radnor	Radn.	Th.	94
Penryn	Cornw.	WFS	54	Ragland	Monm.	——	87
Pensford	Somers.	Tue.	74	Ramfgate	Kent	——	5
Penzance	Cornw.	Th.	34	Ramfay	Hunt.	Sat.	195
Perfhore	Worc.	Tue.	99	Ravenglafs	Camb.	Sat.	142
Peterborough	N.amp.	Sat.	185	Rayleigh	Essex	Sat.	219
Petersfield	Hants	Sat.	26	Reading	Berks	Sat.	51
Peterfham	Surry	——	50	Reapham	Norfolk	——	204
Petherton	Somers.	Tue.	58	Redbourn	Linc.	——	186
Petworth	Suffex	Sat.	29	Redburn	Herts	——	120
Pickering	Yorksh.	Mo.	183	Redruth	Cornw.	——	34

c

Waltham ,				Wheatley	Oxf.	—	82
Crofs	Herts		195	Whetſtone	Midd.	—	119
Wandſworth	Surry	—	25	Whitby	Yorkſh.	Sat.	183
Wansford	N.amp.	—	166	Whitchurch	Hants	Fri.	31
Wantage	Berks	Sat.	78	Whitchurch	Salop	Fri.	128
Warbridge	Cornw.	Sat.	55	Whitehaven	Cumb.	Tue.	141
Ware	Herts	Tue.	193	Whitting-			
Wareham	Dorſet	Sat.	52	ham	N. umb.	—	168
Warminſter	Wilts	Sat.	60	Whittleſea	Hunt.	—	195
Warnford	Hants	—	30	Wickham	Hants	—	46
Warrington	Lancaſ.	Sat.	136	Wickham	Suffolk	—	207
Warſdale	Cumb.	—	141	Wickwar	Gloc.	Mo.	80
Warwic	Warw.	Sat.	109	Wigan	Lancaſ.	M.F.	136
Watchet	Somerſ.	Sat.	63	Wigton	Cumb.	Tue.	144
Watford	Herts	Tue.	114	Willey	Wilts	—	56
Watling ſtreet	Salop	We.	130	Wilton	Wilts	We.	62
Watlington	Oxf.	Sat.	79	Wimborn	Dorſet	Fri.	49
Watton	Norfolk	We.	103	Wincaunton	Somerſ.	We	61
Wavenden	Bucks	—	144	Winchcomb	Gloc.	Sat.	101
Weatherby	Yorkſh.	Th.	167	Winchelſea	Suſſex	Sat.	14
Wedgebury	Staff.	We.	129	Wincheſter	Hants	W.S	43
Weighton	Yorkſh.	—	179	Windſor	Berks	Sat.	73
Weldon	N. amp.	We.	165	Winſlow	Bucks	Tue.	107
Welford	N. amp.	—	148	Winſter	Derbyſ.	—	151
Wellingbo-				Wirkſworth	Derbyſ.	Tue.	156
rough	N. amp.	—	163	Wiſbech	Camb.	Sat.	195
Wellington	Somerſ.	Th	57	Wiſton	Pemb.	Sat.	92
Wells	Somerſ.	W.S	60	Witham	Eſſex	Tue.	206
Wells	Norfolk	—	202	Witney	Oxf.	Th.	82
Welſh pool	Mont.	Mo.	102	Wivelſcomb	Somerſ.	Tue.	63
Welwyn	Herts	—	157	Wivenhoe	Eſſex	—	217
Wem	Salop	Th.	135	Wooburn	Bedf.	Fri.	144
Wendover	Bucks	Th.	107	Woking	Surry	Tue.	29
Wenlock	Salop	Mo.	112	Wokingham	Berks	—	51
Wentbridge	Yorkſh.	—	167	Wolſingham	Durh.	—	182
Weobley	Hertſ.	Tue.	95	Wolverhamp-			
Weſtbury	Wilts	Fri.	74	ton	Staff.	We.	128
Weſterham	Kent	We.	10	Wooler	N. umb	Th.	168
Weyhill	Hants	—	71	Woodbridge	Suffolk	We.	206
Weymouth	Dorſet	TuF	48	Woodford	Eſſex	—	197

I N D E X

TO THE CROSS ROADS.

☞ The Figures refer to the different Pages, in which you will find the Roads leading to, from, or through, the Towns to which they are annexed.

d

₂ *We have to lament, that the ample Communications sent by our accurate Oxford Correspondent, A. S. came too late for Insertion in this Edition; but he may be assured they shall all be carefully noticed in our next; as well as a few Corrections from two or three other Correspondents, which were in the same Predicament.*

I.

GREAT AND DIRECT ROADS

Meafured from LONDON-BRIDGE.

With the ROADS branching from them to
Market and Sea-Port TOWNS,

The Towns printed in CAPITALS are Cities. Thofe printed in *Italics* are
Poft-Towns or Stages. The Letters *r.* or *l.* fhew you are to keep to the
right or left in going to the Town to which they are prefixed.

The Firft Column is the Diftance from one Town to another.
The Second Column is the Diftance from LONDON.

LONDON to *Dover.*			Boughton Blean	$3\frac{1}{2}$	50
To New crofs, *Kent.*		3	Boughton Hill	1	51
Deptford	$\frac{1}{2}$	$3\frac{1}{2}$	Harbledown Turn-		
Blackheath	$1\frac{1}{2}$	5	pike	2	53
Shooter's Hill	3	8	CANTERBURY	3	56
Wellen	$2\frac{1}{2}$	$10\frac{1}{2}$	Bridge Hill	4	60
Crayford	$2\frac{1}{2}$	13	Halfway-Houfe	$3\frac{1}{2}$	$63\frac{1}{2}$
Dartford	2	$15\frac{1}{2}$	Lidden	$2\frac{1}{2}$	66
Northfleet	$4\frac{3}{4}$	$20\frac{1}{4}$	Ewel Turnpike	2	68
Chalk-ftreet	$3\frac{1}{2}$	24	Buckland	2	70.
Gad's Hill	2	26	*Dover*	1	71
Stroud	3	29			
ROCHESTER	1	30	*N. B. The Mile-Stones upon the Road*		
Chatham	1	31	*from London to Dover have been fo*		
Raynham	$3\frac{1}{2}$	$34\frac{1}{2}$	*much lately altered, that at Canter-*		
Newington	$2\frac{1}{2}$	37	*bury the 56th Stone ftands near half a*		
Key-ftreet	1	38	*Mile nearer to Dover than before, occa-*		
Sittingbourn	2	40	*fioned by taking off many angles in dif-*		
Bapchild	$1\frac{1}{2}$	$41\frac{1}{2}$	*ferent Parts of the Road; and the new*		
Green-ftreet	2	$43\frac{1}{2}$	*Turnpike Road, now making from Can-*		
Ofpringe	3	$46\frac{1}{2}$	*terbury over Barham Down, will re-*		
			duce the diftance from Dover fomething		
			more.		

On the right of Blackheath was a fine Seat of the late Sir Gregory Page, Bart. now pulled down; and a little beyond it is Morden College.

On the right beyond Wellen is Danson Hill, Sir John Boyd, Bart. and a new-built House of J. Baring, Esq.

On the left of Wellen, is Belvedere, the fine Seat of Lord Eardley.

Three miles beyond Dartford, to the left of the Road, is Ingress, (or Orme-House) the Seat of the late John Calcraft, Esq. now Charles Lefebure, Esq.

On the r. of 26 is Cobham Hall, the Seat of the Earl of Darnley.

On the left of 27, Hermitage, Sir Francis Head.

On the r. of 46 is Judd's Folly, James Flint, Esq.

On the l. of 49 is Nash, Thomas Hawkins, Esq.

At Harbledown, on the l. Sir Robert Wilmot.

At 55, on the r. Ollantigh, Mr. Sawbridge.

At 56, on the r. St. Lawrence, Mrs. Graham; and Northington House, Richard Milles, Esq.

At Canterbury, a new-erected Cotton-mill for the manufacture of Canterbury muslins, &c.

To the l. of 53 is Bifrons, the Rev. Edward Taylor.

To the r. of 60 is Knolton, Sir Narborough Daeth; Bourn Place, the Seat of Sir Horace Mann; and to the l. Higham, James Hallett, Esq.

On the left of 61, Heden, T. W. Payler, Esq.

On the r. of 63 is Broome, Sir Henry Oxenden; and on the l. Deunehill, Hardinge Stracey, Esq.

At 67 on the r. is Waldershare, the fine Seat of the Earl of Guildford.

To *Dartford*, p. 1	—	$15\frac{3}{4}$
Northfleet	$5\frac{1}{4}$	21
Gravesend	$1\frac{1}{2}$	$22\frac{1}{2}$

To ROCHESTER, p. 1	—	30
Raynham	4	34
Newington Street	3	37
King's Ferry	5	42
Queenborough	$3\frac{1}{4}$	$45\frac{1}{4}$

To ROCHESTER, p. 1	—	30
Raynham	4	34
Newington Street	3	37
Chesnut Street	4	41
l. to Milton	1	42

To Ospringe, p. 1	—	$46\frac{1}{2}$
Feversham	$\frac{3}{4}$	$47\frac{1}{4}$

To CANTERBURY, p. 2	—	56
Littlebourn	$3\frac{1}{2}$	$59\frac{1}{2}$
Wingham	$2\frac{1}{2}$	62
Ash	3	65
Sandwich	2	67
Deal	5	72

Near Littlebourn is Lee, the seat of Thomas Barret, Esq.

Near Wingham is Dene, a Seat of Sir Henry Oxenden; Knolton, Sir Narborough Daeth; Gednestone, Sir Brook Bridges; and St. Alban's, William Hammond, Esq.

Near Sandwich are the ruins of the Roman Castle of Rutupi, or Richborough.

To CANTERBURY, p. 2	—	56
Bridge	$3\frac{1}{4}$	$59\frac{1}{4}$
Barham Down	$2\frac{1}{4}$	$61\frac{1}{2}$
r. to Falkstone	$10\frac{1}{2}$	72

To CANTERBURY, p. 2	—	56
Bridge	$3\frac{1}{4}$	$59\frac{1}{4}$
Elham	7	$66\frac{1}{4}$

LONDON to *Margate.*

To CANTERBURY, p. 2	—	56
l. to Sturry, *Kent*	2	58
r. to Upſtreet	4½	62½
Sarr	2	64½
r. to Monkton*	1½	66
Acol	2½	68½
Margate	4	72½

* *In Summer to Acol.*

A little beyond Canterbury, on left, Hales Place, an elegant Seat of Sir Ed. Hales.

A little before Sarr, crofs Wantſum River, and enter the Ifle of Thanet.

Near Acol is Cleve, late J. F. Farrer, Efq.

Two miles before Margate is Dandelion, an ancient Seat, now a Pleaſure-Houſe much frequented by the Viſitors at Margate.

Near Margate is Kingſgate, a ſingular Seat upon the Sea Coaſt, built by the late Lord Holland.

To Sarr, *above*	—	64½
r. to Monkton •	1½	66
Minſter †	2	68
St. Lawrence	4½	72½
Ramſgate	½	73

† *In Summer to Mount Pleaſant, the Profpect from which furpaffes every other in this Part of Kent.*

To Sarr, *above*	—	64½
Birchington	4	68½

LONDON to *Hithe* and *Folkſtone* by *Rocheſter.*

To ROCHESTER, p. 1	—	30
The Bell	4	34

Boxley Hill	½	34½
Penningden Heath	3½	38
Berſtead	2	40
New England	2	42
Harrietſham	3	45
Sandway	2	47
Hothfield	7	54
Aſhford	3	57
Willeſborough	2	59
Sellinge	5	64
Pedlinſtreet	4	68
Hithe	1½	69½
Folkſtone	4½	74

On the right of 43 is Leeds Caſtle, the Seat of Lord Fairfax.

A mile to the l. of Harrietſham is Stede Hill, Mrs. Turner. Adjoining to Sandway is Chilſon, Th. Beſt, Efq.

At 50 on the right, Cole Hill, Hen. Darell, Efq. and near it Surrenden, Sir Ed. Dering.

At Hothfield is the Seat of the Earl of Thanet.

On the left of 61 is Merſham Hatch, the Seat of Sir Edward Knatchbull, Bart. and a Mile farther, on the right, is Scott's Hall, belonging to Sir John Honywood.

On the l. of 64 is Mount Morris, Matt. Robinſon, Efq.

Near Hithe is Beachborough, the Seat of James Drake Brookman, Efq.

On the r. of 65 is Somerfield Hall, belonging to Mr. Hayman, built by William Gomeldon, Efq. joint Treaſurer with Mr. Morris and Mr. Duncombe to the unfortunate King James II.

On the l. of 67 is Oftenhanger Park, W. H. B. Champnies, Efq.

LONDON to *Hithe* and *Falkstone* by *Maidstone.*

To NewCross, *Kent*, p.1	—	3½
r. *to* Leigh	2½	6
Eltham	2	8
Sedcup	3	11
Foots Cray	1	12
Birchenwood	2	14
Farningham	4	18
Kingsdown	3½	21½
Wrotham	3	24½
Nepeker	1	25½
Wrotham Heath	1	26½
Larkfield	4	30½
Maidstone	4½	35
Bersted	3	38
Ashford, p. 6	17	55
Hithe, p. 6	12½	67½
Folkstone	4½	72

At ¾, on the left, is Leigh-Place, the Seat of Sir Samuel Fludyer.
At Eltham, on the right, is the Seat of Sir John Shaw, Bart.
On the left of 12 is the elegant Italian Villa, Foot's Cray Place, the Seat of Benjamin Harence, Esq.
A little on the r. is Neognall, Lord Sidney.
At 29, to the left of the Road, is the Grange, late Sir Ch. Whitworth.
At Larkfield, on the right, is Bradborn House, late Sir Rog. Twisden's.
At 32, on the l. see Aylesford, Mrs. Milner, a white House in a hollow.
At 33, on the left, is Allington Castle.
Beyond Maidstone, is Mote Park, Lord Romney.

LONDON to *Ashford* by *Aylesford.*

To Kingsdown, above	—	21½
l. *to* Trottesclive	5	26½
Addington	1½	28

Larkfield	3½	31½
Aylesford	2	33½
Allington	2	35½
Fernum Street	3½	39
Bersted	½	39½
Ashford, p. 6	17	56½

At Aylesford, on left, the Friers, Countess Dowager of Aylesford.
At Allington, the Castle.

LONDON to *Maidstone* and *Cranbrook*, continued to *Rye.*

To ROCHESTER, p. 1	—	30
The Bell	4	34
Boxley Hill	½	34½
*Maidstone**	4	38½
Loose	2½	41
Cross Cox Heath to		
Linton	1¼	42¼
Stile Bridge	1½	44
Staplehurst	3½	47½
Cranbrook	4½	52
Hartley-street	2	54
Highgate, *alias*		
Hawkhurst	2½	56½
Newenden	5½	62
Northiam, *Suffex*	2	64
Rye	8	72

**Another Road to *Maidstone*, p. 7.*

A Mile beyond Maidstone, on the left, is Mote Park, the Seat of Lord Romney.

At Linton, on the left, is Linton Place, Sir Horace Mann; and, near Cranbrook, is Siffinghurst Castle, an ancient Seat belonging to Sir Horace Mann.

Another Road to Rye.

To *Wrotham Heath*, p. 7	—	26½
Quarter of a mile from Wrotham Heath, Turnpike turns on the *r. to*		
Offam	1	27½
Teston	4	31½
Farleigh	1	32½
Cross Cox Heath to		
Linton	3½	36
Thence to		
Rye, as p. 8.	29¾	65¾

At Teston, on the l. is the elegant Seat of Mrs. Bouverie.
At Farleigh, —— Perrings, Esq.
At ½ a mile on the l. before you come to Cranbrook, is Swift place, Thomas Adams, Esq.
At Highgate, Fowlers, belonging to Sir J. B. Davies, Knt.

To *Eltham*, p. 7.	—	8
Chislehurst	3¼	11¼
St. Mary's Cray	2¼	13½

At Chislehurst, Lord Camden, Lord Sidney, and Mr. Ch. Townshend

To Wrotham Heath, p. 7.	—	26½
r. to West Malling	3.	29½

To Harrietsham, p. 6.	—	45
Lenham, Kent	2½	47½

To Sandway, p. 6.	—	46½
l. to Charing	2½	49
Wye	7	56

To Wrotham, p. 7.	—	24½
Offam	3½	28

LONDON to *E. Grinstead*, by *Westerham.*

To Bromley, below	—	9¾
A little before the 12 Mile stone, right to		
Holwood Hill	4¼	14
Westerham	7¾	21¾
Eaton Bridge	6¼	28
East Grinstead	6	34
To Grinstead by Croydon, p. 15.		

At Holwood Hill pass through Cæsar's Camp; a little beyond, on the right, the Right Hon. Wm. Pitt.
At Westerham, Mr. Cotton, late Ld. Hillsborough, and Squirries, Mr. Ward.

LONDON to *Rye*.

To New-cross Turnpike, *Kent*	—	3¾
r. to Lewisham	1¾	5½
South End	2	7½
Bromley	2¼	9¾
Mason's Hill	¾	10½
Farnborough	3½	14
Madam's Court Hill	5	19
Riverhead	2¾	21¾
Sevenoaks	1½	23¼
Tunbridge	6¾	30
l. to Wood Gate	5	35
Lamberhurst, *Sussex*	5	40
l. to Stone Crouch, Kent	3	43
Flimwell, *Sussex*	2	45
Highgate alias		
Hawkhurst, Kent	3	48
Newenden	5	53
Northiam, Sussex	2	55
Beckley	1½	56½
Peasmarsh	2½	59
Rye	4	63

At South End, on the right, Francis Flowers, Efq. and Beckenham Place, Mr. Cator.

At the entrance of Bromley, on the left, an Hofpital for Clergymen's Widows.

At the end of Bromley, on the left, a red brick Houfe, bifhop of Rochefter.

From Mafon's Hill, fee, to the right, Hayes, the late Earl of Chatham, now Lord Lewifham.

Entering Bromley Common, on the right, 1. Mr. Jones. 2. G. Norman, Efq. 3. Major Rhode, Efq.

At 13, on the r. near Kefton Mark, is a new Houfe built by Col. Kirkpatrick; and a mile farther, on the road to Wefterham, is Holwood, the Seat of the Right Hon. William Pitt.

About 18, on the left, Halfted, Mr. Serjeant.

On Madam's Court Hill, a moft charming profpect.

At the foot of the Hill, on the r. is Chevening, Earl Stanhope; beyond it, Coomb Bank, Lord Fred. Campbell.

On the left of thefe, Mr. Polhill's, an old Seat among Trees, on the Flat; beyond it fee Montreal and the Pillar in the Park.

On the right of Riverhead is Montreal, the new built Seat of Lord Amherft.

To the right of Sevenoaks is Kippington, the Seat of Sir Charles Farnaby Radcliffe, Bart. and to the left is Knowle Place, a Seat of the Duke of Dorfet.

At the end of Sevenoaks, on the right, a white Houfe, Mr. Lambert's.

At 25½, on left, Henry Woodgate's, Efq.

At Tunbridge, the Caftle.

At 32, on the left, Somerhill, Mr. Woodgate, formerly retired to

and inhabited by the famous Lambert, after the Civil Wars.

At 36, on the right, Bay Hall, a Seat of the Amherfts, and from them the Browns.

At Lamberhurft, on left, Capt. Moreland; a little way off, on the r. Bayham Abbey, a beautiful Place, the Seat of Lord Bayham.

Between 41 and 42, on the left, a large old caftellated Houfe, called Scotney, lately inhabited by the Darells; fince by Mr. Richards, a Mountebank; now Edw. Huffey, Efq.

At 43, on the left, Combwell, the remains of a Priory, belonging to Mr. Champion, once a large Seat of that Family; much of it pulled down a few Years ago.

At 45½, on the right, Mr. Hogarth.

At 47, on the right, a modern-built Houfe, erected by the late John Baker, Efq.

At Highgate, on the l. a new Houfe, of a very particular Conftruction, built by Mr. Turner, late Shopkeeper in that Place; and between 47 and 48, on the right, is the Village of Hawkhurft; Elford, the Seat of Samuel Boys, Efq. and a fmall ancient Building called the Hall Houfe.

At 49, on the left, but not in Sight of the Road, is Tongs, a Seat of the remarkable Sir Thomas Dunk, from whom it defcended to the late Earl of Halifax, and now in poffeffion of William Jenkins, Efq.

At the bottom of the Hill, before you enter Rye, on the right, is Mountsfield, T. P. Lamb, Efq.

To New-crofs, *Kent* —		3¾
l. to Greenwich	1¼	5¼
Woolwich	5	10½

LONDON to *Haſtings.*

To Flimwell, p. 10.	—	45
r. to Hurſt Green, *Suſſ.*	4	49
Robertſbridge	2	51
Battel	6	57
Haſtings	7	64

Another Road, viz.

To *Tunbridge*, p. 10.	—	30
Tunbridge Wells	5	35
Frant, *Suſſex*	2	37
Wadhurſt	4	41
Ticehurſt	4	45
Robertſbridge	6	51
Battel	6	57
Haſtings	7	64

On the l. of Robertſbridge, the Abbey; and 2 miles farther, on the right, Court Lodge, Mr. Nicol.

At Battel, the Abbey, Sir Godfrey Webſter, Bart. formerly Sir Ant. Browne.

Three miles beyond Battel, on the r. is Crowhurſt, Mr. Pelham; and, on the l. Beauport, Gen. Murray.

Another Road to Tunbridge Wells.

Beyond Sevenoaks, at	—	27¼
Turn on r. to Leigh	2	29¼
Penſhurſt	2	31¼
Tunbridge Wells	6	37¼

Beyond Leigh, Mr. Burgeſs, on the r.

At 31, on the r. Redleaf, Mr. Harvey.

At Penſhurſt, Penſhurſt Houſe, late the Sidneys, Earls of Leiceſter, ſince Mrs. Perry's, now in Truſt for her Grandſon, — Shelly, Eſq.

To *Tunbridge*, p. 10.	—	30
Turnbridge Wells	5	35

Rotherfield, *Suſſex*	7	42
Mayfield	2	44
Cat-ſtreet	5	49
Haylſham	9	58
Eaſtbourn	6½	64½

At Mayfield, the remains of a houſe of the Archbiſhop of Canterbury.

At Eaſtbourn, Ld. Geo. Cavendiſh.

Another road to Eaſtbourn, ſee p. 17.

To Wood Gate, p. 10.	—	35
Goudhurſt	9	44
thence to Cranbrook	5	49

To the right of Goudhurſt is Bidgebury, Mr. Cartier.

To Wood Gate, p. 10.	—	35
Goudhurſt	9	44
Milkhouſe-ſtreet	4½	48½
Biddenden	4	52½
Smarden	3½	56

To Wood Gate, p. 10.	—	35
Goudhurſt	9	44
Gofford-Bridge	5½	49½
Tenterden	6½	56
Reding-ſtreet	3½	59½
Appledore	2½	62
Old Romney Mill	6¼	68¼
New Romney	2¾	71

To Old Romney Mill, *as above*	—	68¼
r. to Lydd	3	71¼

To *Rye*, p. 10.	—	63
Winchelſea	4	67

At Winchelſea, the Priory Church, the Friery, and the Caſtle.

To Farningham, p. 7.	—	18
Maidſtone	18	36

Durrington	13	49	Lewes	22	190
Canterbury	15	64	Brighthelmſtone	8	198
Margate	17	81	Lancing	8	206
Kingſgate	3	84	Arundel	12	218
Ramſgate	3	87	Chicheſter	12	230
Sandwich	6	93	Portſmouth	18	248
Deal	5	98	Southampton	16	264
St. Margates	5	103	Wincheſter	12	276
Dover	4	107	Petersfield	18	294
Folkſtone	7	114	Liphook	8	302
Hythe	5	119	Godalming	12	314
Romney	9	128	Guildford	4	318
Rye	10	138	Darking	11	329
Haſtings	12	150	London	25	354
Eaſtbourn	18	168			

II.

GREAT AND DIRECT ROADS

Meaſured from WESTMINSTER-BRIDGE:

With the ROADS branching from them to
Market and Sea-Port TOWNS.

LONDON to *Brighthelmſton,* by *Lewes.*			Wych Croſs	2½	34
			r. to Sheffield Green	2½	36½
			Chailey-ſtreet	6	42½
Brixton Cauſeway	—	3½	Offam-ſtreet	4½	47
Stretham	1½	5	*Lewes*	2	49
l. to Croydon	4¼	9¼	Or, from Wych Croſs,	—	34
l. to Godſtone Green	9½	19	*l.* to Nutley	3	37
New Chapel Green	6	25	*Mareſfield*	3¾	40¾
Fell Bridge, *Suſſex*	2	27	*r.* to Uckfield	2	42¾
*Eaſt Grinſtead**	2	29	*Lewes*	8¼	51
Foreſt Row	2½	31½	Falmer	4	55
Another Road to Eaſt Grinſtead, p. 10.			*Brighthelmſton*	4	59

N. B. *In going to Brighthelmfton the Chailey Road, you may turn to the right at the Direction-Poft, near the Town of Lewes, and avoid it.*

To *Eaftbourn.*

Lewes, p. 16		—	49
Horfebridge		11	60
Eaftbourn		11	71

At Brixton Caufeway, fee before you, on the l. about two miles, Knight's Hill, the New built Seat of Lord Thurlow.

At Stretham, a Seat of the Duke of Bedford, formerly the Howlands, whence one of his titles.

At Croydon was a Palace belonging to the Archbifhop of Canterbury; now fold to, and ufed by, a Callico-Printer.

Two miles beyond Croydon, on the l. as you afcend the Hill, fee Purley, late the Refidence of — Tooke, Efq. whence the etymological Work of John Horne Tooke, Efq. has derived the fingular Title of *The Diverfions of Purley.*

At 17, to the left of the Road, is Marden Park, Sir Robert Clayton.

Juft beyond Godftone, on the r. Mr. Pellatt; the houfe is Sir Robert Clayton's. Over the hill, on the l. Mr. Bridgeman.

At 26½, on the right, is Nelbridge Park, late James Evelyn, Efq. now Sir Geo. Shuckburgh, who married his daughter and heir.

Beyond Grinftead, on the left, near the Road, is Eaft Court, John Cranfton, Efq.

At 32, on the right, is Kidbrook, the Earl of Abergavenny's, inhabited by J. T. Fuller, Efq.

At 36½, Sheffield Park, Ld. Sheffield,

Two miles to the left of Chailey-ftreet, is Pewic Place, Lord Vernon's, let to Lady Fortefcue.

Between Chailey-ftreet and Offamftreet, is Cook's Bridge, the Park adjoining to the Road; to the l. Coney Burrows, Tho. Kemp, Efq.

Before Offam-ftreet, on the right, Combes, Geo. Shiffner, Efq.

At Maresfield, John Newnham, Efq.

Before Uckfield, on the left, Buxted Place, Geo. Medley, Efq.

Five Miles beyond Uckfield, on the left, Plafhet Park.

At 1½, on the right from Lewes, Afh-Coomb, Mr. Boyce.

A Mile beyond Falmer, on the right, Stanmer, Lord Pelham.

At 49, on the right, is Caningfbury, William Kemp, Efq.

Another Road, viz.

To Godftone, p. 15.		—	19
Blue Anchor Turnpike, at 27 turn off to			
Lindfield		18	37
Brighthelmfton		15	52

LONDON to *Brighthelmfton,* the New Road.

To Clapham Common	—	3½
Ballam	1	4½
Upper Tooting	1	5½
Lower Tooting	½	6
l. to Mitcham	2	8
Sutton	3	11
Banftead Downs	1	12
l. to Banftead	1	13
Walton Heath	4	17
Ryegate Hill	2½	19½
Ryegate	1½	21
Woodhatch	2	23
Horley	4	27
Crawley, Suffex	4	31
Peafeporridge Gate	2	33

Filgate Forest on the left		
Hand Cross	2½	35½
Cuckfield	4½	40
Clayton, you ascend the South Downs	7	47
Patcham	3¾	50¾
Preston	1½	52¼
Brighthelmston	1¾	54

At Mitcham Bridge, on the right, is the Seat of Henry Hoare, Esq.

At Walton Heath, on the right, is Tadworth Court, Richard Ladbroke, Esq. a mile left of the Heath, Chepstead, Mr. Fanshawe.

At 19, on the left, Upper Gatton, Mark Currie, Esq. and below it Gatton Park, late Sir George Colebrooke's, now Robert Ladbroke's, Esq.

At Ryegate, on the right, late Sir John Cotton, now Mr. Jones.

At Woodhatch, Mr. Carter, on r.

Beyond Hand Cross, on the r. is Slaugham Park, Mr. Tericauton.

Beyond Cuckfield, on the right, Cuckfield Place, Francis Sergison, Esq.

To the r. of Clayton, Hurst Peirpoint, Mr. Campion.

At Patcham, on r. John Paine, Esq.

At Preston, on r. Nathaniel Kemp, Esq.

LONDON to *Brighthelmston* by *Horsham*.

To Lower Tooting, p. 18.	—	6
r. to Merton Abbey	1	7
Morden	2¼	9¼
Ewell	3¾	13
Epsom	1½	14½
Ashted	2½	17
Leatherhead	1½	18½
Mickleham	2	20½
Westhamble	1¼	21¾
Darking	1¼	23
Capel	6	29
Warnham	2	31
Horsham	5	36
Henfield	10	46
Brighthelmston	10	56

At Merton, on the left, late Sir Richard Hotham's, and on the right you see Wimbledon, Earl Spencer's, and a little beyond it Mr. Rush.

At Morden, on the left, late Charles Garth, Esq. late let to Alderman Sainsbury.

At 10, on the right, late Mr. Conway, now Mr. Polhill.

At 12, on the right, see Combe, late the Harveys, now Earl Spencer's; inhabited by Mr. Tollemache.

Adjoining to Epsom is Durdans, a fine Seat formerly of the Earl of Guilford; a Seat of Mr. Northey's; Woodcote, late Lord Baltimore's, now Mr. Teissier; and at the End of the Town, on the right, a white House, Mr. Pattle.

At 16, on the left, is Ashted Park, Mr. Howard.

At the End of Leatherhead, on the right, is Mr. Boulton's; nearly opposite is Mr. Norman. A little farther on l. Geo. Fuller, Esq.

At 20, is Norbury, late the Tryons, now Mr. Lock, on the Hill.

In Mickleham, on the r. Sir Charles Talbot, Bart.

At 21, on the left, Juniper Hill, on the Hill, Sir Lucas Pepys; and just beyond, in the Bottom, late Sir Cecil Bishop, now Mr. Jenkinson.

At Westhamble, on the left, under Box-Hill, is the Seat, late of Mr. Eckersall, now Mr. Colville; and a little beyond it the Grove. late Mr. Vaughan, now Mr. Bocket.

See over Darking Town a new Houfe late of the **Duke** of Norfolk, now Sir Will. **Burrell**, and behind it Chart Park, a beautiful Seat of the late **Henry** Talbot, Efq. now Captain Cornwall, who married his daughter.

At the entrance of Darking, on the left, late Mr. Nafh, now Mr. Eld; a little farther, on the left, Shrub Hill, late John Bugden, Efq. now Lord Leflie.

Towards the end of the Town, on a Hill upon the right, fee Denbighs, formerly the Seat of Jonathan Tyers of Vauxhall, late of Ld King, and now of Mr. Dennifon.

At $34\frac{1}{2}$, on the left, Warnham Place, By fhe Shelley, Efq.

At $35\frac{1}{2}$, over Horfham, fee Denn Park, late Sir Charles Eversfield, now Mrs. Eversfield, his fifter.

At 36, on the right, Mr. Blunt; on the left, late Sir Thomas Broughton, now W. Smith, Efq.

At Horfham, Hills, a Seat of Lady Irwin.

At Weft Grinftead, late Sir Meyrick Burrell, now Mrs. Wyatt.

Near Steyning, on the right, Wifton, Sir Charles Goreing.

LONDON *to Newhaven* and *Seaford.*

To *Lewes*, p. 16.	—	49
Ilford	2	51
Piddinghoe	4	55
Newhaven	1	56
Bifhopfton	2	58
Seaford	$1\frac{1}{4}$	$59\frac{1}{4}$

LONDON to *Arundel.*

To *Horfham*, p. 20.	—	36
Steyning	14	50
Finden	5	55
Arundel	8	63

At Finden, late Mr. Green, now Mr. Richardfon.

At Arundel, the Caftle, a Seat of the Duke of Norfolk. Whoever poffeffes this Seat, as Owner, becomes Earl of Arundel, without any Patent or Creation from the Crown. No other Spot in England poffeffes this peculiar Dignity. It was given by the Emprefs Maud to William de Albani, as a Recompence for his Defence of it againft King Stephen. It defcended to the Norfolk Family in 1579.

Another Road to Arundel.

To Petworth, p. 29.	—	49
Fittleworth	$3\frac{1}{2}$	$52\frac{1}{2}$
Bury	$3\frac{1}{2}$	56
Arundel	4	60

Another Road to Arundel, *made and kept by the Parifhes as far as* Pulborough, *and as good as a Turnpike. From* Pulborough *it is Turnpike Road.*

Horfham, p. 20.	—	36
Slinfold	4	40
Billingfhurft	4	44
Pulborough	5	49
Hardham	1	50
Cold Waltham	1	51
Watersfield	1	52
Bury	2	54
Arundel	4	58

Lymister	1	59	Buckman Corner	$3\frac{1}{2}$	39
Wick	2	61	*Billingshurst*	1	40
Little Hampton	1	62	Mulsey	2	42

Or, turn off at Warnham, p. 20.
and come into the above Road
before Slinfold, missing Horsham.

Pulborough Common	2	44
Wickford-Bridge	1	45
Wickenholt	2	47
Parham	2	49
Amberley	1	50

A little beyond Horsham, on the l. Lady Irwin; farther on, on the r. Mr. Shelley; before Billingshurst, on l. a new House, Mr. Betsworth. At Pulborough, Mr. Spragg; before Hardham, on r. see under the Hill, Stopham, Mr. Smith. On the l. of Bury, see Parham, Sir C. Bishopp, a white house under some woods.

This is not a Road for Carriages beyond Stone-street, except in a dry Summer; hardly for Horses in wet weather.

At Stone-street, the Roman Causeway, for 2 Miles.

On the Causeway, a House, late Col. Clarke.

On the l. Evershed, Mr. Witts; on the r. Jays, late Mrs. Steere, now also Mr. Witts, and Leith-Hill, Mr. Thompson.

On the left of 49 is Parham Park, the Seat of Sir Cecil Bishopp, Bart.

To *Croydon*, p. 15.	—	$9\frac{1}{2}$
Blechingly, *Surry*	$10\frac{1}{2}$	20

To *Steyning*, p. 22.	—	50
Tarring, *Sussex*	7	57

To *Steyning*, p. 22.	—	50
New Shoreham	6	56

LONDON to *Amberly.*

To *Darking*, p. 20.	—	23
Over the Holmwood Stone-street	$7\frac{1}{2}$	$30\frac{1}{2}$
Okewood Bridge	$1\frac{1}{2}$	32
r. to Rowhook, *Sussex*	$2\frac{1}{2}$	$34\frac{1}{2}$
r. through a Coppice to Arun River	1	$35\frac{1}{2}$

To *Bognor*, or *Hothamton*, a new Bathing-Place.

To *Arundel*, p. 22	—	58

Quit the Chichester Road in the Bottom, beyond the second Public-House.

Eastergate	5	63
Aldingbourn	1	64
Bursted	4	68
Hothamton	$\frac{1}{2}$	$68\frac{1}{2}$
Or to *Chichester*, p. 28.		61
Hothamton	7	68

III.

GREAT AND DIRECT ROADS

Meafured from the Stone's End in the BOROUGH.

With the ROADS branching from them to
Market and Sea-Port TOWNS.

N. B. *The Mile ftones on the* Portfmouth *Road have been lately al-
tered as far as Sheet Bridge, and the Meafure taken from the Stone's
End, inftead of the Standard in Cornhill; by which Means the 29th
Mile-ftone ftands within the Town of* Guilford; *and the other
Roads branching therefrom are confequently fhorter than heretofore reckoned when the Meafurement was taken from Cornhill, according to which the Mile ftones are ftanding in many Places.*

LONDON to *Portfmouth.*		
To Newington, *Surry*	—	$\frac{1}{2}$
r. *to* Vauxhall	1	$1\frac{1}{2}$
Wandfworth	4	$5\frac{1}{2}$
Putney Heath	2	$7\frac{1}{2}$
Kingfton	4	$11\frac{1}{2}$
Thames Ditton	$2\frac{1}{2}$	14
Efher	2	16
Cobham-ftreet	$3\frac{1}{4}$	$19\frac{1}{4}$
Ripley	$4\frac{1}{4}$	$23\frac{1}{2}$
Guilford	6	$29\frac{1}{2}$
l. to Catharine Hill	1	$30\frac{1}{2}$
Godalming	3	$33\frac{1}{2}$
Milford	$1\frac{1}{2}$	35
Over the Heath to		
Hind-Head Hill	6	41
r. *to* Lippock, *Hants*	5	46
r. *to* Rake, *Suffex*	$2\frac{3}{4}$	$48\frac{3}{4}$
Sheet Bridge, *Hants*	$3\frac{3}{4}$	$52\frac{1}{2}$
Peterfield	1	$53\frac{1}{2}$
Horndean	$7\frac{1}{2}$	61
Bere Foreft	$2\frac{1}{2}$	$63\frac{1}{2}$
Purbec Heath	1	$64\frac{1}{2}$
Portfdown	2	$66\frac{1}{2}$
Cofham	$\frac{1}{2}$	67
Portfey Bridge	$\frac{1}{2}$	$67\frac{1}{2}$
Portfmouth	$4\frac{1}{2}$	72

On the left, entering Putney Heath,
is a Houfe built by Lady Rivers,
now Mr. Rucker's; and on the
right, a Houfe built by Sir William
Fordyce, on Part of the Common
inclofed by him.

A little farther, on the left, is Wimbledon Park, Earl Spencer's; and,
on the right, a new Avenue to the
late Sir Jacob Downing's.

From 9 to 11, on r. Richmond Park.

At 11, on a Hill upon the left, is Combe, late the Harveys, now Earl Spencer's, inhabited by Mr. Tollemache.

At 12, on the l. Mr. Sherers; and on the r. late Mr. Farren, of Covent Garden Theatre.

At Thames Ditton, on the right, is Ember Court, late Lord Onflow, now Sir James Ford.

At Efher, on the right, is Efher Place, late Henry Pelham, Efq. now Mifs Pelham; and beyond it, on the left, Claremont, late D. of Newcaftle's, now Earl of Tyrconnel.

A little beyond Cobham, fee on the r. Burwood-Park, late Sir John Dalling's, now Mr. Chamberlayne's; and, on the left, the beautiful Gardens called Pain's Hill, laid out by Mr. Hamilton; late Benjamin Bond Hopkins, Efq.

To the l. is Pointers, Mr. Page, and Hatchford, Mr. Ramfay.

Before Ripley, on the left, is Ockham, Lord King's.

Crofs Ripley Green, on the r. Rev. Mr. Onflow.

Two Miles before Guilford, on the right, Send Grove, late General Evelyn's, now Lady Drake.

One Mile and Half before Guilford, on the right, Sutton Place, a noble feat of the Weftons.

Half a Mile before Guilford, on the right, is Stoke, late Jeremiah Dyfon, Efq. now Mr. Alderfey.

Two Miles beyond Guilford, on the right, behind, fee Lofely, Mifs Molyneux; inhabited by Mr. Strode.

Before Godalming, on the l. on a Hill, Mr. Parry.

At Godalming Bridge, on the right, Weftbrook Place, late Gen. Oglethorpe, now Mr. Godbold.

Near Godalming, a Mile fouth, Eufbridge, late, Sir Robert Barker, now Capt. Webb.

At Milford, on the left, late Mr. Smith, now Mr. Webb; and on the right, upon the Heath, fee Pepper-Harrow Park, Lord Vifc. Midleton's.

At 48, on the left, Milland Church, below which is Milland Houfe. late Sir Thomas Ridge, now Mr. Richardfon's.

At Petersfield, late John Joliffe, Efq. Houfe pulled down; and, beyond it, Mapple Durham, late Henry Bilfon Legge, Efq. now Lord Stawell, his Son.

On the right of Portfdown is Southwic, the Seat now of Mr. Thiftlethwaite, late of Richard Norton, Efq. who by a Will in 1753 (afterwards fet afide) left his Eftate to Parliament to pay public Debts.

LONDON to CHICHESTER.

Godalming, p. 25.	—	33½
Milford	2	35½
Brook Green	2½	38
Grayfwood	2½	40½
Haflemere	1½	42
Suffex Bells, Suffex	1	43
Fernhurft	2	45
Henley Green	1½	46½
Midhurft	3¼	49¾
Cocking	2¼	52½
Singleton	2¾	55¼
E. Lavant	3¾	59
CHICHESTER	2	61

At Milford, Mr. Webb.

On the right of 35 is Pepper-Harrow Park, Lord Vifcount Midleton's.

At Midhurft is Cowdry, late Lord Vifc. Montagu, now Mr. Poyntz, who married his Sifter and Heir, Houfe burnt down in 1793. Near Chichefter, on l. Goodwood, Duke of Richmond.

On the right of 56 is West Dean, Sir James Peachey.

Another Road to Midhurst, viz.

To *Godalming*, p. 25.	—	33½
Busbridge	2	35½
Hambledon	2½	38
Chiddingfold	2	40
Cripple Crouch, *Sussex*	3	43
Lecford Bridge	3½	46½
Bexley Hill	1½	48
Eastbourn	2	50
Midhurst	1	51

Another Road, viz.

To Hind-Head Hill, in the *Portsmouth* Road, p. 25.	—	41
l. to Sussex Bells, *Suss.*	3	44
Midhurst, as above	6¾	50¾

To Milford, p. 25.	—	35
Witley	2	37
Chiddingfold, *as above*	3	40
North Chapel	4	44
Petworth	5	49

At Witley, on l. Mr. Chandler.
Before 43, catch a sight of the House at Shillingly Park, amongst the Woods, on l. Earl of Winterton's.
About 45, on r. see Blackdown, Mr. Yalden, on a dip of the Hill, marked by some high trees.
At Petworth, an elegant Seat and large Park, formerly the Duke of Somerset's, now Earl of Egremont's.

To Ripley, p. 25.	—	23½
Woking	3½	27

At Woking, is Hoebridge, late Serjeant Forster's, since Capt. Cornwallis.

To *Petersfield*, p. 26.	—	53½
Warnford, *Hants*	9½	63
Exton	2¼	65¼
Waltham	4	69¼

To *Petersfield*, p. 26.	—	53½
Horndean	7½	61
l. to Havant	3½	64½

To *Portsmouth*, p. 26.	—	72
Cowes (Isle of Wight) by Water	14	86
Newport	5	91

Above the Town of W. Cowes, on an Eminence, commanding a most extensive Prospect, stands Belle Vüe, a Seat of George Rogers, Esq.

A Mile beyond Newport is Carisbrook Castle.

Seven Miles beyond Newport is Appledurcomb, Sir Rich Worsley.

About 3 Miles farther is Steephill, a romantic Cottage of the late Hans Stanley, now Mr. Doyley's, who married his sister; inhabited by Mr. Tollemache.

To *Portsmouth*, p. 26.	—	72
Cowes (Isle of Wight) by Water	14	86
Newton	7	93
Yarmouth, *Hants*	6½	99½

Near Cowes, Captain Christian.
Near Newton is Westover, Mr. Holmes; and Swaynston, Sir Fitzwilliams Barrington.

IV.
GREAT AND DIRECT ROADS

Meafured from HYDE-PARK-CORNER.

With the ROADS branching from them to Market and Sea-Port TOWNS.

LONDON *To the Land's End in Cornwall.*					
To Kenfington, *Mid.*	—	1½	Little Anne	1	66
Hammerfmith	2½	4	Abbots Anne	1	67
Turnham Green	1	5	*l.* to Middle Wallop	5	72
Brentford	2	7	LobcombCorner, *Wilts*	3	75
Smallbury Green	2	9	The Hutt	1½	76½
Hounflow	¾	9¾	SALISBURY	6½	83
l. to Powder Mills	2	11¾	Or,		
Belfont	1½	13¼	From *Bafingftoke*	—	45½
Staines	3½	16¾	*l.* to Popham Lane	6	51½
Egham, *Surry*	1¼	18	*l.* to Cranburn	7½	59
New-England Inn	3¼	21¼	Sutton	1	60
Bagfhot Heath	1¾	23	*Stockbridge*	7	67
Bagfhot	3½	26½	LobcombCorner, *Wilts*	7	74
Golden Farmer	1	27½	The Hutt	1½	75½
r. to Blackwater, *Hants*	3	30½	SALISBURY	6½	82
Hartford Bridge	5½	36	Combe Baffet	2¾	84¾
Hartley Row	½	36½	*Woodyate's Inn,* Dorf.	6¾	91½
Murrel Green	2	38½	Cafhmoor	5¼	97
Hook. *	1¾	40	Tarrant Hinton	2	99
Newnham	1½	41½	Pimperne	3	102
Mapledorewell Hatch	2½	44	*Blandford*	2	104
Bafingftoke	1½	45½	Brianftone	½	104½
r. to Worting	3½	49	Whitchurch	4½	109
Overton	5½	54½	Milbourn	3	112
Whitchurch	3½	58	Piddle Town	3	115
Hurfhorn	3	61	*Dorchefter*	5	120
Downe Houfe	2	63	Winterborn	5	125
Andover	2	65	*Bridport*	10	135
			Chidiock	2	137
			Charmouth	4½	141½
			Axminfter, Devon.	5½	147

Wilmerton	5½	152½
Honiton	4	156½
Fenny Bridges	3½	160
Rockbere	6½	166½
Honiton Clyſt	2½	169
Heavy Tree	3	172
EXETER †	1	173
Adderwater	2	175
Lilly Bridge	4	179
Cheriton Croſs	3½	182½
Crockern Well	1	183½
South Zeal	7½	191
Okehampton	4	195
Bridiſtow	6	201
Lyſton	9	210
Newport 4½ } *Corn.*		214½
or *Launceſton* }	4	214
Hackſhaw Mill	4½	218½
Trerithick Bridge	1	219½
Trewent	2	221½
Enter Temple Moors		
Palmer's Bridge	2½	224
Temple	4½	228½
Moor Ends	2	230½
Bodmin	4	234½
Ford	2	236½
Belovely	5½	242
Summer Court	6	248
St. Michael	1½	249½
St. Erme	4	253½
Treſpean	½	254
Buckſhead	1½	255½
Truro ‡	1½	257
Sticken Bridge	6	263
Meneby	8	271
Trevenhan	1	272
Helſtone	2	274
Briage	2¾	276¾
Golzenna	5	281¾
Merazion, *alias* Jew Market	1¼	283
Penzance	3½	286½
Newlyn	1½	288
Trevelloe	2	290
St. Burien	2½	292½
Treſede	1½	294
Senan	3	297
Land's End	1	298

Another Road, viz.

To *St. Michael*, p. 33.	—	249½
Redruth	13	262½
Penzance	18½	281
Land's End, *as above*	11½	292½

* *A new Road from Hook, miſſing Newnham and the long Water, and coming in a Mile before Mapledore, being a Mile and a Quarter nearer.*

† *To Exeter, by Shaftſbury, p.* 41.

‡ *To Truro, by Taviſtock, p.* 42.

At Kenſington is one of his Majeſty's Palaces.

At 2, Holland Houſe, the Seat of the late Lord Holland, now Edward Bearcroft, Eſq.

To the left of Turnham Green is Chiſwic Houſe, late Earl of Burlington's, now Duke of Devonſhire's; alſo the late Earl of Grantham's.

At 6, on the right, is Gunnerſbury Houſe, Seat of the late Princeſs Amelia, now Col. Ironſide.

Entering Brentford, to the left, is Kew Bridge, on the other ſide of which is Kew, ſometimes the Summer Reſidence of their Majeſties.

At 8, on the left, Sion Houſe, Duke of Northumberland's; and on the right, nearly oppoſite, is a Seat of the Duke of Marlborough; and about a Mile farther up the Lane is Oſterley Park, late Lady Ducie, now Earl of Weſtmorland.

On the r. of Smallberry Green, late Mr. Biſcoe, now Sir Joſ. Banks.

About a Mile to the left of Hounſlow is Whitton, a Seat of the late Archibald, Duke of Argyll, now Mr. Goſtling's of Doctor's Commons, and near it is Whitton Dean, the Seat of Col. William Campbell

To the left of 12 is Hanworth Park, late the Seat of Lord Vere, now Duke of St. Albans.

To the r. of 15 is Stanwell Church and Houſe, Sir Will. Gibbon.

At 21, on the left, St. Anne's Hill, Right Hon. C. J. Fox. Chertſey and Try's Hill.

At 21½, on the right, is Windſor Park; and at 22, Shruh's Hill, the late Duke of Cumberland's Lodge.

At 25, on the left, Mr. Woodford, and Mr. Leiceſter.

At 26, Bagſhot Park, late Lord Keppel, now the Prince of Wales.

At 30, on the left, the Houſe of the late Hawley Norris, Eſq. to whom the Obeliſk on Bagſhot Heath belonged, now inhabited by Mrs. Digby; and on the r. a ſhell of a Houſe, Mr. Lodge.

At 35, on the left, Everton, Sir H. Gough Caltrop; beyond this, Dogmersfield, Sir Henry St. John Mildmay, (5 Miles off,) and, on the right, Bramſhil, Sir John Cope.

At 37, on the right, a Mile out of the Road, late Gen. Hawley, now Mr. Hawley, but inhabited by Gen. Sloper, and, on the left, Winchfield, Lady Geo. Beauclerc.

At 39, on r. Tylney Hall, late Lord Tylney, inhabited by Wel. Ellis, Eſq.

At 44½, on the left, ſee Hackwood, Duke of Bolton's.

At 49, Worting, Mr. Edwards.

At 49½, on the r. ſee Mr. Tarrant's.

At 52½, on the left, Bramſtone Park, Mrs. Bramſtone.

At 52, on the right, Mr. Harwood.

At 52½, on the left, Aſh Park, Mrs. Bouverie.

At 56, Freefolk, Mrs. Portal.

At 61, Down Hurſborn, a Seat of the E. of Portſmouth, who has another at Early Wallop near Baſingſtoke.

At Andover, Mr. Pollen, and to the left is Wherwell, Mr. Ironmonger.

About 67, on the l. Red Rice, in a Wood, Mr. Errington. Beyond it, on a Point of a Hill, Dunbury Camp.

To the left of the Hutt is Winterſlow Houſe, Lord Holland's.

At the Entrance of Saliſbury, on the right, Mr. Wyndham.

On the r. of Blandford is Stepleton, Peter Beckford, Eſq. and near it Ranſton, Peter William Baker, Eſq.

On the l. Langton, Mr. Snow.

A Mile beyond Blandford, on the r. Down-Houſe, Lord Camelford.

One Mile beyond Woodgate, on the l. lies Winborn St. Giles, Lord Shaftſbury, and Mr. Templer.

To the r. of Caſhmoor Inn, Mr. Chaſſin; and, to the r. of Caſhmoor, Critchill-Houſe, Charles Sturt, Eſq.

At Brainſtone, on the r. going over Blandford Bridge, Henry William Portman, Eſq.

At Milbourn, Edmund Morton Pleydell, Eſq.

At 109, on the r. Whatcombe, Mr. Pleydell, jun.

On the right of **Milbourn** (112) is Milton Abbey, **Lord Milton.**

At 116, on the right, Dulifh, Mr. Michael, and Mr. Gundry.

At 118, on the left, Kingston House, Lord Rivers.

At 119, on left, Stinsford, a Seat of Lord Ilchester, inhabited by Mr. Obrien.

At the End of Dorchester, on r. Mr. Churchill, and on left Mr. Damer.

At 124, on the r. Sydling, Sir John Smith, Bart.

Two Miles beyond Axminster, on right, Coryton, Mr. Tucker; and one Mille farther, on left, Shute, Sir John de la Pole.

A little beyond Honiton, on the right, Tracey House.

Five Miles beyond Honiton, on the right, is Escott, late Sir Geo. Yonge.

At Okehampton, the Castle and Park, a Seat formerly of the ancient Earls of Devonshire, now of Lord Viscount Courtenay.

To the r. of 253½, is Trutham, Mr. Williams.

To the r. of 254½, Treworgan, Mr. Collins.

To the l. of 256, Mr. Polwhele.

Beyond Helstone, on the r. Godolphin, Duke of Leeds.

To the r. of Newlyn, Castle Horneck, Dr. Borlace.

To the r. of Trevelloe, Kerries, Mr. Pearce.

LONDON to *Plymouth.*

To Exeter, P. 33.	—	173
Alpington	2	175
r. to Shillingford	1½	176½
Chudleigh	6½	183
Bickington	6	189
Ashburton	3½	192½
Buckfastleigh	2½	195
Dean Court	1½	196½

Harburton Ford	1½	198
Brent	2	200
Bideford	3	203
Ivy Bridge	2	205
Woodland	1	206
Lee Mill	1½	207½
Ridgeway	4	211½
Plymouth	4½	216
Plymouth Dock	2	218

Another Road, viz,

To Exeter, P 33.	—	173
Alphington	2	175
l. to Kenford	2	177
Hall Down	2	179
Red Lion	6½	185½
Newton Bushel	2½	188
Totness	8	196
Modbury	12	208
Yealmpton	5½	213½
Brixton	1½	215
Plympton Earle	2½	217½
Plympton St. Mary	½	218
Plymouth	4½	222½

Or,

From Totness	—	196
To Wanton	4½	200½
Ivy Bridge	5½	206
Plymouth, as above.	11	217

A little beyond Alphington, on the right, Mr. Coxe.

A little farther, on left, Mr. Cooke; a little beyond Kenford, on the left, Mr. George Templer; in a Bottom, hanging Woods and Plantations.

Going up Hall-Down Hill, at 3½ Miles from Exeter, on the right, Hall-Down House, Sir R. Palk, Bart.

At 4, upon a Hill, on the left, is Castle Lawrence, built in honour of the late General Lawrence.

On the Top of the Hill, ſee the City of Exeter; Topſham, Powderham Caſtle. Lord Viſc. Courtenay; beyond it the Woods of the Earl of Liſburne, and the River to the Sea.

On Hall-Down, ſee on the farther Hill, towards the right, Hightor Rocks, one on a point of a Hill, the other in the Center of a Dip in the Hill; they accompany you all the way to Totnes; but, as you go on, appear almoſt cloſe together. They form a Sea-Mark.

At 9½, from Exeter, on the right, ſee Lord Clifford's Park and Kitchen-Garden; Houſe in a Bottom, not ſeen.

At 11, ſee before you Stover Houſe, Mr. James Templar; on the right, Bovey Tracey, beyond Dartmoor.

At 12, croſs the River Teign by a long narrow Bridge and Cauſeway.

On the l. of Newton Buſhel is Knoles, and, a little beyond, on the r. Broadridge, which, with ſeveral other Points near them, afford ſome of the moſt pleaſing and picturesque Prospects that can any where be found.

Another Road, viz.

To EXETER, p. 33.	—	173
Pocomb	2½	175½
Longdown End	1½	177
Crew	1	178
Morton Hampſtead	7	185
New Houſe	7	192
Dart River	6¾	198¾
Merrivale Bridge	3	201¾
Taviſtoc	4¼	206
Whitechurch	1½	207½
Hara Bridge	2	·09½
Nackerſhole	7½	117
Plymouth	3	220

Another Road, viz.

To Okehampton, p. 33.	—	195
Sourton	4½	199½
Lidford	4½	204
Brent Tor	3½	207½
Taviſtoc	5½	213
Robarrow Downs	7	220
Plymouth	7	227

At Lidford is a moſt remarkable Bridge, and a natural Caſcade.

Brent Tor is a Church on a piramidal Hill, which ſerves as a Sea-Mark to thoſe entering Plymouth-Sound.

To Morton·Hampſtead, p. 39.		—	185
Chegford,	Devon	3½	188½

To Plymouth, p. 38.	—	216
Croſs Crimble Paſſage over Tamer River, to Looe, (Eaſt and Weſt)	16	232
Fowey	8	240

On the other Side Tamer River, to the left, is Mount Edgcumbe, the Seat of the E. of Mount Edgcumbe.

To Plymouth, p. 38.	—	216
Weſton	2¾	218¾
Croſs Tamer River to Saltaſh, Cornwall	1¾	220½

To Plymouth, p. 38.	—	216
Croſs Crimble Paſſage to Milbrook	3	219
Craſthole	4¼	22¼

Join Landreck Road	4½	227¾
Catchfrench	1	228¾
Coldrinnick	2	230¾
Catuther	2½	233¼
Leskard	1½	334¾

N. B. *The Crimble-Passage is now much disused, being nearly 3 Miles farther than by Torpoint Passage.*

At the Passage, Mount Edgcumbe.

Between 5 and 6 Mile Stones, fine View from the Passage.

View down the Lyner, at 9 miles from the Passage.

LONDON to EXETER, by *Shaftsbury*.

To SALISBURY, p. 52.	—	83
Mount Harnham Hill *r.* over the Plain	1	84
By the Race-Ground	4	88
Fovent Hutt	5½	93½
White-Sheet Hill	3½	97
Ludwell, *Dorset*	4	101
Shaftsbury	1	102
Stour East-over	4	106
Stour West-over	2½	108½
Milborn Port, Som.	6½	115
Sherborn, Dorset	2½	117½
Babylon Hill	4½	122
Yeovil, Som.	1	123
West Coker	3	126
East Chornoc	1½	127½
Hasilbeer	2½	130
Crewkerne	2½	132½
Chard	8	140½
Stockland	6	146½
Honiton, Devon. thence to	6	152½
EXETER, p. 33.	19	171½

Three Miles beyond Salisbury, on the right, is Wilton, a noble Seat of the Earl of Pembroke.

On the right, a few Miles on this Side Shaftsbury, are Wardour Castle, the Seat of Lord Arundel, and Font-Hill, a fine Seat, built by the late William Beckford, Esq. Alderman of London.

A little on this Side of Milborn Port, to the left of the Road, is Stalbridge, the Seat of the late Mr. Walter; now the Earl of Uxbridge.

At Sherborn is Sherborn Castle, the beautiful Seat of Lord Digby.

Three Miles to the right of Crewkerne is Hinton. St. George, the Seat of Earl Poulett.

At Ford, is Ford Abbey, the Seat of —— Gwyn, Esq.

LONDON to *Truro*, by *Tavistoc*.

To *Tavistoc*, p. 39.	—	206
Newbridge	3½	209½
Renny Mills	8¾	218¼
Combron	1¼	219½
Leskard	1½	221
Lestwithiel	12	233
St. Blaise	5	238
St. Austle	4	242
Penhall	4	246
Grampound	4½	250½
Storne	1	251½
Probus	1	252½
Tresillon	2	254½
Truro	4	258½
Truro by Launceston, p. 33.		

On the left of Renny Mills is Newton, a Seat of the late Sir John Croyton.

Near Lestwithiel is Reformel Castle, and the beautiful Grounds belonging to Francis Gregor, Esq. M. P. for that County.

On the left, this side of Lestwithiel, is Boconnoc, the Seat of Tho. Pitt, Esq. now Lord Camelford, first Cousin to the late Earl of Chatham.

On l. of Storne, Seat of Mr. Williams.

To *St. Arstle*, p. 42.	—	242
Tregony	7½	249½
Philligh	5	254½
St. Maws	5½	260

To *Tavistoc*, p. 39.	—	206
Killington, *Corn.*	11	217

To *Penzance*, p. 34.	—	281
St. Just, *Corn.*	6	287

To *St. Michael*, p. 33.	—	249½
Redruth, *Corn.*	13	262½
St. Ives	14	276½

LONDON to WINCHESTER and *Poole*, by *Basingstoke*.

To *Basingstoke*, p. 31.	—	45½
l. to Popham Lane	6½	52
Popham	1	53
E. Stretton	3	56
New Inn	3	59
Worthy	2½	61½
WINCHESTER	2	63½
Pitt	2¼	65¾
Hursley	3	68¾
Ansield	2¼	71
Rumsey	3	74
l. to Oux Bridge	3	77
Enter New Forest	3	80
Ragged Row	¼	80¼
Castle Malwood	1¾	82
Bonner	8	90
Ringwood	1	91
St. Leonard's Bridge	3¼	94¼
New Bridge	¾	95
Ham	3	98
Kingston	1	99
How Corner	1	100
Poole	5	105

At 50, on left, a House, late Mr Delaney, now the Prince of Wales.

At East Stretton, is a Seat of the Duke of Bedford.

At 57, see on the right, Micheldever. —— Bristow, Esq. Not far off, Avington, the Duchess of Chandos.

Beyond 60, on r. Sir Chaloner Ogle.

A Mile beyond Hursley is Hursley Lodge, the Seat of Sir William Heathcott, Bart.

At Ainfield, Mr. White.

At Rumsey, on l. Lord Palmerston.

At 77, on r. Paulton's, Mr. D'Oyley.

LONDON to WINCHESTER, by *Farnham*.

To *Bagshot*, p. 31.	—	26½
Golden Farmer	1½	28
l. to Frimley	2½	30½
Farnborough	1½	32
Farnham †	6½	38½
Bentley Green, *Hants*	4	42½
Moyle	1½	44
Hollyburn	2½	46½
Alton	1	47½
Chawton	1	48½
Ropley Dean	5	53½
Bishop's Sutton	2½	56
Alresford	1	57

| Steward's Bridge | 1 | 58 |
| WINCHESTER | 6¼ | 64½ |

† *Another Road to Farnham.*

| To *Guilford*, p. 25. | — | 29½ |
| *Farnham*, | 10½ | 40 |

At Frimley, on the r. Capt. Beckford.

At Farnborough, on the left, Farnborough Place, Mr. Wilmot.

Two Miles beyond Guilford, on the left, fee Lofely, Mifs Molyneux.

On the r. fee Henley Park, on a fmall Hill, Mr. Halfey.

Five Miles beyond Guilford, on the left, Puttenham, Admiral Cornifh.

A Mile and Half farther is Hampton, late Mr. Parker, now Mr. Snell; fome Water by it.

At 9, on left, Moor Park, near which lies Waverley Abbey, late Sir Robert Rich, now Sir Charles (Boftock) Rich, Bart. LLD. who married his daughter.

At Farnham, Farnham Caftle, the Bifhop of Winchefter's.

At 42, on l. the Woods of Holt Foreft for two Miles.

Beyond Bentley Green, on l. late Mr. Sainfbury, now Mr. Oliver; and, on r. Mr. Rothwell.

Beyond 43, on the right, 1. Mr. Watkins, a brick Houfe. 2. Mrs. Nicholas, white Houfe. 3. Sir Thomas Miller, a white Houfe.

At Chawton, Mr. Knight.

At Old Alresford, a white Houfe, Col. Sheriff; a red Houfe by the Church, Lord Rodney.

Beyond Alresford, on the r. Mr. Harris.

At 59, on r. Overington, late Mr. Armftrong, now Mr. Standerwick; next the Church is the Parfonage.

About 62, on r. fee Sir Chaloner Ogle's, a white Houfe, fheltered by woods.

LONDON to *Gofport.*

To *Alton*, p. 44.	—	47½
Chawton	1	48½
Farringdon	1½	50
Eaft Tifted	2	52
Falmer Hill	4½	56½
Weft Meon	2½	59
Warnford	2¼	61½
Exton	2¼	63½
Meon Stooke	1	64½
Droxford	1	65½
Soberton	1½	67
Wickham	4	71
Fareham	3½	74½
Forton	3	77½
Gofport	1	78½

At 49, on the left, Mr. Knight.

At 52, Rotherfield Park, Capt. Poulett.

About 2 Miles to the left of W. Meon is a Roman Camp, called Old Winchefter, on the Point of a Hill, looking over Meon Stooke and Droxford.

At Warnford, Marq. of Clanrickard.

At Wickham, on the left, Mr. Garnier.

To the left of Fareham is Cams, Lady Betty Delmé.

A nearer Way to Gofport is by Portfmouth, whence there is but a fhort Ferry to Gofport.

LONDON to *Southampton.*

To *Alresford*, p. 44.	—	57
Seward's Bridge	1	58
l. over Longwood		
Down to Morftead	6	64
Twyford	2	66
Albrook	2	68

Swathling	4	72
Portſwood	1	73
Southampton *	2	75

* *This is not a Turnpike Road, and you do not turn off to Long-wood Down till near the 60 Mile Stone.*

At Twyford, Capt. Vane.
At Swathling is the Seat of the late Tho. Lee Dummer, Eſq. lately Lord Hawke, now Will. Chamberlayne, Eſq.
About a Mile farther, to the left, Portſwood Houſe, Gen. Stibbert.
Near it is Bevis Mount, Edward Horne, Eſq.
A little farther is Belle Vüe, late N. St. André, Eſq. now Rear Admiral Sir Richard King; and a little farther, on the l. is Proſpect-Place, the Seat of Capt. Dixon.

Another Road, viz.

WINCHESTER, p. 43.	—	$63\frac{1}{2}$
St. Croix	1	$64\frac{1}{2}$
Compton	$1\frac{1}{2}$	66
Otterborne	2	68
Southampton	$8\frac{1}{2}$	$76\frac{1}{2}$

N. B. 78 *Poſt Miles are charged.*

At St. Croix, the Hoſpital.
Before Compton, ſee Twyford, on the left, 1. A white Houſe, Mr. Hore. 2. A red Houſe, Mr. Shipley. 3. In the Bottom, Shawford Houſe, Mrs. Mildmay.

LONDON to *Lymington.*

Otterborne, *as above.*	—	68
Redbridge	9	77
Totton	$\frac{1}{2}$	$77\frac{1}{2}$

Lindhurſt	$4\frac{1}{2}$	82
Brockenhurſt	$2\frac{3}{4}$	$84\frac{3}{4}$
Battramſley	$2\frac{1}{2}$	$87\frac{1}{4}$
Lymington	$2\frac{1}{2}$	$89\frac{3}{4}$

At Lyndhurſt is a Houſe of the King, uſed, when in the Foreſt, by the Duke of Glouceſter, as Lord Warden. The King, Queen, and two elder Princeſſes, were here eight or nine days in 1789.
Alſo Fox Leaſe, late the Seat of Sir Philip Jennings-Clerke, Bart. now of Iſaac Pickering, Eſq.
About a Mile from Lyndhurſt, on r. is Mount Royal, that Name being given it by the King when he was at Lyndhurſt, it being before called Notherwood. It is the Seat of Robert Ballard, Eſq.
To the left of Brockenhurſt, Edward Morant, Eſq.
A Mile beyond Lymington, late Sir Harry Burrard-Neale; and a little farther is Pilewell, Mr. Robins.

To Caſtle Malwood, P. 44.		82
Fordingbridge	$5\frac{1}{2}$	$87\frac{1}{2}$

To *Ringwood,* p. 44.	—	91
Chriſt Church	7	98

At Chriſt Church, the Priory, late Guſtavus, now John Brander, Eſq.
Between this and Lymington is High Cliffe, late the Earl of Bute; advertiſed in July, 1795, to be ſold for the materials.

LONDON to *Weymouth.*

To *Dorcheſter,* p. 32.	—	120
Monkton	2	122
Melcomb	$7\frac{1}{2}$	$129\frac{1}{2}$
Weymouth	$\frac{1}{2}$	130

At Monkton, on the l. is Harrington, Mr. Williams; and, on the right, Maiden Castle.

LONDON to *Cranbourn* and *Poole*, by SALISBURY.

To SALISBURY, p. 32.	—	83
Coombe	2	85
Tipput	5	90
Cranbourn, Dorset	3½	93½
Stanbridge Chapel	6¾	100¼
Wimborn Minster	2½	102¾
Poole	7¼	110

N. B. *A nearer Way by Winchester and Ringwood*, p. 43, 44.

Two Miles from Cranbourn is Wimborn St. Giles, the Seat of the E. of Shaftsbury; and a few Miles farther, on the left is Woodlands, the Seat of Edward Seymour, Esq.

On the right, beyond Wimborn Minster, is Charborough, the Seat of Thomas Drax Grosvenor, Esq.

LONDON to *Hampton-Court*, *Sunbury*, and *Shepperton*.

To Brentford, p. 31.	—	7
At 7¾ turn to the left to Isleworth	1½	8½
Twickenham	1¾	10¼
Teddington	1¾	12
Enter Bushy Park	½	12½
Through the Park to the Palace of Hampton Court	1¼	13¾
Hampton	1	14¾
Sunbury	2	16¾
Lower Hanworth	2¼	19
Shepperton	½	19½

At Hampton, Mrs. Garrick, Widow of the late David Garrick, Esq.

At Sunbury, a fine Seat late of the Earl of Pomfret, late Mr. Chandler; after, Mr. Richardson.—Kempton Park, Sir Philip Musgrave, Bart.—A Seat of Lord Hawke, and several others, beautifully situated on the Banks of the Thames.

LONDON to *Ham*.

To Brompton	—	1
Walham Green	2	3
Fulham	1	4
Cross the Thames to Putney, *Surry*	½	4½
r. to Richmond	4	8½
Petersham	1	9½
Ham	1	10½
Another Road, viz.		
To Wandsworth, p. 25.	—	5½
r. to Richmond	5½	11
Petersham	1	12
Ham	1	13

To *Hounslow*, p. 31.	—	9¾
Feltham	3½	13¼
Littleton	3¾	17
Chertsey, Surry	3	20

At Littleton, Thomas Wood, Esq.

At Chertsey, the Abbey, Mr. Weston.

Near Chertsey is St. Anne's Hill, on the Side of which is a Seat, late Lady Trevor, now Right Hon. C. J. Fox.

And near that is Botleys, a new-built Seat of Sir Joseph Mawbey, Bart.

LONDON to *Reading*, by *Egham*.

To Egham, p. 31.	—	18
Through Windfor Park to Braknell, *Berks*	10	28
Okingham, alias *Wokingham*	4	32
London Bridge	3	35
Reading	4	39

Or,

From Egham to Warfield	10	28
Reading	10	38

N. B. *To Reading by Maidenhead*, p. 63.

At 35½, on left, Early, the late Gov. Birt, now Mr. Golden.

A little farther is White Knights, late Sir Henry Englefield, now Mr. Martin.

To Hartford Br. p. 31.	—	36
Hartley Row	½	36½
Odiham, *Hants*	5½	42

At Odiham, Dogmersfield, Sir Hen. St. John Mildmay.

To *Bafingftoke*, p. 31.	—	45½
Kingfclear, *Hants*	9¼	54¾

To *Stockbridge*, p. 32.	—	67
Broughton	4	71
Weft Tytherley	3	74
Eaft Dean, *Wilts*	2	76
Dunkton or Downton	7	83
Tipput	7	90
Cranbourn, *Dorfet*	4	94

Another Road, p. 49.

To *Cranbourn*, p. 49.	—	93½
Wimborn, *Dorfet*	11	104½
Wareham	10	114½
Corfe Caftle	5½	120
Swanage	6	126

Three Miles beyond Wareham, on the r. is Grange, Mr. Bond; and three Miles beyond Corfe Caftle, on the r. is Encomb, Will. Morton Pitt, Efq.

To *Blandford*, p. 32.	—	104
Bere Regis, *Dorfet*	9	113
Wareham	6	119

Six Miles beyond Bere Regis, on the r. is Lulworth Caftle, the admired Seat of Edward Weld, Efq. It is near the Sea.

To *Blandford*, p. 32.	—	104
Milton Abbey	7¾	111¾
Cerne Abbey	9¼	121
Sydling	2	123
Beaminfter	10	133

At Milton Abbey is the Seat of Lord Milton.

At Sydling, Sir John Smith, Bart.

To *Dorchefter*, p. 32.	—	120
Abbotfbury	7½	127½

Remains of the Abbey—a (Decoy or) Swannery.

To *Dorchefter*, p. 32.	—	120
Frampton	6	126

To *Bridport*, p. 32.	—	135
Lime	8½	143½
Culliton, *Devon*	6½	150
Ottery St. Mary's	6	156

To Bridport, p. 32.		—	135
Lime		8½	143½
Colyford,	Devon	6½	150
Sidford		9½	159½
Newton Poppleford		3	162½
Woodbury		5	167½
Topsham		3	170½
thence to			
EXETER		3½	174

To Lime, as above		—	143½
Colyford		6½	150
Sidmouth,	Devon	8	158

To Sidmouth, as above		—	158
Otterton		6	164
Exmouth		5½	169½

At Otterton, a Seat of Mr. Rolle.

To EXETER, p. 33.		—	173
Alphington		2	175
l. to Kinford		2	177
Hall Down		2	179
Teignmouth		8¾	187¾
Or,			
Alphington, as above		—	175
Powderham		5	180
Star Cross		2	182
Dawlish		3	185
Teignmouth		3	188

Near Hall Down, Sir Robert Palk.
At Powderham, the Castle, Lord Viscount Courtenay.

To Stour Eastover. p. 41		—	106
Stalbridge,	Dorset	5	111

At Stalbridge is the Seat late of Edward Walter, Esq. now of the Earl of Uxbridge.

To Stour Eastover, p. 41.		—	106
Sturminster,	Dorset	5	111

To Crewkerne, p. 41.		—	132½
Chard,	Somers.	8½	141

To Newton Bushel, p. 38.		—	188
Comb		5	193
Crupland		9	202
Dartmouth		2	204
Dodbrook		15½	219½

Near Comb is Stoke Common which affords a very extensive and picturesque Prospect. Skirting this Eminence, is a Road to Shaldown, and thence, by a Ferry across the Mouth of the Teign, to Teignmouth.

By going to Dartmouth from Newton, you have the Harbour to cross, which is avoided in going by Totnes, only 2 or 3 Miles round.

To Dartmouth, as above	—	204
Kingbridge	14½	218½

To Plymouth, p. 38.		—	216
Over Crimble-Passage to			
St. Germain's,	Corn.	8	224

To Tavistoc, p. 39.		—	206
Berealstone,	Devon.	5	211

To Truro, p. 33.		—	257
Penryn		9	266
Falmouth		2	268

LONDON to *Padstow*.

To *Newport* or *Launceston* } p. 33	—	214
St. Stephen's Down	1½	215½
Egglesherry	1¼	216¾
Kett's Moor	4¾	221½
Hall Drunkard	1½	223
Davidstow	1½	224½
Camelford	4	228½
Tregmaney	1	229½
Helson	1	230½
Knert's Mill	1¼	231¾
St. Theath	¼	232
Tregear	2½	234½
Peadogget	1	235½
St. Endellion	1½	237
r. to S. Minver	3	240
l. to Tredeffic	1	241
Fredilly	1	242
Cross the River Camel to *Padstow*	1½	243½

To Hall-drunkard, *as above*	—	223
Boscastle, *Cornw.*	7	230
Bossiney	3	233

To St. Theath, *above*	—	232
Warbridge	9½	241½
St. Columb, Cornw.	7½	249
St. Michael	7	256

LONDON to *Stratton* in *Cornwall.*

To EXETER, p. 33.	—	173
Newton St. Cyres	4½	177½
Crediton	3	180½
Coleford	4	184½
Bow	3½	188
North Tawton	4	192
Stamford Courtenay	2½	194½
Jacobstow	3	197½
Hatherleigh	3½	201
Houlsworthy	13½	214½
Stratton, Cornw.	7	221½

To *Hatherleigh*, above	—	201
Shepwash	4½	205½

To EXETER, p. 33.	—	173
Crediton, *Devon.*	7½	180½
Chawleigh	12	192½
Chimleigh	1	193½

LONDON to *Barnstaple*, continued to *Hartland*.

To *Andover*, p. 31.	—	65
r. to Wey Hill, *Hants*	3	68
Mullen Pond	1½	69½
Harradon Hill, *Wilts*	6	75½
Ambersbury	2¾	78¼
Winterton Stoke	4¾	83
Deptford Inn	4	87
Willey	¾	87¾
New Inn	4¾	92½
Chicklade	1	93½
Willoughby Hedge	3	96½
Kilmington, *Somers.*	5½	102
Bruham	4	106
Bruton *	3	109
Castle Carey	3	112
King Weston	7	119
Somerton	3	122
Langport	5	127
Curry Rivel	2	129
Rook House	4	133
Wrantage	1	134
Taunton Dean	6	140
Ramwell	3	143

Buckland	2	145
Chesson	½	145½
Wellington	1½	147
Upwell Green	1	148
Bluet's Cross, *Devon.*	3	151
Maiden Down	1	152
Sampford Peverell	4	156
Halberton	2	158
Tiverton	3	161
Caverleigh	2½	163½
South Moulton †	16	179½
Southalla	2	181½
Philley	1½	183
Swimbridge	3½	186½
Lankey	2¼	188¾
Newport	1¼	190
Barnstaple	1	191
Bideford	8½	199½
Harton	11½	211
Hartland	2	213

* *Another Road to Bruton*, p. 62.
† *Another Road to S. Moulton*, p. 59.

At r. at Weyhill, Mr. Gawler. More on r. Chute Lodge, Mr. Freeman.
See before you, on a Hill, a white Object, a Summer-House of Mr. A. Smith, at Tidworth, which is near the Road beyond Ludgershall.
About 70, is Rednam, Sir John Pollen, Bart.
At Ambersbury is a Seat of the Duke of Queensberry and Dover.
At 80, on the right, Stonehenge, one of the most remarkable remains of Antiquity in the Kingdom.
At 85, on the r. a large and strong Intrenchment.
At 102, on l. is Stourton, the beautiful Seat and Gardens of Sir H. Colte Hoare, Bart.
On l. of Bruton is Bruton Abbey, Seat of the late Ld. Berkley, of Stratton, now belonging to Sir H. C. Hoare, and pulled down by him.
At Tiverton is the Seat of Sir Tho Carew, Bart. which formerly belonged to the ancient Earls of Devonshire.
At Philley is a Seat of Lord Fortescue.
A Mile beyond Bideford, on the r. is Daddon, George Bulk, Esq.
At King Weston, on r. William Dickenson, Esq.
Before Somerton, on l. Mr. Howe.
At 130, on r. Burton Pynsent, Countess Dowager of Chatham, and the Obelisk, built by the late Lord Chatham, in memory of Sir R. Pynsent.
On the l. Earnshill, R.T. Combe, Esq.
At 144, on r. Heatherton Park, Sir T. Gunstone.

LONDON to *Taunton*.

To *Yeovil*, p. 41. *Som.*	—	123
Preston	1	124
Odcomb	2	126
Montacute	1	127
Stoke	2	129
Petherton Bridge	1½	130½
White Lackington	5	135½
Ilminster	1½	137
Horton	1¾	138¾
Ashill	2	140¾
Hatch	3	143¾
Taunton	5¾	149½

Near Odcomb, on the l. is Brimpton, Earl of Westmorland.
At Montacute, Edward Philips, Esq.
Near White Lackington is Dillington, Lord North.
At Hatch, the Seat of John Collins, Esq.

LONDON to *South Moulton* by *Bridgewater*.

To *Bruton*, p. 56.	—	109
Cole	1	110
Ainsford	2	112
Clanvil	1	113
Alford	1½	114½
Lidford	2	116½
Kingſweſton	3½	120
Aſcot	7½	127½
Knowle	5½	133
Bridgewater	4	137
Durlay	1½	138½
Faulty	1½	140
Enmore	1	141
Water Pitts	2	143
Weſt Bagborough	3	146
Willet	3½	149½
Rawlin's Croſs	4	153½
Holwelſlade	1½	155
Wilcot	3¼	158¼
Heal Bridge	4	162¼
Dulverton	1¾	164
Durly Ford, *Devon*.	6	170
Buſh Bridge	6	176
South Moulton	1	177

N. B. *This Road not Turnpike farther than Bridgewater. See the Turnpike Road*, p. 57.

At Kingſweſton, Will. Dickinſon, Eſq.

At Enmore is a Seat of the Earl of Egmont.

A little beyond Willet is Harrow-Houſe, belonging to the Family of Lacy.

LONDON to *Frome*, continued to WELLS.

To *Andover*, p. 31.	—	65
Amberſbury, p. 56.	13¼	78¼
Shrewton	5¾	84
Chiltern	5	89
Heyteſbury	4	93
Boreham	2½	95½
Warminſter	1½	97
Or,		
Amberſbury		
Deptford	10	
Warminſter	1½	
Buckley	1	98
Corſley Heath	3	101
Frome	3	104
Whatley	3	107
Little Elham	1	108
Mendip Hills		
WELLS	12	120

At 80, Stonehenge, one of the moſt remarkable remains of Antiquity in the Kingdom.

At Shrewton, the Earl of Ilcheſter.

At Chiltern, Mrs. Mitchell.

At Heyteſbury is a Seat late of the Family of Aſhes, but now of Wm. A'Court, Son of late General A'Court.

At Norton, Mr. Parry.

At Biſhopſtone, Mrs. Temple.

At 100, on the left, is Longleat, the Marquis of Bath.

Four or Five Miles beyond Frome on r. Plantations and Park of Mr. Horner of Wells.

From Mendip Hills, ſee on l. Mr. Hoare's Tower at Stourton, and the Torr at Glaſtonbury, a conical Hill, with a Tower on the Top.

To *Warminſter*, as above	—	97
Samborne	1	98
Croſs Sheer-Water	1¾	99¾
Maiden Bradley	4¾	104½
Yarnfield	1	105½
Kilmington	1	106½

Bruham	4	110½
Bruton	3	113½

To Bruton, by Willey, p. 56.

At Maiden Bradley is a Seat of the Duke of Somerset.

To *Shaftsbury*, p. 41.	—	102
Gillingham	4½	106½
Wincaunton	6½	113
Bruton	5	118

Half a Mile beyond Shaftsbury, on the r. Mr. Whitaker.

At the End of Gillingham, Mr. Frelse.

Between Wincaunton and Bruton, on the l. Lord Ilchester, his Plantations running towards Alfred's Tower on the right.

To Willoughby Hedge, p. 56.	—	96½
At one Mile farther *l. to Mere*, Wilts	3¾	100¼
Wincaunton, *Som.*	8	108¼

A Mile beyond Mere, on l. is Zeal's House, Wm. Chaffin Grove, Esq.

To Wincaunton, *as above*	—	108¼
Holton	2	110¼
Thackeston	1	111¼
South Cadbury	2	113¼
Sparkford	3	116¼
Ilchester	6	122¼

At North Cadbury, Mr. Newman.

Just beyond Cadbury Hill, a large Intrenchment.

LONDON to *Bruton*, by SALISBURY.

To SALISBURY, p. 32.	—	82
Fisherton	½	82½
Wilton	2½	85
Ugford	1	86
Barford	1¾	87¾
Tessont	4½	92¼
Chilmark	1¼	93½
Fonthill	2¼	95¾
Hindon	1½	97¼
Willoughby Hedge	2¾	100
Bruton, p. 56.	12½	112½

At Wilton is a noble Seat of the Earl of Pembroke.

At 91, on the left, Dinton House, Wm. Penruddock Wyndham, Esq.

At Fonthill is a fine Seat, built by the late William Beckford, Esq. Alderman of London.

To *Amersbury*, p. 56.	—	78¼
East Lavington	10	88¼
Or,		
Market Lavington	10	88¼
Devizes	6	94¼

A Mile and a Half from East Lavington is West Lavington, late the Seat of the Earl of Abingdon, now pulled down, and the Property of the Duke of Marlborough.

To *Frome*, p. 60.	—	104
Shepton Mallet	10½	114½

To *Bruton*, p. 56.	—	109
Pitcomb	1	110
Castle Carey, *Som.*	2	112
Ilchester	11½	123½
Petherton	8	131½
Ilminster	6	137½

To *Bridgewater*, p. 59.	—	137
Cannington, *Som.*	3½	140½
Nether Stowey	4½	145
Hoverd	2¾	147¾
Doniford	4½	152¼
Watchet	1¼	153½
Dunster	5	158½
Minehead	2½	161
Porlock	6	167
Comb Martin, *Devon*	9	176
Ilfracomb	5	181

At Dunster is a Castle belonging to the Family of Lutterell.

To West Bagborough, p. 59.	—	146
Wivelscomb, *Som.*	8½	154½
Bampton	8	162½

To *S. Moulton*, p. 57.	—	179½
Torrington, *Devon*	15	194½

LONDON to BATH, by *Chippenham.*

To Kensington, *Mid.*	—	1½
Hammersmith	2½	4
Turnham Green	1	5
Brentford	2	7
Hounslow	2¾	9¾
r. to Cranford Bridge	2½	12¼
Longford	3	15¼
Colnbrook, *Bucks*	2	17¼
Slough	3¼	20½
Salt-Hill	1	21½
Maidenhead Bridge	3½	25
Maidenhead, Berks	1	26
l. to Hare Hatch	6	32
Twyford	2	34
Reading *	5	39
Calcot Green	3	42
Theal	1¾	43¾
Woolhampton	5¾	49½
Thatcham	3½	53
Newbury and Speenham Land	3	56
Speen	1	57
Half-way House	3	60
Hungerford	4½	64½
Froxfield, *Wilts*	3	67½
Marlborough Forest	4¼	71¾
Marlborough	2¾	74½
Marlborough Field	2½	77
Overton	1¼	78¼
West Kennet	1½	79¾
Silbury Hill	¾	80½
Beckington	1	81½
r. to Calne	6	87½
Studley	2	89½
Chippenham	4	93½
l. to Upper Peckwic	4½	98
Box	3¾	101¾
Bath Easton	2½	104¼
Walcot	1¾	106
BATH	1	107

* *To Reading by Egham*, p. 51.
For Remarks on this Road from London to Hounslow, see p. 34, &c.

On the right of Cranford Bridge is Cranford, a Seat of Earl Berkeley.

At 15, on left, Stanwell, the Seat of the late Alex. Hume Campbell, Esq. and Stanwell Place, the Seat of Sir William Gibbons, Bart.

At 18, on right, is Langley Park, late Duke of Marlborough, now Sir Robert Bateson Harvey, Bart.

To the left of 20 is Windsor Castle; and to the right, Stoke Park, the Seat of Sir George Howard.

At 21, on r. Baylis, late Lord Godolphin, now Lord Chesterfield.

At 21½, on the r. Stoke Houſe, John Penn, Eſq.

At 25, on r. is **Taplow,** a Seat of the Earl of Inchiquin.

Beyond the **Bridge,** on the r. is Sir Iſaac Pococke.

On left, entering Maidenhead, is the Seat of **Pennyſton Powney,** Eſq.

On the r. of Maidenhead, Hicks, the late Mr. Ambler; and, on the r. at ſome diſtance, Sir Will. Eaſt, and Biſham Abbey, Mr. Vanſittart.

On Maidenhead Bridge, on the r. you have a fine View, up the River, of Cliefden, another Seat of the Earl of Inchiquin, the Reſidence of the late Prince of Wales.

At Maidenhead Thicket, on the l. ſee the Spire of Shotterbrook Church; cloſe to which is the Seat of Arthur Vanſittart, Eſq.

At 31½, on the r. is a fine Seat of Mr. Ximenes.

At 31¾, Killgreen, on r. Mrs. Phillips; on l. Mr. Parrot.

At 32, on left, Mr. Girdler and Mr. Young.

At 33½, on a Hill, is Hurſt, the Seat of Rt. Hon. Sir James Eyre, Knt.

At 35, on right, ſee Shiplake on the Hill, late Lord Harrowby, now E. Biſcoe, Eſq.

At 37, on right, is Sunning, belonging to the Family of Sir —— Rich, Bart. and on l. John Bagnal, Eſq.

Before 38, to the l. is White Knights, late Sir Henry Englefield, Bart. now Wm. Byam Martin, Eſq. And near it, late Admiral Hotham, now the Right Hon. Henry Addington, Speaker of the Houſe of Commons.

At 39, on r. **Caverſham,** late Lord Cadogan, now Mr. Marſac.

At 40, on l. Coley, late Miſs Thompſon.

At 41, on the right, Edmund Powers, Eſq.

At 42, on the right, John Belgrave, Eſq.

At 45, on r. Englefield Houſe, Rd. Benyon, Eſq.

At 47, on left, is Padworth, the Seat of the late Chriſtopher Griffiths, Eſq. now his Widow.

At 48, on the left, is Aldermaſton Houſe, now inhabited by E. Long, Eſq.

At 49, on the left, John Mount, Eſq. and Sir Robert Mackreth.

At 50, on the right, Mr. Poyntz.

Before Thatcham, on the right, is Dunſden Houſe, a Seat of Sir Archer Croft, now inhabited by —— Waddington, Eſq.

At 56½, on right, Sir Joſeph Andrews, and at 57, alſo on r. a Seat late of his Brother, Mr. Andrews, late Mr. Brummell; and Donnington Caſtle, Mr. Baſket, late the Packers, from them Mr. Hartley's. Formerly the famous Chaucer. Alſo, in the Bottom, Mr. Cowſlad.

On the left of 58 is Hamſtead Marſhall, and Benham Park, a Seat of Lord Craven.

Before 62, on l. Mr. Dundas.

At 64¼ from Hungerford Bridge, on the r. ſee Chilton Lodge, late Gen. Smith.

At Froxfield, a large Hoſpital for Clergymens' Widows, founded by the Ducheſs of Somerſet.

At 67, on right, is Littlecot, the Seat of Mrs. Popham; and a little beyond it is Ramſbury, late Sir Will. Jones, Bart.

At 71, on the left, is Tottenham, the Seat of the Earl of Ayleſbury.

At 73, on l. is the Earl of Ayleſbury's Avenue through Severnake Foreſt.

In going out of Marlborough, on the l. is a large Houſe, formerly a Seat of the Duke of Somerſet, but now the Caſtle Inn.

Silbury Hill, a remarkable Barrow.
On the r. lies Abury, a Remain of the Druids.
On the right of 85 is Compton Baffet, John Walker Heneage, Efq.
On the left of 86, Blacklands, Thomas Maundrell, Efq.
At Studley, —— Brown, Efq.
Before Calne, on l. a white Horfe, lately cut out of the Hills.
At 90, on the left, about half a Mile off the Road, is Bow Wood, the Marquis of Lanfdown.
On the l. after leaving Chippenham, Ivy Houfe, the Seat of Matthew Humphrys, Efq.
About 94, before Bath, on r. Shoeerwic, Mr. Wiltfhire.
At 94, on the right, Rowdford, Mr. Delmé.
Near Bath is Prior Park, a Seat of the late Ralph Allen, Efq. now Mr. Smith, who married the the Widow of Bifhop Warburton.

LONDON to *Bath* by *Windfor*.

To Windfor, p. 73.		22
Binfield	9	31
Reading	9	40
BATH, p. 64.	67	107

This Road is travelled in the Summer Time, on Account of the many rural Profpects it affords.

At 1, on the left from Windfor, is Windfor Great Park.

At 2, on the right, St. Leonard's Hill, the Seat of General Harcourt, and Sophia Farm, the Seat of —— Birch, Efq.

At 3, on the left, is Cranbourn Lodge, the Seat of his Royal Highnefs the Duke of Gloucef-

ter; near which is Fern Hill, late the Seat of Lady Knowles. On the r. is New Lodge, the Seat of General Hodgfon; alfo the Seats of Sir Alexander Crawford, Standluke Batfon, and James Bannifter, Efqrs.

On Wingfield Plain is a free Grammar School; endowed by Vifcount Ranelagh.

At 4, on the left, is Afcot Place, the Seat of the late Andrew Lindegren, Efq. and Afcot Heath, where his Majefty's Stag-Hounds are kept, and his Majefty's Plate of one hundred Guineas annually run for.

Adjoining to this are the celebrated Wells of Sunning Hill, called by many the Montpelier of England.

At 5 is Wingfield Church.

At 6, on the right of Harley Green, is the Seat of Admiral Bowyer; and, a little to the left, is the Seat of John Walfh, Efq.

Near 7, on the right, is the Seat of —— Parry, Efq. and on the left is Swinley Lodge, the Seat of the Mafter of his Majefty's Stag-Hounds, and where the Deer are kept for his Majefty's hunting.

At 9, is the pleafant Village of Binfield. On the left, is the Seat of Lord Kinnaird, late the Refidence of William Pitt, Efq. alfo the noble Manfion of John Elliot, Efq. and Binfield Place, the Seat of —— Goodenough, Efq. Adjoining is the Seat of Admiral Vernon.

On the left of Binfield Place, on the Foreft, is the Place where Julius Cæfar was encamped. The Entrenchments are intire to this Day.

Near 10, is the Seat of —— Angle, Esq. and, to the right, is Billingbear, the Seat of the Earl of Abergavenny, late the Earl of Portsmouth's.

Near 11, on r. is Belle Hill, the Seat of the late Admiral Lev. Gower; and on the left, about Half a Mile, is the Town of Oakingham.

Near 15, is the river Loddon, over which is a free Bridge; Half a Mile beyond it is Reading Race-Ground, and Half a Mile farther is Early Common. On the left, is Maiden Early, the Seat of —— Golding, Esq. and White Knights, the Seat of William Byam Martin, Esq.

At 19, the old Bath Road joins and enters the Town of Reading.

To BATH, *by Devizes.*

To Beckington, p. 64.	—	81½
l. to Wansditch	3	84½
l. to Devizes	4	88½
r. to Melsham	7½	96
Shaw	1	97
Atford	2	99
Horse and Jockey	1½	100½
Kingsdown Hill	2	102½
Bathford, *Som.*	1½	104
Enter Chippenham new Road	½	104½
Bath Easton	½	105
Walcot	1¾	106¾
BATH	1	107¾

Beyond Devizes, on the l. under the Hills, see Earlstoke, late Mr. Delmé, now Mr. Joshua Smith.

At Melsham, late William Long, Esq. now Miss Thresher.

Before Shaw, on the l. Shaw House, late —— Neale, Esq.

At 98, on the r. a new-built House of the Rev. Dr. Walter.

Going down Kingsdown Hill, in the Vale, beyond Bathurston, on the r. the Villa of Sir John Miller, Bart. On r. Shockerwic, Mr. Wiltshire.

To BATH, *by Sandy Lane.*

To Beckington, p. 64.	—	81½
l. to Wandsditch	3	84½
r. to Sandy Lane	5½	90
Rawdon Hill	2	92
Laycoc	1½	93½
Corsham	3	96½
Lower Pickwic	1	97½
Box	2½	100
Bath Easton, *Som.*	2½	102½
Walcot	1¾	104¼
BATH	1	105¼

Beyond 89, on r. Whetham, Colonel Money; on the l. Wand's House.

At Sandy Lane, on r. is Beau-Wood, Marquis of Lansdown; and on the l. Spy Park, late a Seat of the Bayntuns, and since of the Rolts, who have taken the Name of Bayntun.

At 92, on the right, Bowdon House, Ezekiel Dickenson, Esq.

At 93, Laycoc Abbey, John Talbot.

At Corsham, Corsham House, the Seat of Paul Methuen, Esq.

To *Melksham*, p. 69.	—	96
l. to Holt	3½	99½
Bradford	2½	102

Another Road to Bradford, viz.

To Hilperton, p. 72.	—	97½
Staverton	1½	99
Bradford	1½	100½

Or,

To *Trowbridge*, p. 72.		—	98½
Bradford		2	100½

Before Holt, on the right, is Holt Well, Dr. Jones.

Entering Bradford, on the left, late Duke of Kingston.

LONDON to BATH, by *Andover*.

To *Andover*, p. 31.		—	65
Weyhill		3	68
Ludgershall,	*Wilts*	4	72
E. Everley		4½	76½
W. Everley		1½	78
Uphaven		3¾	81¾
Rushal		1	82¾
Charlton		¾	83½
Conoc		3½	87
Nursteed		3	90
Devizes		1	91
BATH, p. 69.		19⅓	110¼

On the r. of Weyhill, Mr. Gawler; and Chute Lodge, Mr. Freeman.

At Ludgershall, a Castle, Mr. Astley's.

At E. Everley, late Sir John Astley, now Mr. Astley.

At Rushal, John Poore, Esq.

At Conoc, John Powell, Esq.

Before Devizes, on left, South Broom House, Josiah Eyles Heathcote, Esq. and on the r. a Park, Mr. Sutton.

LONDON to BRISTOL.

To *Chippenham*, p. 64.		—	93½
r. to Wraxhall,	*Wilts*	8	101½
Marshfield,	*Gloc.*	1	102½
Tug Hill		3	105½
Wyck		2	107½
Warmley		2	109½
St. George		2	111½
BRISTOL		2	113½

Before Tug Hill, on left, Hamswell, the Seat of Thomas Whittington, Esq.

At 108, on the left, Highfield, —— Parrot, Esq.

At 112, on left, are Mr. Champion's Copper-Works.

LONDON to *Sodbury*.

To *Chippenham*, p. 64.		—	93½
Yatton Kenel		4	97½
Castlecomb		1½	99
Nettleton		3	102
Acton Turvil,	*Gloc.*	5	107
Cross Hands Inn		2	109
Chipping Sodbury		3	112

A Mile beyond Chippenham, on the right, Harden Hewish, —— Davenport, Esq.

To the right of Acton Turvil is Badmington Park, Duke of Beaufort.

LONDON to WELLS.

To Beckington, p. 64.		—	81½
l. to Wansditch		3	84½
l. to Devizes		4	88½
Seend		4	92½
l. to Hilperton		5	97½
Trowbridge		1	98½
Studley		1	99½
Southwich		1½	101
Road,	*Som.*	2¼	103¼
Beckington		1¼	104½
Frome		3	107½
Whatley		3	110½
Little Ellam		1	111½
Mendip Hills			
WELLS		12	123½

Another Road to Trowbridge.

To Conoc (called Coule) p. 71.	—	87
Eaſterton	3	90
Market Lavington	1	91
- to Worton		
Buckington		
r. to Hilperton	10	101
Trowbridge	1	102

Another Road branches off from this by Seend to Melksham.

At Devizes, Charles Garth, Eſq. and, on the Green, South Broom Houſe, Joſiah Eyles Heathcote, Eſq.

At Seend Green, Ld. Wm. Seymour; and, in the Town, Mr. Awdry; beyond, on r. a new Houſe, Mr. Robſon.

Seend Cleve, Mr. Lock.

Seend Head, Mr. Baniſter.

At Farley is Farley Caſtle, formerly Lord Hungerford.

One Mile from Old Down, on the Briſtol Road, is Stone Eaſton, Richard Hippeſley Coxe, Eſq.

To Colnbrook, p. 63	—	17½
l. to Datchet	2¼	19½
Croſs the Thames, and keep to the left round Windſor Little Park, to		
Windſor, Berks	2½	22

Before Datchet, on right, Ditton Park, Lord Beaulieu.

LONDON to Great Marlow.

At 23, on the Bath Road, p. 63.	—	23
r. to Burnham	1	24

Hedſor	3	27
Bone End	1	28
Little Marlow	2	30
Great Marlow	1¼	31¼

At 26, on the left, is Cliefden Houſe, a Seat of the Earl of Inchiquin.

To Reading, p. 63.		39
Pangbourn, Berks	5	44
Compton	7½	51½
Eaſt Ilſley	2	53½

By Pangbourn, Purley Hall, the Rev. Dr. Wilder's.

To Hungerford, p. 64.	—	64½
Aldbourn	8½	73

To Hungerford, p. 64.	—	64½
Great Bedwin, Wilts	6	70½
Burbage	3	73½

To Devizes, p. 69.	—	88½
Weſtbury, Wilts	13	101½

Another Road to Weſtbury.

To Market Lavington, p. 75.	—	91
Weſt Lavington	1	92
Weſtbury	9	101

To Bath, p. 64.	—	107
Keynſham, Somer.	8	115

To Bath, p. 64.	—	107
Pensford, Somer.	10½	117½

To Bath, p. 64.	—	107
Chewton, *Somer.*	13½	120½

To Bristol, p. 71.	—	113½
Wrington, *Somer.*	12	125½

To Bristol, p. 71.	—	113½
Bedminster, *Somer.*	1½	115
l. to Perry Bridge	9¼	124¼
Langford	1¼	125½
Cross	4½	130
East Brent	7	137
Highbridge	4	141
Huntspill	2	143

To Langford, *above*	—	125½
Axbridge	6¼	131¾

To Wells, p. 72.	—	123½
Polsham	3	126½
Glastonbury	2½	129

Near Wells is the Cavern, called Wookey Hole.

At Glastonbury, fine ruins of the Abbey.

LONDON to Oxford, by *Henley.*

To *Maidenhead*, p. 63.	—	26
r. to the Thicket	3	29
Hurley Bottom	2	31
Henley	4	35
Nettlebed, Oxfordsh.	5	40
Hunterton Common	2	42
Beggar's Bush	2	44
Benson	2	46
Shilingford	2	48
Dorchester	1½	49½
r. to Nuneham	3½	53
Sandford	2	55
Littlemore	1½	56½
Oxford	1½	58

Another Road to Oxford, by Wycomb, p. 82.

On the right of 29 is Bisham Abbey, late the Seat of Sir John Hoby, Bart. now of Mr. G. Vansittart.

At 30, on right, see Harleford, Mr. Clayton, a Brick House, in Bucks: And Hurley Place, late Mr. Wilcock's, a white House, in Berks.

On right of 33, Rose Hill, the Seat of the Hon. F. West.

On the left of 34 is Park Place, late Lord Archibald Hamilton, Gen. Conway.

Near Nettlebed is a Windmill, said to be on the highest Ground South of the Trent.

Near Nettlebed is Newington, Mr. White.

About a Mile to the left of 45 lies the Town of Wallingford.

At Nuneham, on left, Earl Harcourt; on the right, Belden House, C. Willoughby, Esq.

LONDON to Glocester, by *Cirencester.*

To *Dorchester*, p. 75.	—	49½
l. to Burcot	1½	51
Clifton	1¼	52¼
Collum Bridge	2¾	55
Abingdon, Berks	1	56
Shipton	2	58
Tupney Warren	2	60
Fifield	1½	61½
Kingston Inn	1½	63
Farringdon *	8	71
r. to Buscot	4	75
St. John's Bridge	1	76

Lechlade,	*Gloc.*	1	77
Fairford		3½	80½
Poolton		3½	84
Eaſington		1½	85½
Cirenceſter		3½	89
Along a Roman Road to			
Birdlip		10	99
Whitcomb		2	101
Brockworth		1	102
Hucclescot		1	103
Barnwood		1	104
Wotton		1	105
GLOCESTER †		1	106

. * *Another Road to Farringdon,* by *Wantage,* p. 78.

† *Another Road to Glocefter, by Oxford and Burford,* p. 82.

On r. of 59 is Oakley Houſe, H. E. M'Cullock, Eſq.
On r. of 60, Tubney Lodge, S. Law-rance, Eſq.
On left of 62 is the Seat of A. W. Blandy, Eſq.
At 65, on the left, is Puſey-Houſe, the Hon. Ph. Puſey.
To the right of 66 is Buckland, Sir John Throckmorton; and, a Mile and a half farther on the right, Caſtle Surby, Mr. Southby.
To the left of 69 is Wadley, —— Stead, Eſq.
At Farringdon, Wm. Hailet, Eſq.
At 73 is Buſcot Park, Loveden Loveden, Eſq.
At Lechlade, on the r. a new Houſe, Sir Thomas Wheate, Bart.
At Fairford is the Seat and fine Garden of John Raymond Barker, Eſq. and a great deal of curious painted Glaſs in the Church.
Beyond Eaſington, on r. Ampney, S. Blackwell, Eſq.
At Cirenceſter, the magnificent Seat and fine Woods of Earl Bathurſt.

A fine Window of painted Glaſs in the Abbey-Church.
At 100, Birdlip Hill, two Miles long; at the bottom on the left, Whitcomb, Beach Hicks, Eſq.
At Hucclescot, on l. Wm. Colcheſter, Eſq. and a little beyond it, Sir Wm. Stretcham.
A little before Glocefter, on the left, are Margaret and Maudling Hospitals, built by two Siſters.

Another Road to Glocefter, viz.

To Fairford, p. 77.	——	80½
Barnſley	6	86½
Perrots Bridge	3½	90
Birdlip	10	100
GLOCESTER, p. 77.	7	107

A Barnſley, James Muſgrave, Eſq.

LONDON to *Farringdon,* by *Wantage.*

To Hunterton Common, p. 75.		42
l. to *Wallingford,* Berks	4	46
Brightwell	2	48
Harwell	6	54
Great Hendred	2	56
Wantage	4	60
Eaſt Challow	2	62
Stanford	2½	64½
Stanford Plain	1	65½
Farringdon	2½	68

Another Road, p. 76.

At two Miles and a half beyond Wallingford, on r. Whittenham Hill, a Plantation of the late Sir Henry Oxendon, in an old Camp. A Plantation near it, seen all the way from Wantage.
At Lockings, about three Miles on this Side Wantage, Mr. Baſtard, and Part of the Oxfordſhire Ickineld Street.

At Challow, late John Bunce, Efq.
On the left of Stanford Plain is Shel-
lingford Caftle, ·Earl Spencer,
rented by Mr. Bridges : · And on
the right is Hatford, Mr. Tyrrel.

To *Nettlebed*, p. 75. ·	—	40
r. to Watlington	5¾	45¾

To *Abingdon*, p. 76.	—	56
Fifield, *Berks*	5	61
Bampton, *Oxfordfh.*	8½	69½

To *Wantage*, p, 78.	—	60
Lamburn	6	66
Albourn	6	72

Other Roads to Lambourn and
Albourn, viz.

To *Newbury*, p. 64.	—	56
Welford, *Berks*	5½	61½
Great Shefford	2½	64
Lambourn	4	68

Near Lambourn is Afhdown Park,
Lord Craven.

To *Hungerford*, p. 64.	—	64½
Aldbourne, *Wilts*	8½	73

To *Farringdon*, p. 76.	—	71
Colefhill	4	75
Highworth, *Wilts*	2	77
River Ray	5½	82½
Purton	2½	85
Guerfden Green	6	91
Guerfden	1½	92½
Milbourn Green	1½	94
Malmfbury	1	95

At Malmfbury, the Abbey.

To *Farringdon*, p. 76.	—	71
Shrivenham	5½	76½
Hackron Bridge	2	78½
Swindon, *Wilts*	5	83½
Wootton Baffet	6	89½
Chriftian Malford	8	97½

Near Shrivenham is Becket, Lord
Vifcount Barrington.

To *Farringdon*, p. 76.	—	71
Colefhill	4	75
Highworth	2	77
Cricklade	6½	83½
Charlton	10	93½
Malmfbury	2	95½

At Charlton, Earl of Suffolk.

To *Cirencefter*, p. 77.	—	89
Tetbury	10	99
Durfley	8½	107½

To *Cirencefter*, p. 77.	—	89
Tetbury	10	99
Didmarton	5	104
Wickwar	7	111

To *Cirencefter*, p. 77.	—	89
Minchin Hampton	10	99
Stanley	5½	104½
Berkeley	8½	113
Hill	3	116
Thornbury ·	5	121
Alliftone	1	122
Briftol	10	132

Berkeley Caftle is a Seat of the Earl
of Berkeley.
Thornbury Caftle, Mr. Howard.

To *Cirencester*, p. 77.	—	89
Minchin Hampton	10	99
Wootton Underedge	9	108

To *Cirencester*, p. 77.	—	89
Bisley	9	98
Painswic	3	101

To *Cirencester*, p. 77.	—	89
Minchin Hampton	10	99
Stroud	3	102
Painswic		
GLOCESTER	10	112

V.

GREAT AND DIRECT ROADS

Measured from TYBURN TURNPIKE.

With the ROADS branching from them to Market and Sea-Port TOWNS.

LONDON to OXFORD, GLOCESTER and St. DAVID'S.

To Bayswater, *Mid*	—	1
Kensington Gravel-Pits	1	2
Shepherd's Bush	1½	3½
Acton	1½	5
Hanwell	3	8
Southall	1¼	9¼
Hayes	4	13¼
Hillingdon	¾	14
Uxbridge	1	15
Gerard's Cross, *Bucks*	5	20
Beaconsfield	3	23
Low Water	4	27
High Wycombe	2	29
West Wycombe	2	31
Stoken Church, *Oxf.*	5	36
Tetsworth	6¼	42¼
Wheatley Bridge	5¾	48
At 48¾ *l. to* Wheatley	1	49
Shotover Hill	3	52
OXFORD*	2	54
Eynsham	5	59
Witney	5	64
Burford	7	71
Northlech, *Glo.*	9	80
Frogmill	7	87
Little Whitcomb	7½	94½
Brookworth	1½	96
Hucclescot	1	97
Barnwood	1	98
GLOCESTER †	2	100
Huntley	7½	107½

Longhope	2½	110
Michael Dean	2	112
Colford	11	123
Redbrook	2½	125½
Monmouth, Monm.	2½	128
r. to Rochfield	2½	130½
Llangaddoc	1¾	132¼
Llandilo Cruſſency	3¾	136
Llanvapley	2½	138½
Kevenhedagor Hill	3½	142
Abergavenny ‡	1¼	143¼
Llanwenarth	1¾	145
Llangranach	2½	147½
Crick Howell, *Breck.*	1¾	149¼
Tretower	1¾	151
Bwlch	3	154
Llanſanfraid	1½	155½
Llanhamlog	3	158½
Brecon	3½	162
Llanſpetheid	2½	164½
Croſs the Uſke at Rheed-Brue	5½	170
Trecaſtle §	2½	172½
Enter *Caermarthenſh.*	3½	176
Llandovery	5	181
Llanurda	4	185
Abermarles	2	187
Landilo Faur	6	193
Rhuraddor	3	196
Croſs Inn	2¼	198¼
Cothy Bridge	3¾	202
White Mill	2½	204½
Abergwilly	1½	206
Caermarthen	2	208
St. Clear	9½	217½
Landowrer	2	219½
Tavern Spite, *Pemb.*	5	224½
Noah's Ark	3	227½
Narbeth	3	230½
Robinſon	2	232½
Cannaſton Bridge	1½	234
Mid-County Houſe	2½	236½
Haverfordweſt	5½	242
Trecoed	4	246
Newgal Sands	4¾	250¾
Solva	3¾	254½
St. DAVID's	3¼	257¾

* *To Oxford, by Henley*, p. 75.

† *Gloceſter, by Cirenceſter*, p. 76.

‡ *Another Road to Abergavenny*, p. 87.

§ *Another new Turnpike Road from Trecaſtle to Llandovery, called Cwymdwr Road, and now univerſally travelled, as it avoids the Mountains, and is equally near.*

On l. from Bayſwater to Kenſington Gravel-pits, are Kenſington Gardens.

On the r. at Wytham, 2 Miles beyond Oxford, the Seat and Woods of the Earl of Abingdon.

Beyond Hillingdon, on the right, is a white Houſe, late Mrs. Talbot, now the Marchioneſs of Rockingham's.

On the r. of 16 is Denham, Sir William Bowyer, Bart.

On l. of 20 is Bulſtrode Houſe and Park, the D. of Portland.

At 22½, on r. late Mr. Baſil, now Mrs. Dupré.

On the left, near Beaconsfield, Edmund Waller, Eſq. and on the r. the Rt. Hon. Edm. Burke.

On l. of High Wycombe, the Marquis of Lanſdown; and on the left of Weſt Wycombe is the late Lord le Deſpencer, now Sir John Daſhwood King, Bart. his Brother; and near it, on the top of a Hill, is Weſt Wycombe Church, on the Tower of which is a Ball that will contain fix People, and may be feen from a little beyond Beaconsfield.

A few Miles to the left of Stoken Church is Sherburn Caftle, the Earl of Macclesfield.

From Stoken-Church Hill fee in the bottom, before you, Afton, General Calliaud.

At 41, on l. Lord Cha. Spencer.

On the r. Thame Park, Lord Vifcount Wenman.

At 48, on r. Water-Stock, Sir William Henry Afhhurft.

At Wheatley, on the right, Waterperry, John Barnabas Curfon, Efq.

A little farther, Holton-Houfe and Park, Henry Whorwood, Efq.

At 50, on the l. Mr. Schutz.

At 52, on the r. Headington-Houfe, W. Jackfon, Efq. and, a little farther, Capt. Lloyd, late Sir Banks Jenkinfon.

Beyond Eynfham, fee Eynfham-Hall, Mrs. Duberley.

Before Burford, on r. fee Swinford Mr. Fettiplace.

At Burford is the Lenthalls.

Three Miles and a Half beyond Burford, on r. is Barrington Park, late the Brays, now Lord Dynevor; and Two Miles and a Half farther on r. is Lord Sherborn, built by Inigo Jones.

Before Northlech, on the l. fee Stowell Park, Lord Chedworth; and to the right, Farmington, Edmund Waller, Efq.

At the end of Northlech, one of the new County Bridewells.

About a Mile beyond Frogmill, to the r. is Sandywell Park, Mrs. Tracey, and a little beyond it, Dowdefwell, —— Rogers, Efq.

From the Hill beyond Frogmill, fee the Vale of Evefham, Cheltenham, Tewkefbury, and Worcefter.

At 91½, to the right, is the famous faline mineral purgative, Cheltenham Spa-Water Wells.

Four Miles and a half beyond Frogmill are the Seven Wells, which give birth to the Thames; and to the left hereof is Cobberley, Lord Chedworth.

To the left of 96 is Cree Place, —— Campbell, Efq.

At Huccelfcot, on l. Rich. Colchefter, Efq. a little beyond it Sir William Stretcham.

A little below Glocefter, on the left, are Margaret and Maudlin Hofpitals, built by two Sifters.

Two Miles beyond Glocefter, on the right, is Highnam, late Mr. Cooke's.

Four Miles and a half before Monmouth, on l. is High Meadow, Lord Vifcount Gage.

A Mile before Monmouth, fee on the left, acrofs the River, Troy-Houfe, Duke of Beaufort; which is again feen about a Mile beyond Monmouth, on left.

At the foot of Bwlch-Hill, on l. in the bottom, Buckland, Mr. Gwynn.

Beyond Llanfanfraid, on r. Skethe-rog, late a Seat of the Vaughans, now Mr. Socket.

At Llanhamlog, Mr. Powell.

At Brecon, the Caftle, the Priory, and pleafant Walks by it.

At Abermarles, a Seat, late the Cornwallis's.

A Mile beyond, on l. in the bottom, is Danyralt, Admiral Lloyd.

At 2, on the r. from Abermarles, is Tally Aris, Lord Robert Seymour.

Before Llandilo, on the l. Mr. Hemming.

At half a Mile on the l. from Llandilo Faur, is Dynevor Caftle, the moſt beautiful Seat in South Wales, belonging to Lord Dynevor.

At 4, on the l. from Llandilo Faur, is the Village of Langathan and Berithlandwell, a beautiful Seat of Richard Jones Llwyd, Eſq. Alſo Aberglaſſiny, —— Dyer, Eſq.

Two Miles beyond Rhuraddor, on the left, is Golden Grove, John Vaughan, Eſq.

At Croſs Inn, on the r. Courthenry, William Philips, Eſq.

At a Diſtance from the Road, on the Summit of the Hill, is Penylan, William Davies, Eſq.

At 12, on the r. is Merlin's Cave.

At Abergivilly, on the l. is the Palace of the Biſhop of St. David's. Alſo Cliſtandy, Richard Thomas, Eſq. and Caſtlepiggin, the Seat of Tho. Blome, Eſq.

At the entrance of Caermarthen, on the l. are the Iron and Tin Mills of John Morgan, Eſq. and the Smelting-Houſe of John Campbell, Eſq.

At 3 Miles on the l. from Cannaſton Bridge, is Picton Caſtle, Lord Milford.

Another Road to Abergavenny.

To *Monmouth*, p. 83.	—	128
At the Turnpike, *on l.*		
Dynyſtow Church	$3\frac{1}{2}$	$131\frac{1}{2}$
Dynyſtow Court	$\frac{1}{2}$	132
At $5\frac{1}{2}$ left to		
Ragland	4	136
Clyder	3	139
Abergavenny	6	145

Dynyſtow Court, Mr. Drake.

At Ragland, the Caſtle.

At $2\frac{1}{2}$, from Ragland, on right, ſee Llanarch, Mr. Jones.

At Clyder, Mr. Jones, and a little farther, on l. ſee Mr. Hooper's, a brick Houſe.

Farther on, a brick Houſe, on l. Capt. Lewis.

At $6\frac{1}{2}$ from Ragland, ſee a Farm houſe caſtle-wiſe, a View from Mr. Hanbury Williams's Seat at Coalbrook, at 7 on right.

LONDON to *Cardiff*, continued to *Haverfordweſt*.

To *Monmouth*, p. 83.	—	128
l. to Glogheker	$4\frac{1}{2}$	$132\frac{1}{2}$
Trelagh	1	$133\frac{1}{2}$
Devordon	4	$137\frac{1}{2}$
New Church	$2\frac{3}{4}$	$140\frac{1}{4}$
Throggy River	$2\frac{1}{2}$	$142\frac{3}{4}$
Coylegny	$3\frac{3}{4}$	$146\frac{1}{2}$
Catts Aſh	$1\frac{1}{4}$	$147\frac{3}{4}$
Chriſt Church	2	$149\frac{3}{4}$
Newport	$2\frac{3}{4}$	$152\frac{1}{2}$
Stow	$\frac{1}{2}$	153
St. Melen's	7	160
Rompeny Bridge	$1\frac{1}{4}$	$161\frac{1}{4}$
Roth, *Glam.*	$1\frac{3}{4}$	163
Cardiff	1	164
Elay River	$2\frac{1}{2}$	$166\frac{1}{2}$
St. Nicolas	$3\frac{1}{2}$	170
Treſimon	2	172
Cowbridge	4	176
Ewenny	2	178
Cornton	$3\frac{1}{2}$	$181\frac{1}{2}$
New Inn Bridge	2	$183\frac{1}{2}$
Over the River Ogmore		
The Pile-Inn	5	$188\frac{1}{2}$
Margam	$2\frac{1}{2}$	191
Aberavon	4	195
Baglan	2	197
Neath	$3\frac{1}{2}$	$200\frac{1}{2}$
Swanſea	$4\frac{1}{2}$	205

Trahere	1/2	205 1/2	At Raglan, on r. Mr. Jones.
Pont Lew	2 3/4	208 1/2	Beyond on l. Lord Vernon.
Pont Brenin	1 1/2	209 3/4	On an Eminence near Neath, is the
Lloghor	1 1/4	211	Gnole, a beautiful Seat of Lady
Llanelly	5	216	Mackworth.
Pont Spuddore	6 1/2	222 1/2	At Neath, on r. Mr.
Kidwelly	2	224 1/2	On left of Lloghor is Lloghor Castle
A Ferry to Carmarthen	9	233 1/2	
[Llanstephan*	5	229 1/2	To GLOCESTER, p. 82.——100
Llaugharn	3 1/3	233	Keep to the left over
Eglois Kemen	4 1/2	237 1/2	Corselawn . 6 106
Llanguido, Pemb.	5 1/2	243	Ledbury, Heref. 10 116
Cannaston	6	249	To the l. at 42 1/4 is Hope End, Sir
Mid-County House	2 1/2	251 1/2	Harry Tempest, Bart.
Haverfordwest]	4 1/2	256	The View from this Seat is extensive and picturesque.

* *That Part of the Road included between two Crotchets, is out of use.*

About a Mile beyond Monmouth, on the left, is Troy-House, a Seat of the Duke of Beaufort.

Before Coylegny, on l. are the Ruins of Stogle Castle.

Two Miles beyond Newport, is Tredeagar, Sir Charles Morgan, Bart.

About St. Melens, on r. see Ruperra, Col. Morgan.

At St. Nicolas, on r. is Cotterells, Mrs. Gwynnett.

Beyond Cowbridge, see Penline Castle, another Seat of Mrs. Gwynett.

On the left, 3 miles before Cowbridge, is Llanthithed, Sir John Aubrey, Bart.

At Ewenny, the Priors; over the Ogmore, see Ogmore Castle.

At Margam is Margam House and Park, the Seat of Mr. Talbot.

LONDON to Chepstow.

To GLOCESTER, p. 82.	——	100
Minsterworth	4	104
Westbury	4 1/2	108 1/2
Newnham	3 1/2	112
Blakeney	3	115
Lidney	3 1/2	118 1/2
Aylburton	1	119 1/2
Alvington	1	120 1/2
Woolaston	1	121 1/4
Chepstow	5 1/2	127

At 3, on the right, High Grove, Sir Cha. Barrow, Bart.

At Westbury, M. Colchester, Esq.

Before Aylburton, on right, Tho. Bathurst, Esq.

At Piersfield, near Chepstow, are the Seat and fine Gardens made by Mr. Morris, late Mr. Smith's.

To Monmouth, p. 83.	——	128
Uske, Monm.	12	140

Caerleon	7½	147½
LANDAFF, *Glam.*	18½	166

Eight Miles from Monmouth, on r. the Ruins of Ragland Caftle.

To *Monmouth,* p. 83.	—	128
Ufke, *Monm.*	12	140
Ponty Pool	6	146
Caerphilly, *Glam.*	12	158
Llantriffent	8½	166½
Bridgend	11	177½

At Ponty Pool, the Seat of —— Hanbury, Efq.
At Caerphilly, the Caftle.

To *Swanfea,* p. 88.	—	205
Penrice, *Glam.*	14	219

To Trecaftle, p. 83.	—	172½
Llangadoc, *Carm*	13	185½
Llandilovaur	8¾	194¼

A Crofs Road.

Llandyby	5
Pontardulas	9
Swanfea	9

A Crofs Road

To *Caermarthen* by *Swanfea,* p. 88.	—	205
Pontardulas	9	214
Lanon	4	218
Langardaim	6	224
Caermarthen	6	230

LONDON to *Cardigan,* continued to St. DAVID's.

To *Llandovery,* p. 83.	—	181
Kavo	6	187

Pynfant	1½	188½
Llanbeder, *Card.*	8½	197
Red Owen	10	207
Tredrair	8	215
Cardigan	10	225
St Dogmel's, *Pemb.*	1¼	226¼
Velindree	6¼	232½
Newport	3	235½
Fifkard	7	242½
Merth	6	248½
Gorid Bridge	8¼	256¾
St. DAVID's	1¾	258½

Another Road to St. David's, p. 84.

To Tredrair, *above*	—	215
Newcaftle, *Carm.*	4	219
Killgaren, *Pemb.*	8	227

To *Llanbeder,* as above	—	197
Llanarth, *Card.*	15	212

LONDON to *Pembroke.*

To *Caermarthen,* p. 83.	—	208
St. Clear	8½	216½
Tavern Spite, *Pemb.*	7	223½
Pembroke	14	237½

To Cannaftan Bridge, *Pemb.* p. 84.	—	234
Wifton	4	238

To Tavern Spite, p. 83.	—	224½
Narbarth	5	229½

To Tavern Spite, p. 83.	—	224½
Tenby	13	237½

To *HighWycombe*, p. 81.	—	29
Riſborough, *Bucks*	8	37
Thame, Oxfordſh.	8¼	45¼

Near Thame, to r. is Kingſey, the
Seat of the Herberts; and to l. is
Thame Park, Ld Viſc. Wenman.
About Two Miles Weſt of Thame is
Rycot Park, the Earl of Abing-
don.

Another Road, viz.

To Ayleſbury, p. 114.	—	38
Thame	7	45

To OXFORD, p. 82.	—	54
Woodſtoc	8	62
Charlebury	6	68

Adjoining to Woodſtoc is Woodſtoc Park and Blenheim Houſe,
the Duke of Marlborough.
At Charlebury is Blandford Park,
the Duke of Beaufort.

To Northlech, p. 82.	—	80
Frogmill	7	87
At ½ Mile from Frog-		
mill turn to the r. to		
Dowdeſwell	1½	88½
Cheltenham	4	92½
Tewkſbury	9	101½
Upton, *Worceſt.*	7	108½
Kempſey	7	115½
WORCESTER	2½	118

At Dowdeſwell, on l. Edward Rogers, Eſq.
At 91½ is Charlton Kings, Doddington Hunt, Eſq.
Near Cheltenham is the ancient Family of Delabere.
At ½ a Mile weſtward of Cheltenham, on an Eminence, Lord Fau-
conberg, near which is a Spring,
diſcovered by his preſent Majeſty,
of the ſame kind of Water as the
celebrated Spa, but of a ſtronger
Nature.

LONDON to *Radnor*, by HE-
REFORD and *Kington* or *Kyneton.*

To GLOCESTER, p. 82.	—	100
Huntley	7½	107½
l. to Durley Croſs	1½	109
Lea, *Heref.*	2	111
Weſton	2	113
Roſs	2	115
Croſs the River Wye to		
Wilton	1	116
Peterſtow	2	118
Over Pitcher Common to		
Harewood End	3	121
Great Birch	2½	123½
Callow	2½	126
HEREFORD *	4	130
Manſel Lacy	7	137
Foxley Hill	1	138
Yazor	½	138½
Eccles Green	2¼	140¾
Wonton	3¼	144
Wonton's Aſh	1½	145½
Holmes	½	146
Lion's Hall	¼	146¼
Penreſs	1½	148¼
Kington or *Kyneton*	1¼	149½
Radnor	7	156½

* *See a new Road from Hereford to*
Brecon, p. 95.

At Weſton, on the l. J. Nourſe, Eſq.
A Mile beyond Peterſtow, on the r.
Pengethly, Tho. Symonds-Powell,
Eſq.
At Harewood, on the right, Sir
Hungerford Hoſkins, Bart.

One Mile from Harewood, on the Banks of the Wye, beautifully fituated, is Aramftone, John Woodhoufe, Efq.

Four Miles to the right of Hereford is Sufton Court, Sir James Hereford, whofe Family has poffeff.d the fame ever fince 1223, the 7th. of Henry the Third.

On Foxley Hill, R. Price, Efq.

Near Kyneton is Compton-Houfe, Lord Willoughby, through whofe Park the Road goes.

At the fifth Mile-ftone from Kyneton to Radnor, on the r. is Downton, Edward Lewis, Efq.

Another Road to Kington or Kyneton.

To HEREFORD, p. 94.	—	130
Tillington	5	135
Brinfop Court	$1\frac{1}{4}$	$136\frac{1}{4}$
Weobley	$5\frac{1}{4}$	$141\frac{1}{2}$
Bond's Green	4	$145\frac{1}{2}$
Lion's Hall	$1\frac{1}{2}$	147
Pentrefs	$1\frac{1}{2}$	$148\frac{1}{2}$
Kington or *Kyneton*	$1\frac{1}{2}$	$149\frac{3}{4}$

To HEREFORD, p. 94.	—	130
Weft Hope	$8\frac{1}{2}$	$138\frac{1}{2}$
Stretford Bridge	$2\frac{1}{2}$	141
Pembridge	$4\frac{1}{4}$	$145\frac{1}{4}$
Comb	$5\frac{1}{4}$	$150\frac{3}{4}$
Prefteign	$2\frac{1}{2}$	$153\frac{1}{4}$

To Prefteign, by Worcefter, p. 99.

LONDON to *Brecon* by HEREFORD and *Hay.*

To HEREFORD, p. 94	—	130
White Crofs	1	131
King's Acre	1	132
New Ware	$2\frac{1}{2}$	$134\frac{1}{2}$
Bridge Sollers	$1\frac{1}{2}$	136
Garnons	$1\frac{1}{2}$	$137\frac{1}{2}$
Portway	1	$138\frac{1}{2}$
Hammer's Crofs	$1\frac{1}{2}$	140
Bradwardine	2	142
Clocknill	3	145
Hardwic Court	2	147
Hay, Brecon	2	149
Glafbury	4	153
Bruntlis	4	157
Brecon	7	164

For the Continuation of this Road to St. David's, fee p. 83, 84.

From Hereford to Hay is a very beautiful Ride through a rich enclofed Country, fertile in Corn; but not abounding fo much with Hops and Apples as the eaftern Part of Hereford.

On the r. fee Credinall Hill and Park, at the Foot of which is a good Houfe belonging to Mr. Eckley.

On the l. of New Ware is a Houfe lately built by Will. Parry, Efq.

Beyond Bridge Sollers is Kenchefter, a Roman Station, where feveral Antiquities have been found.

On the l. at the 6 Mile-ftone, a View of the Wye; Shipton Hill on the right, whence is a fine View to the South over a Valley fruitful in Corn, watered by the Wye, and terminated by Mountains covered with Oak. See in this Valley the Churches of Prefton upon Wye and byford.

At Garnons, John Green Cotterell, Efq. and, more to the left, is Stanton upon Wye.

On the l. on the fouth Side the Wye, is Moccas Court, Sir George Cornwall, Bart.

North of the Wye is Morning, almoft oppofite to Moccas, lately purchafed of Mr. Heywood by Sir

George Cornwall. This was the Eftate of the famous Owen Glendour, in the Time of Henry IV. who is faid to have retired here, and was buried in the Church.

At the ten-mile ftone, where the Road divides to Kington, pafs over Tin Hill, from which you have a fine View to the right.

At Bradwardine was formerly a Caftle, but now deftroyed, but the Foundations remain near the Church.

After paffing the Wye at Bradwardine, leave Burbridge Hill to the South; a fine Valley to the North, watered by the Wye, on the north Bank of which are Winforton, and Letton Court, formerly belonging to the Booths, now the Eftate of —— Freeman, Efq. who is much improving the Place. Weft of Winforton, is Whitney, formerly the Seat of the ancient Family of Whitney, now of Tomkins Dewe, Efq.

Beyond Bradwardine, pafs over a high Hill, called Penna Park, in the Parifh of Clifford, belonging to Sir George Cornwall. Here are the Ruins of a Caftle, which was the Eftate of, and gave Name to, the Lord Clifford, afterwards Earls of Cumberland; but was exchanged by them with the Crown, temp. Edw. I. for Skipton in Yorkfhire, ftill enjoyed by their Defcendants.

On the r. of the Road, in the Parifh of Clifford, is the More, now —— Penoyre, Efq.

Enter Brecon at the Hay, a Market-Town on a Hill, South of the Wye, where has been a Caftle, now nearly deftroyed, and a Houfe is now built on the Seite, belonging to Richard Wellington, Efq.

On the Road from Hay to Brecon is Marflough, feated on the north Bank on the Wye, Gov. Wilkins.

On the l. of Glafbury is the Lodge, Sir Edward Williams.

Farther to the l. fee Talgorth Church, Hill, and Foreft, where are the Remains of an ancient Caftle.

On the l. of Bruntlis is Tregunter, a good Houfe, lately built by Mr. Harris.

Leave the Turnpike Road, about feven Miles from Hay, down a narrow gloomy Lane to the left, which leads to Trevecka, noted for the late Lady Huntingdon's Methodift College, which contains eleven Students, with their Tutor.

Another Foundation is alfo here by Howel Harris, Efq. now in the Hands of his Executors, where feventy Men and Boys are fed, and clothed, and employed in the following Manner: At four in the Morning, Prayers and Preaching; then to work on the Turnpike Road; Breakfaft at eight, Prayers, &c. again, and fo on, Prayers and Work alternately.

LONDON to *Aberiftwith*.

To Wheatley Br. p. 82.	—	48
r. to Foreft Hill	2	50
Stanton	1¼	51¼
Iflip	4¾	56
Blechingdon	2¾	58¾
Enflow Bridge over Cherwell River	1¾	60½
Glimpton	4	64½
Chequer Inn and Kiddington Turnpike	1¼	65¾

H

Or, From LONDON to OXFORD, p. 82.	—	54
Yarnton	4	58
Begbrook	2	60
Woodſtoc	2½	62½
Chequer Inn and Kiddington Turnpike	4¼	66¾
Enſtone	2½	69¼
Chapel Houſe	3¾	73
Wheelbarrow Caſtle	5	78
Four-Shire Stone.	2¼	80¼
l. to Morton in Marſh, *Gloceſt.*	2¼	82½
Bourton on the Hill	1¾	84¼
Broadway	5¾	90
Wickenford Bridge	5½	95½
Perſhore, Worceſt.	6½	102
Stouton	4	106
WORCESTER*	5	111
Broadway	5½	116½
Bridge over Temb. R.	2½	119
Bromyard Heath *Heref.*	4	123
Bromyard	2	125
Bridenbury	3	128
Hockly	2¾	130¾
Eaton	5¼	136
Leominſter	1	137
Kingſland	4	141
Eaſterton	2½	143½
Comb	4½	148
Preſteign, Radn	1½	149½
New Radnor	7¾	157¼
Penybont	10	167¼
Rhayadergowy	10	177¼
At Ecomiſtwith Brook enter *Candiganſhire*	8½	185¾
Mowen Glowth	5¾	191½
Pentre Brunant	1¼	192¾
River Ridal on the *r.*	8½	201¼
Aberyſtwith	1½	202¾

At Blechingdon is the Seat of Arthur Anneſley, Eſq. and a little more to the right is Kirtlington, Sir Henry Watkin Daſhwood, Bart.

Adjoining to Woodſtoc is Blenheim Houſe and Park, a moſt magnificent Seat of the Duke of Marlborough.

To the left of Kiddington is Ditchley Park, the late Earl of Lichfield, now Lord Dillon, his Nephew.

At the foot of Enſtone Town, on r. curious Water-works.

Two Miles beyond Enſtone, to the r. is Heathorpe, Earl of Shrewſbury.

Near Perſhore is Flatbury Hill, commanding a fine View of the Vale of Eveſham.

One Mile to the r. of Kingſland, in Aymeſtice Vale, is Yatton-Court, John Woodhouſe, Eſq.

To the l. of Eaſterton is Shobton-Court, the Seat and fine Plantations of Lord Viſcount Bateman.

Two Miles on the r. of Preſteign is Kynſham, Mrs. Harley, the Widow of the late Biſhop of Hereford.

Between Morton and Broadway, Northwich Park, Sir John Ruſhout, Bart.

At 202, ſee on r. the Town of Llanbader Vawr.

Three Miles from Aberyſtwith is Nantcos, Thomas Powell, Eſq. and 3 Miles farther is Croſſwood, Earl of Liſburne.

* *Another Road to Worceſter*, viz.

To *Enſtone*, p. 99.	—	69¼
A little before 73, left, to *Chipping Norton*	4¾	74
Salford	2	76
Salford Hill	1	77
Four-Shire Stones	3	80

Right cross Fosse way to		
Darnton	2	82
Campden	4½	86½
Willersley	3	89½
Bengworth	4½	94
Cross Avon River to		
Evesham, Worcest.	¾	94¾
Piddle	5¼	100
r. to Speckley	5	105
WORCESTER	4	109

At Campden are the Remains of a noble House, built by Sir John Baptist Hickes, burnt down in the Civil Wars to prevent its being made a Garrison for the Parliament's Army.

To *Oxford*, p. 82.	—	54
Wolvercot	2	56
Yarnton	1¾	57¾
Begbrook	2¼	60
Woodstoc	2	62
Kiddington Turnpike	4	66
Enstone	2	68

To Wheatley Br. p. 82.	—	48
Islip, p. 98.	8	56
Blechingdon	3	59
Enslow Bridge	1½	60½
Deddington	9	69½

To *Morton*, in Marsh, p. 99.	—	82½
Winchcomb, *Glocest.*	10½	93

To WORCESTER, p. 99.	—	111
Fennel Green	3	114
Droitwich	4¼	118¼

To *Presteign*, p. 99.	—	149½
New Radnor	7½	157
Builth, Brec.	14	171
Bringwin	12	183
Dole Goch, *Card.*	8½	191½
Tregarron	11	202½

Near Radnor, a Cascade, called Water-break-neck.

To *Presteign*, p. 99.	—	149½
Knighton	5½	155

LONDON to *Montgomery*, *Welsh Pool*, *Harleigh*, and *Caernarvon*, continued to *Holyhead*.

To WORCESTER, p. 99.	—	111
Hallow Park and Village	3	114
Hundred House	6¼	120¼
Stocton	3	123¼
Lynbridge	2½	125¾
Newnham Bridge	1¾	127½
Tenbury	3	130½
Burford, *Shropsh.*	1	131½
Ludlow	6½	138
Oniberry	5	143
Newton	2½	145½
Barford's Gate	2¾	148¼
Bishop's Castle	4	152¼
Bishop's Mott, *Mont.*	2	154¼
Red House Inn	2¾	157
*Montgomery**	4	161
Welsh Pool †	8	169
Golway Mountain	2½	171½
Llanvaier	5½	177
Cann's Office	7	184
Howel's House	4½	188½
Dynasmouthy, Mer.	7½	196
Vronseth Hill	8	204
Dolgelly	1	205

Llaniltid	1½	206½
Flowerlec Hill	7½	214
Llandura	3	217
Llanbeder	3½	220½
Llanvaier	1½	222
Harleigh	1	223
Crofs the Sands	4	227
Crofs the Sands	3	230
Penmanruay	3	233
Dalbenmer, *Caern.*	2½	235½
Llanlaveney	7½	243
Llanuda	4	247
Newbridge	1½	248½
Caernarvon	3	251½
Crofs Abermeney Ferry to		
Newburgh, *Anglefea*	6	257½
Aberfraw	5½	263
Boddedar	4½	267½
Holyhead	8½	276

*See the direct Road from London
to Holyhead,* p. 119.

* *Another Road to Montgomery,*
viz.

To *Shrewfbury,* p. 129.	—	154
Lockerton	6	160
Wefpry	2¾	162¾
Montgomery	12¼	175

† *Another Road to Welfh Pool,*
viz.

To *Shrewfbury,* p. 129.	—	154
Crofs Gates	5	159
Rowton	2	161
Trefnant	5	166
Buttington Br. *Mont.*	4	170
Welfh Pool	2	172

LONDON to *Aberyftwith,*
Cardiganfhire.

To *Shrewfbury,* p. 129.	—	154
Welch Pool	18	172
Llanvaier	7	179
Cann's Office	8	187
Mallwyd	12	199
Penegofs	11	210
Machynlleth	1	211
Aberyftwith	20	231

Before Llanvaier, a beautiful View.
A Mile beyond Towyn, on l. Ynyf-
maen gwyn, Edward Corbet, Efq.

LONDON to *Towyn,*
Merionethfhire.

To Machynlleth, *as above.*	—	211
Towyn	12	223

*A Road is made from Towyn to
Barmouth, or Dolgelly.*

LONDON to *Barmouth,*
Merionethfhire.

To Mallwyd, *as above*	—	203
Dolgelly	12	215
Barmouth	10	225

Near Gofylehan, in the Parifh of
Llanerfyll, and about 3 Miles
from Cann's Office, on the Pool
Road, is the Roman Caufey,
which formerly led from Caerfw's
to Caulleon, or the City of Le-
gions, now called Weft Chefter.
It croffes the Roman Road at this
Place, which formerly led from
Uriconium, or Wroxcter, to Se-
gontium, otherwife Caer Segeint,
now called Carnarfore.

On the Church-yard of Llanerfil is a Stone Monument with a Roman Inscription.

Near the Village of Llanerfil stands Llwyfin, with an extensive Park, formerly the Lords Herberts, Ancestors of the present Earl of Powis.

At Cann's Office is a noted Tumulus, or Barrow, which is supposed to be the Monument, and contains therein the interred Body of an antient British Chief. It is surrounded with the remains of an antient Fortification.

☞ The Traveller, on Horseback, who wishes for a most exquisite Prospect, may have it by going from Shrewsbury to Welsh Pool by another Way. Go to Wespry 8¼ Miles on the Montgomery Road, there turn by the Inn on the right Hand, keep a track over the Hill, inclining to the right, and go down to Buttiugton, known by a small Church, and, just beyond it, a wooden Bridge over the Severn. From the Brow of the Hill see the Vale, Powis Castle and Park, the Town, River, &c.

At 3¼ Miles on the left, Onslow, Rowland Wingfield, Esq.

To the l. of the Road, on the River Team, 2 Miles from Ludlow, the fine Seat of Lord Clive, late Lord Powis. Not far from there, Mr. Walpole. Four Miles farther to the l. is Downton Castle, the noble Mansion and fine Walks of Richard Payne Knight, Esq.

At Rowton, on the right, Richard Lyster, Esq.

One Mile beyond Welsh Pool is Powis Castle and Park, Earl of Powis.

From Montgomery to Welsh Pool a new Turnpike Road is made, only 7¼ Miles; it passes Lord Viscount Hereford's, crosses the Severn by Mr. Jones's, and then comes into the other Road.

Cann's, or Cannons Office, now an Inn in Montgomeryshire, was so called, either from having formerly been an Ecclesiastical Office, or else (and indeed more probably) a Military Office, from the Fortifications around it.

To Newton, p. 102.	—	145½
r. to Little Stretton	6	151½
Church Stretton	1½	153

To *Montgomery*, p. 102.	—	161
Newton, *Montgom.*	8	169
Llanydlos	11	180
Machynelth	18	198

To *Shrewsbury*, p. 129.	—	154
Crofs Gates	5	159
Albrefbury	3½	162½
Llandrinis Br. *Montg.*	4½	167
Llanfaint fraid Bridge	5	172
Llanvylling	6	178
Bala, *Merioneth.*	16	194

At 163, on the r. is Loton, Sir Robert Leighton, Bart.

At 166, on the l. Brithen Hill, on the lofty summit of which was erected, in the Year 1782, a pillar in honor of Lord Rodney.

At 176, on the left, is Bayngwyn, William Mostyn Owen, Esq.

At the Entrance of Llanvylling, on the left, is Llwn, Mr. Humffreys.

To *Harleigh*, p. 103.	—	223
Crickieth, *Caern.*	13½	236½
Puthely	7	243½
Newin	6	249½

LONDON to *Stratford on Avon*, by *Banbury*.

To *Uxbridge*, p. 81.	—	15
At 18, *r.* to Chalfont St. Peter's, *Bucks*	6	21
Chalfont St Giles	2	23
Amerſham	3	26
Little Miſſenden	2½	28½
Great Miſſenden	2½	31
Wendover	4	35
Ayleſbury＊	5½	40½
Hardwic	3½	44
Whitchurch	1	45
Winſlow	5½	50½
Padbury	4	54½
Buckingham	2¾	57¼
Tinſwic	2¾	60
Finmore, *Oxfordſh.*	1	61
Honk's Houſe	3	64
Barley Mow, *Northampt.*	1	65
Croughton	1½	66½
Aynho	2	68½
Nell Bridge	1½	70
Adderbury, *Oxf.*	1½	71½
r. to Weeping Croſs	1½	73
Banbury	2	75
Drayton	2	77
Wroxton	1	78
Edge Hill, *Warw.*	4½	82½
Pillerton	4½	87
Upper Eatington	2	89
Stratford on Avon	5	94

Another Road to Stratford on Avon, p. 110.

＊ *Another Road to Ayleſbury*, p. 114.

At 17, on r. Denham, Mr. Way.
At 19, on r. Mr. Churchill.
At one Mile from Chalfont, St. Peter's is Newland Park, Sir Henry Gott; and, on the r. is the Vatch, Sir Hugh Palliſer, Bart.
At Amerſham, on a Hill to r. of the Market-houſe, is the Parſonage.
Beyond, on the left, is Shardeloes, William Drake, Eſq.
At Great Miſſenden, on the right, the Abbey, late Mr. Gooſetrey, now Mr. Oldham. Three Miles l. of Great Miſſenden is Hampden, the ancient Seat of the Family.
About 36, on the right, under the Hill, is Halton Houſe, late Sir John Daſhwood King, Bart.
On l. of 45, Oving, Mr. Hopkins.
At Winſlow, Mr. Lowndes.
Near Buckingham, Stowe, Marquis of Buckingham.
Near 65, to the r. Imley, Mr. Baſſet.
At Aynhoe, Mr. Cartwright.
At Adderbury, Duke of Buccleugh.
At Wroxton, Earl of Guilford.
A Mile before Edge Hill, on l. Upton, late Lady Ducie, now Earl of Weſtmorland; on the right, under Edge Hill, Radway, Mr. Miller; on the Hill, a Tower built by him. From Edge Hill a moſt extenſive Proſpect.

To *Amerſham*, p. 107.	—	26
Cheſham, *Bucks*	3	29

To *Buckingham*, p. 107.	—	57¼
Bracley, *Northamp.*	6¾	64

On the left, between Amerſham and Cheſham, Hyde Lodge, Rev. Mr Hubbard.

Three Miles beyond Buckingham, to the right, is Stowe, the Seat and elegant Gardens of the Marquis of Buckingham.

To *Banbury*, p. 107.	—	75
Kineton, *Warw*	13	88

To *Stratford* on Avon, p. 107.	—	94
Bitford, *Warw.*	6¼	100¼

To *Broomsgrove*, p. 111	—	115
Stourbridge, *Worceſt.*	9½	124½

Near Stourbridge is Hagley, the noble Seat of the late Lord Lyttleton, now Lord Weſtcote.

To *Kidderminſter*, p. 111	—	125
Bewdley, *Worceſt.*	3	128
Cleobury, *Shropſh.*	8	136

LONDON to *Birmingham*, by *Warwic*.

To *Banbury*, p. 107.	—	75
Warmington	4	79
Gaydon	5	84
Warwic *	9	93
Knowle	10½	103½
Solihull	2½	106
Birmingham	7½	113½

* *Another Road to Warwic*, p. 132

From *Banbury* to *Warwic*, another Road, viz.

UpperEatington, p107	—	89
R. by Welleſburn, Montfort, and Hartford Bridge to *Warwic*	10	99

Beyond Hartford Bridge, on the left, Shirburn, Mr. Webb.

At Warwic, the Caſtle, Earl of Warwic; and the Priory, Mr. Wiſe.

LONDON to *Birmingham*, the Coach Road.

To OXFORD, p. 82.	—	54
Yarnton, *Oxfordſh.*	4	58
Regbrook	2	60
Woodſtoc	2½	62½
Kiddington	4¼	66¾
Enſton	2½	69¼
Chapel Houſe	3¼	73
Compton Hill	3	76
Long Compton, *War.*	1	77
Burmington	4	81
Barcheſton	1	82
Shipſton, Worceſt.	1	83
Honington, *Warw.*	2	85
Thridlington	2	87
Newbold	2	89
Stratford on Avon	5	94
Wotton	6	100
Henley in Arden	2	102
Boxtrees	5	107
Shirley Street	4	111
Birmingham	5	116

At Woodſtoc is Blenheim-Houſe and Park, the Duke of Marlborough.

At Enſton, the Waterworks.

Two Miles beyond Enstone, to the r is Heathorpe, the Earl of Shrewsbury.

On the r. of Compton Hill is Weston, Sir William Sheldon, Bart.

At Honington, J. Townsend, Esq. and behind it, on the Hill, is Idlicot, Robert Ladbroke, Esq.

At 88, on the right is Lower Eatington, Mr. Shirley's.

At 89, on the left, Miss Parker.

At 91, Oscot Park, Mrs. West.

Half a Mile beyond Stratford, on the r. is Clopton House, Mrs. Partridge.

At 100, Mr. Ulford.

LONDON to *Birmingham*, by *Wycomb.*

To *Chapel House,* p. 110.	—	73
Thence to *Birmingham,* above .	43	116

Other Roads to Birmingham, p. 109 and 110.

LONDON to *Shrewsbury* and *Holywell,* by *Bridgenorth.*

To *Stratford,* p. 107.		—	94
Aulcester,	*Warw.*	8	102
Coughton		2	104
Crab's Cross,	*Worc.*	3½	107½
Tardbec		4½	112
Broomsgrove		3	115
Chedderley		5	120
Winterford		1½	121½
Stone		1½	123
Kidderminster *		2	125
Alam Bridge,	*Shropsh*	7	132
Quat		2½	134½
Quatford		2	136½
Bridgenorth		2½	139

Morvil		3	142
Wenlock		5	147
Harley		2	149
Cressedge		2	151
Cound		2	153
Shrewsbury †		6	159
Sim Hill		5½	164½
Harmer Hill		1	165½
Cockshut		5½	171
Ellesmere		4	175
Overton		4¾	179¾
Dee Bridge,	*Denb.*	2	181¾
Pontfroud		3¼	185
Wrexham		2½	187½
Queenhope,	*Flintsh.*	6	193½
Mould		7	200½
Prin Calon Digry		2½	203
Holywell		8½	211½

Another Road to Holywell, p. 122.

* *Another Road to Kidderminster, p. 113.*

† *Another Road to Shrewsbury, p. 129.*

Another Road to Wrexham is by Whitchurch, p. 127, whence there is an exceeding good Turnpike Road to Wrexham, crossing the Dee at the village of Bangor.

A Mile to the left of Aulcester is Ragley, Marquis of Hertford.

At Coughton, Sir John Throckmorton.

Near Broomsgrove is Hewel, Earl of Plymouth.

At one Mile, on the r. from Morvil, Sir Richard Acton, Bart.

At Cound, Miss Cressett.

Two Miles beyond Cressedge, on the right, is Eyton, formerly the Earls of Bradford.

7

At one Mile on the r. this Side of Ellesmere, is Oatley Park, Mrs. Vaughan; on the l. Birch Hall, belonging to the Family of the Leeds; and near it, on the left, Hardwicke, Major Halliday.

To the South, one Mile and a Half from Wrexham, is Erthig, Philip Yorke, Esq. and one Mile to the North lies Acton, Sir Forster Cunliffe, Bart. formerly the Jeffries, of which Lord Chancellor Jeffries was a younger Son.

On the l. of Queenhope is Cargurrel's Castle; and two Miles farther is Trevalin, late Sir John Trevor, Knight, Secretary of State to Charles II.

Three Miles on this Side of Holywell is Mostyn, Sir Roger Mostyn, Bart. and near it Mr. Williams.

From Bridgenorth *to* Shrewsbury, *far the best Way, and now by much more the common Road, is*

To *Bridgenorth*, p. 111.	—	139
Iron Bridge cross the Severn	8½	147½
Leighton	4½	152
Atcham	4	156
Shrewsbury	3½	159½

At Leighton is Sir Rob. Leighton, Bart.

LONDON to *Kidderminster*, by *Birmingham.*

To *Birmingham*, p. 110	—	116
Hales Owen	8	124
Hagley	3½	127½
Stourbridge	2½	130
Kidderminster	4	134

Another Road, p. 109.

Before Hales Owen is the Leasowes, the famous Mr. Shenston's, late Major Halliday.

At Hagley, late Lord Lyttelton, now Lord Westcote.

LONDON to *Bicester*.

At the Turnpike, *r. to* Paddington, *Midd.*	—	¾
Kilburn	2	2¾
Hyde	3½	6¼
Edgeware	1¾	8
Stanmore	2	10
Bushy, *Herts*	3	13
Watford	1½	14½
Hunton Bridge	3¼	17¾
Kings Langley	1¾	19½
Two Waters	2	21½
Boxmoor	1½	23
Bourn End	1	24
Berkhamstead	2	26
Tring	5	31
Aston Clinton	3	34
*Aylesbury**	4	38
Waddesdon	5	43
Ham Green	3	46
Black-Thorn Heath	5	51
Bicester	3¼	54¼

* *Another Road to Aylesbury*, p. 107.

From Edgware to Stanmore, on l. is Cannon's Park, where the late Duke of Chandos's Father built a most magnificent House, which after his Death, was pulled down, and sold by piecemeal: the Park became the Property of the late Mr. Hallet, an Upholster in London, who built an elegant House near the same Spot where the Duke's stood, which has been lately sold; now Mr. O'Kelly.

At Stanmore on the l. late Mr. Drummond, Banker.

Before 11, on the r. late Col. Chauvell, and a little farther, almoft adjoining, is late Mr. Capadocia, now Major Torriano; on the l. a Houfe built by Mr. Duberley, and now occupied by the Marquis of Abercorn. In the Bottom, a large Houfe, called Thieves Hole, built by Mr. Gray, a Brickmaker.

A little beyond Watford, on the left, is Cafhiobury Park, the Earl of Effex.

Near 17, on the l. the Grove, Earl of Clarendon; on the r. Ruffel Farm, Dowager Countefs of Effex; a little beyond, on the l. Langly Bury, Sir John Filmer, Bart.

At 23, Boxmoor Hall, built by Mr. Almon, Bookfeller.

At the End of Boxmoor, on the l. is a Seat of P. L. Luard, Efq.

At 30, on the r. is Penley Hall, Mr. Harcourt's.

At 30½, on the r. is Tring Grove, Mr. Scare's.

At 31, on the l. is Tring Park, a moft beautiful Seat of Mr. Drummond Smith's.

At 32, on the l. is Terret Houfe, Colonel Leake's.

At 45, on the l. is Lady Saye and Sele's.

At 47, on the left, is Wotton Underwood, Lord Grenville.

To Watford, p. 114.	—	14½
Hunton Bridge	3½	18
Belfwains	2½	20½
Hemel Hempftead	2	22½
Ivingho, Bucks	9½	32

Another Road, viz.

To K. Langley, p.114.	—	19½
Two Waters	2	21½
r. to H. Hempfted	1½	23
Ivingho, Bucks	9½	32½

To Watford, p. 114.	—	14½
l. to Ricmanfworth	3	17½

Another Road to Ricmanfworth.

To Stanmore, p. 114.	—	10
l. to Hatch End	2	12
Pinner Green	2	14
Right beyond Windmill over the Common to		
North Wood	2	16
Bacher Heath	1	17
By Moore Park to Ricmanfworth	1½	18½

At Stanmore, on the left, late Mr. Drummond, Banker.

At 15, on the right, Pinner's Hill, Mr. Cochran.

Moore Park, Sir Thomas Dundas, Bart.

At Ricmanfworth, Bury Park, W. Field, Efq.

LONDON to Harrow on the Hill.

To Paddington	—	¾
l. to Weftern Green	¾	1½
Kinfel Green	1½	3
Holfden Green	1¾	4¾
Fortune Gate	½	5¼
Wembley Green	1¾	7
Harrow	3	10

At Weftern Green, — Colfton, Efq.

One Mile before Harrow on r. —— Halliday, Esq. and just beyond him the Right Hon. Thomas Orde.

LONDON to *St. Albans*, by *Edgeware*.

To *Edgeware*, p. 114	—	8
Brocley Hill	2	10
Elstree (or Idlestree)	1	11
Radlet	3	14
Colney Street	2¼	16¼
Frogmore	1	17¼
St. Stephen's	1	18¼
St. Albans	1½	19¾

St. Albans by Barnet, p. 119.

At Elstree, Mrs. Reeves.

At 13, on the right, Kendall's Hall, Mr. Phillimore.

A little before St. Stephen's, on the l. St. Juliens, Mrs. Ashhurst.

At St. Albans is Holloway House, late Duchess of Marlborough, now Countess Dowager Spencer's.

LONDON to Hampstead, Hendon, and Mill-Hill.

From Holborn Bars to Battlebridge	—	1
Pancras	½	1½
l. to Mother Red-Cap's	¾	2¼
Haverstoc Hill	¾	3
Hampstead	1¼	4¼
Northend	¾	5
Goulders Green	1	6
Hendon	1	7
Mill Hill	2	9
Or, From		
Tottenham Court to Mother Red-Cap's	—	1
l. to Hampstead	2	3
Hendon, *as above*	2¾	5¾
Mill-Hill	2	7¾

At Hampstead, see, on the right, Caenwood, Earl of Mansfield; and Fitzroy Farm, Lord Southampton.

III.

GREAT AND DIRECT ROADS

Meaſured from HICKS'S HALL:

With the ROADS branching from them to Market and Sea-Port TOWNS.

LONDON to CHESTER and *Holyhead*.

To Iſlington, *Midd.*	—	1
Holloway	2	3
Highgate	1¼	4¼
Whetſtone	4¾	9
Barnet, Herts	2	11
The Obeliſk, *Mid.*	¾	11¾
l. to Kitt's End	½	12¼
South Mims	2¾	15
Colney, *Hertf.*	3¼	18¼
*St. Albans**	3	21¼
Redburn	4¼	25½
Market Street	4	29½
Dunſtable, Bedf	4	33½
Hockliff	4¼	37¾
Brickhill, *Bucks*	5¼	43
Fenny Stratford	2	45
Hartford Bridge	2	47
Shenley End	1½	48½
Stoney Stratford	3½	52
Old Stratford, *N.amp.*	½	52½
Potters Pury	2½	55
Heavencott	4	59
Towceſter	1	60
Foſter's Booth	3½	63½
Weedon	4½	68
Daventry	4	72
Drayton	1	73
Braunſton	2	75
Berry Bridge	½	75½
Willoughby	1½	77
Dunchurch, *Warw.*	3	80
Dunſmore Heath	2¾	82¾
Croſs Foſſe Way	1¾	84½
Knightly Croſs	½	85
Ryton	1½	86½
Ryton Bridge	1	87½
COVENTRY †	3½	91
Auſley	3	94
Meriden	4	98
r. to Coleſhill	5	103
Curdworth Bridge	2½	105½
Wiſhaw Green	2	107½
l. to Baſſet's Pole, *Staff.*	4½	112
Weeford	2½	114½
Swinfen	1½	116
LICHFIELD	2¾	118¾
r. to Longdon Green	3¼	122
Longdon	¾	122¾
Bruerton	2	124¾
Rugeley	1¼	126
Wolſeley	2¼	128¼
l. to Millford	3¾	132
Stafford	3½	135½

Great Bridgeford	3¼	138¾
Walton	1¾	140½
Eccleshall	2	142½
Broughton	5¼	147¾
Muckleston	3¾	151½
Knighton	2	153½
Wore, *Shropsh.*	1½	155
Or,		
From *Rugeley*, p. 120, to Wolseley	2¼	128¼
Right across the Trent to Colwich	¾	129
Great Haywood	1½	130½
Shirleywich	2½	133
Sandon	3	136
Stoke	2¾	138¾
Stone	1	139¾
Darlaston	1¾	141½
l. to Sandiford	2	143½
l. to Stableford Bridge	3	146½
l. to Pipe Yate, *Shrop*	5½	152
Wore	1	153
Bridgemore, *Chesh.*	2	155
Walgherton	3	158
Stapley	1¾	159¾
Nantwich	2¼	162
Acton	1	163
Hurlstone	1¼	164¼
Bar Bridge	1¼	165½
Highway Side	2½	168
Tarperley	3	171
Utkinton	1½	172½
Clotton	1	173½
Dudden	1	174½
Tarvin	1½	176
Stanford Bridge	1½	177½
Boughton	3	180½
CHESTER ‡	1	181½
Bretton, *Flintsh.*	4½	186
Hawarden	2	188
Pantry Bridge	3	191
Northorp	2	193
Holywell ‖	6	199
ST. ASAPH §	11	210
Abergeley, Denb.	8	218
Conway, alias *Aberconway*, Carn.	12	230
Over Penman Ross, and Penman Mawr Mountains, to Llandegay	12	242
BANGOR	4	246
Bangor Ferry	2	248
Llangavenny, *Angl.*	7½	255½
Gwyndu	5	260½
Holyhead	12½	273

Other Roads to Holyhead, p. 102, 125, *and* 126.

* *To St. Albans, by Edgware*, p. 117.

† *Lord Aylesford having turned the Road which used to go by Packington through his Park, it is now twelve Miles from Coventry to Coleshill, instead of eleven as formerly.*

‡ *Another Road to Chester*, p. 127.

‖ *Another Road to Holywell*, p. 111.

§ *Another Road to St.* ASAPH, viz.

To Northorp, *as above*	—	193
Caerwis	10	203
St. ASAPH	5	208

At Kitt's End, on r. G. Bing, Esq. and Mr. Barouneau.

At 13, on the r. Dancer's Hill, Capt Allen; and, a little before it, Governor Hornby.

On the l. of Kitt's End is Derehams, formerly the Earl of Albemarle, now of Capt. Bethel.

Before Mims, on r. Mr. Vincent.

Beyond 15, to the right, is North Mims, Duke of Leeds.

To the r. of 17, Tittenhanger Park, the Earl of Hardwicke.

At St. Alban's is Holloway House, a Seat belonging to the late Duchess of Marlborough, now to Countess Dowager Spencer.

On the left of 23, Gorehambury, Lord Viscount Grimstone.

Near Market-Street, on r. is Market Cell, Mr. Coppin, formerly a Nunnery of Benedictines.

On the left of Dunstable is Eaton Bray, Mr. Beckford.

Beyond Hockliff, on l. T. Gilpin, Esq.

At 39, on the r. is Battlesden, the late Sir Gregory Page, Bart.

At Old Stratford, on the r. is Losgrove, Mr. Mansell's.

Beyond Potter's Fury, on l. Wakefield Lodge, the D. of Grafton.

At Havercourt, on the r. is Stoke-Park, Mrs. Jolliffe.

On the r. of Towcester is Easton Neston, the Earl of Pomfret.

At 1½ from Towcester, on the l. is Braddea, Mr. Ives.

At 2 Miles from Foster's Booth, on the r. is Rugbroke, Mr. Warren's; and ½ Mile farther is Lower Heyford, Rev. Henry Jephcott's

At 67½, on r. is Flower, Mr. Kirby; on left, Stowe, Dr. Lloyd.

On the left of Daventry is Fawsley, a Seat of the antient Family of the Knightleys.

Near Daventry is Burrow Hill, a Roman Camp.

At Daventry, on the right, is Norton, Mr. Breton's; and just beyond it, on the left, is Arbury Hill, Mr. Parkhurst's.

At 1 Mile from Drayton, on the r. is Welton, Mr. Clark's.

At 82½, Dunsmore Heath, where Guy, Earl of Warwic, killed the Dun Cow, is inclosed.

At 93, Ansley, Mr. Neal.

At Meriden, on the l. opposite the Inn, W. Digby, Esq.

At 99, on r. is Packington Hall, Earl of Aylesford.

At Coleshill, Wriothesley Digby, Esq.

At 105½, on the r. is Ham's Hall, C. Adderley, Esq.

At 106½, on the r. is Moxhull Hall, A. Hacket, Esq.

Two Miles beyond, on the r. is Middleton Hall, Lord Middleton.

At 113, on the r. is Canwell Hall, Sir R. Lawley, Bart.

At 116½, Swifen Hall, J. Swifen, Esq.

At 122, on r. a House of Mr. Cobb.

Before Wolseley Bridge, on the l. is Hagley, Mr. Courzon.

At Wolseley Bridge is Wolseley Hall, Sir Wm. Wolseley, Bart. Opposite is a handsome Brick House, Mr. Sneyd.

Beyond Wolseley Bridge, on l. is New Hall, or Oak Hedge, late Mr. Whitby's, now Mr. Anson.

Farther on the r. is Shuckborough, Mr. Anson, a fine Building, with a great Variety of Wood and Water.

To the l. a Mile beyond Haywood, is Tixall, Mr. Clifford.

At Sandon, late Lord Arch. Hamilton, now Lord Harrowby. About four Miles off is Chartley, the antient Seat of the Ferrers.

A Mile farther, left, Ingestree Hall, Earl Talbot.

On the left, a Mile beyond Nantwich, is Woodnay, the Family of Wilbraham.

On the right, about 6 Miles from Nantwich, is Marton-Sands, Sir Thomas Fletewood, Bart.

At Sandiford, on the right, Trentham Hall, Marquis of Stafford's.

Three Miles beyond St. Asaph, on the r. Kinmel House and Park, David Roberts, Esq.

To Holywell, p 122.			199
Newmarket,	Flintfh.	7	206
Rudland	.	5	211
Abergeley,	Denb.	5	216

LONDON to Bangor and Holyhead, by Shrewsbury.

To Shrewfbury, p. 129.			154
Montford Bridge		4	158
Enfdon		2	168
Nefcliff		2½	162½
Ofweftry		9½	172
Llangollen,	Denb.	12	184
Corwen		12	196
Kenniogga		13	209
Llanrooft		11	220
Conway		12	232
Bangor Ferry		17	249
Crofs to Anglefea			
Gwyndy		12½	261½
Holyhead		12½	274

N. B. *The above is hard, fmooth, level, Road, and extremely pleafant. A Coach goes conftantly the above Road from Shrewfbury, it being paffable at all Times.*

Road from Ofweftry to Cynfel, viz.

To Ofweftry, above		172
Llangollen	14	186
Corwen .	10	196
Bala	13	209
Cynfel	16	225

One Mile on the r. beyond Shrewf-bury, fee acrofs the Severn, Ber-wic, Thomas Jeff Powis, Efq.

At 14½, on the l. is Afton, Rev. Mr. Lloyd.

On the l. about four Miles beyond Ofweftry, is Chirk Town and Caftle, the Seat of Richard Myddleton, Efq.

Near Llangollen, on the r. is Caftle Dinas Bran, famous in Hiftory.

About two Miles from Llangollen, on the r. are the Ruins of a very large Abbey, well worth the Notice of the curious in Antiquity.

About a Mile farther, on the r. are the Ruins of the Palace of Owen Glyndwr; and alfo Llanfillio, the Seat of Thomas Jones, Efq.

About a Mile farther, on the right, the Village of Llan St. Praid.

On the r. Half a Mile this Side of Caer y' Drudion, is the famous Citadel of the Druids, whereto Caractacus retired after his Defeat at Caer Caradoe.

Between Corwen and Kenioge-Mawr is a famous Stone Cheft of the Druids; near Kenioge, the Seat of —— Kenryck, Efq.

At Llanrwft is a Bridge over the River Conway, built by Inigo Jones, and faid to be his Mafter-Piece.

On the left of Llanrwft is Gwyder, a Seat of the Duke by Ancafter.

Another Road to Holyhead, viz.

To Northorp, p. 122		193
Cravatelough	1½	194½
The Smelt Mills	5½	200
Pontriffith Br. Denb.	5	205
Denbigh	3	208
Hen Llan	2½	210½
Llanwith	3½	214
Pontgwithy Bridge	2	216
Bettws	3	219
Dolven Bridge & Mill	1½	220½
Crofworth	6	226½
Conway Ferry	1½	228

Aberconway, Caern.	¾	228¾
When the tide is out, keep to the r. over a Skirt of Penman-Vechan Mountain, and along the Sands to Meney Straits, where you ferry over to		
Beaumaris, Angl.	12	240¾
Tincohet	5¼	246
Hildravaught Mill	3½	249½
Llangaveney	1½	251
Massalan	4½	245½
Rudbrand Bridge	2¼	257¾
Boddedar	2¼	260
At 1¼ Mile farther the Road divides, where you keep to the r. over Clevenk Sands, if the Tide is out; otherwise turn to the left, or pass straight over the Rocks and Sands to		
Holyhead	8¾	268¾

LONDON to *Parkgate by the Coach Road to* CHESTER.

To Meriden, p. 120.	—	98
l. to Bacon's Inn	6½	104½
Castle Bromwich	1½	106
Over Sutton Colefield Heath to		
Swan and Harp Inn at Stonal, *Staff.*	10	116
Norton	5	121
Straitway	2½	123½
Four Crosses Inn	1	124½
Ivetsey Bank	7½	132
Weston	2	134
Parney Corner	2	136
Woodcot, *Shrop.*	1½	137½
Chetwyn Aston	1½	139
Newport	1	140
Stafford Bridge	4	144
Hinstoc	2	146
Shackeford	2	148
Stocke Heath	2	150
Ternhill	2	152
Blatchley	1¼	153¼
Sandford	2¾	156
Whitchurch	5	161
Grindley Bridge	1½	162½
Red Lion Inn, *Chesh.*	3	165½
Hampton	1½	167
Broxton	3	170
Barnhill	1	171
Hendley	2	173
Golbourn Bridge	1	174
Hatton	1½	175½
Rowton	2	177½
Cristleton	1½	179
CHESTER *	2	181
Mollington	2½	183½
The Yacht	2¾	186¼
Enderton	4½	190¾
Great Neston	1	191¾
Parkgate	1¼	193

* *Another Road to Chester*, p. 119

At Castle Bromwich, an old Seat of Sir Henry Bridgeman, Bart. and two Miles farther, on the r. Pipe Hall, David Davies, Esq.

On the r. of the Heath are Sutton Colefield Park and Woods, and Four Oaks Hall, Hugh Bateman, Esq.

At Norton, on r. Rich. Gildart, Esq.

At 129, on right, Stretton, the Rt Hon. Thomas Conolly.

At Weston, a Seat of Lord Bradford.

At Woodcot, on left, Woodcot Hall, John Coates, Esq.

Before Newport, on left, a Seat of the late Earl Talbot.

One Mile and a Half beyond Newport, on r. Chetwyn, late Robert Pigot, Efq. and two Miles farther, on the left, Stanford Hall, R. Bayley, Efq. At Sandford, on r. Sandford Hall, Rev. Tho. Sandford.

Before Broxton, on l. Broxton Hall, Philip Egerton, Efq.

Beyond Henley, on l. Calvely Hall, Philip Egerton, Efq.

At Chriftleton, on r. R. Townfhend, Efq.

Road from Whitechurch to Feftiniog.

To Whitechurch, p. 128.	—	161
Wrexham	16	177
Davondowy	6	183
Bala	12	195
Feftiniog	16	211

LONDON to *Shrewfbury.*

To Meriden, p. 120.	—	98
Ivetfey Bank, p. 127.	34	132
Wefton	2	134
Oaken Gates, *Shrop.*	6½	140½
Watling-Street	2½	143
Atcham	7½	150½
Shrewfbury	3½	154

Another Road, viz.

To Meriden, p. 120.	—	98
Elmdon	5	103
Birmingham*	7	110
Wednefbury, or Wedgbury, *Staff.*	8	118
Bilfton	3	121
Wolverhampton †	3	124

King's Tetnal	2	126
Shiffnal	10½	136½
Watling-Street	6½	143
Atcham	7½	150½
Shrewfbury	3½	154

Another Road, p. 111.

* *This Road to Birmingham is fhady and good in Summer, bad in Winter; other Roads, p. 111. and 113.*

† *Another Road to Wolverhampton, p. 131.*

At 120, on r. Earl of Dartmouth.

At 123, on left, Patfhull, late Lord Pigot.

At 128, on r. Wrottefley Hall, Sir John Wrottefley.

At 130, on the l. is Patterfhall, Sir Robert Pigot.

At 133, on the r. Tong Caftle, Mr. Durant.

Between Shiffnal and Watling-ftreet, three Miles to the l. the Iron Works, and the Iron Bridge in Coalbrook Dale.

At Shefnall, on r. Haughton Hall, Mr. Brooke.

At 144, on the right, Orleton, Mr. Cludd.

Before Atcham, on the right, Attingham, Tern Hall, Lord Berwic.

N. B. *There is a Road from Shefnal to Shrewsbury by the Iron Bridge.*

LONDON to *Shrewsbury*, and beyond, through *Birmingham.*

To Birmingham, p. 110	—	116
Wolverhampton	14	130
Shiffnal	12	142

K

Hay Gate －	8	150
Shrewsbury	10	160
Llanhyod	26	186
Llangunog ‧	6	192
Bala	11	203
Festiniog ‧	16	219

LONDON to *Wolverhampton*, by *Walsall*.

To Meriden, p. 120.	—	98
Bacon's Inn, *War.*	6½	104½
Castle Bromwich	1½	106
Over Sutton Colefield Heath to		
Walsall *Staff.*	10	116
Willenhall	3	119
Wolverhampton	3	122

To *Birmingham*, p. 129	—	110
Smethwic, *Staff.*	4	114
Oldbury	3	117
Dudley	3	120
Kinver	8	128

On l. of Smethwic is Hales Owen, Seat of the late Lord Dudley.
Near Dudley is Dudley Castle, Viscount Dudley and Ward, who has a Seat at Himley.

Castle Bromwich, p 127	—	106
Sutton Colefield	5	111

LONDON to *Manchester*, by *Macclesfield*.

To Sandon, p. 121.	—	136
Hilderston	3½	139½
Cellar Head	8½	148
Cheddleton	3½	151½
Leek	3	154½

Bosley, *Chesh.*	7½	162
Macclesfield	9½	171½
Hope Green	6	177½
Poynton	1	178½
Norbury	1	179½
Stocport	4	183½
Manchester, Lanc.	6½	190

At 5 Miles from Macclesfield, on the l. is Adlington Hall, a Seat of the late John Lee, Esq.

At Poynton, on the r. is a Seat of Sir George Warren.

Another Road, viz.

To Holmes Chapel, p. 136.	—	165
Knutsford	8	173
Bucley Hill	3	176½
Altringham ‧	4	180½
Cross Street	3½	183½
Manchester＊	3½	187½

＊ Another Road to Manchester, by Derby, p. 144.

Near Altringham is Dunham Hall, a Seat of the Earl of Stamford.

To Four Crosses Inn, p. 127.	—	124½
Spread Eagle, *Staff.*	2½	127
r. to Penkridge.	2½	129½

To Four Crosses Inn, p. 127.	—	124½
Brewood, *Staff.*	5	129½

To *Dunstable*, p. 119.	—	33½
Ampthill	12	45½

To *Dunstable*, p. 119.	—	33½
Leighton Buzzard	7½	41

To *Daventry*, p. 120.	—	72
l. to Southam, *War.*	11	83
Warwic	10	93

Another Road, p. 110.

To Wishaw Green, 120	—	107½
r. to Tamworth, *Staff.*	6½	114
Elford	4½	118½
Wichnor Bridges	4½	123
Branston	4½	127½
Burton upon Trent	2	129½
Horninglow	1½	131
Tutbury	3	134

Another Road to Burton, viz.

To COVENTRY, p. 120	—	91
Nuneaton	8¼	99¼
Manchester	3	102¼
Atherston	2	104¼
Sheepy, *Leicest.*	3	107¼
Twycross.	2¼	109½
Snareston	3½	113
Crichet's Inn	3½	116½
Over Seal	1½	118
Castle Greasley, *Derb.*	2	120
Stapenhill	3	123
Burton, Staff.	1	124

Another Road to Atherston, p. 148.

Other Roads to Tamworth, p. 148.

At Manchester, Oldbury, Mr. Okeover, and a Roman Station.

To Snareston, *above*	—	113
Ashby de la Zouch, Leicest.	6	119

Another Road to Ashby de la Zouch.

To *Leicester*, p. 145.	—	98
Grooby	4	102
Markfield	3	105
Huclescote	4½	109½
Raunston	2½	112
Ashby de la Zouch	3	115

At Raunston, Mr. Fisher.

To LICHFIELD, p. 120	—	118¾
Abbots Bromley	10½	129¼
Uttoxeter	6¾	136
Checley	5½	141½
Cheadle	4½	146
Leek	10	156

To Cheadle, *as above*	—	146
Ipstones, *Staff.*	4½	150½
Onecote	4	154½
Longnor	7½	162
Buxton, *Derb.*	5	167

To *Eccleshall*, p. 121.	—	142½
Drayton, *Shropsh.*	11½	154

Near Eccleshall, the Bishop of Lichfield and Coventry has a Seat, called Eccleshall Castle.

To *Leek*, p. 131.	—	154½
Pool End	1½	156
Congleton, Chesh.	8	164

To Swan and Harp Inn, at Stonal, p. 127	—	116
Cannoc, *Staff.*	7½	123½

To *Whitchurch*, p. 128.	—	161
Malpas, *Cheſh.*	5	166
To CHESTER, p. 128.	—	181
Star-Chamber Ale-houſe, *Flintſh.*	7¼	188¼
Flint	5	193¼
To *Shrewſbury*, p. 130.	—	154
Wem, *Shrop.*	10½	164½
To *Wrexham*, p. 112.	—	187½
Ruthyn, *Denb*	18	205½
To Tarperley, p. 121.	—	171
r. to Frodſham, Cheſ.	11	182
Haulton	2½	184½

LONDON to CARLISLE.

To Darlaſton, p. 121.	—	141½
Right over the Heath to		
Titenſor	2	143½
Trentham, *Staff.*	1½	145
Newcaſtle under Line	3¾	148¾
Cheſterton	2¾	151½
Talk	2¼	153¾
Lawton	2¼	156
Ordrode, *Cheſh.*	2	158
Knoles	2¼	160¼
Bruerton Green	3¾	164
Holmes Chapel	1	165
Carnage Green	1¼	166¼
Left over the Heath to		
Stublage	2½	168¾
Loſtoc	½	169¼
Lach Green	1¾	171
Laſtocke	1	172
Grulam	1	173
Budworth	1	174
Whitley	2¼	176¼
Stocks	¾	177
Oliſt Hill	3	180
Stocken	1¼	181¼
Warrington, Lanc.	1¾	183
Or,		
From Holmes Chapel	—	165
to Carnage Green	1¼	166¼
r. to Alloſtoc	1½	167¾
Knutsford	5¼	173
Mere	2¼	175¼
High Legh	2¼	177½
Latchford	5½	183
Warrington	1	184
Langford Bridge	1	185
Holme	1½	186½
Winwic	½	187
Newton	2	189
Aſhton	2½	191½
Gooſe Green	2½	194
Wigan	2¼	196¼
Standiſh	3	199¼
Coppen Moor	1¾	201
Welch Whittle	1¼	202¼
Euxton	3	205¼
Cureden Green	3½	208¾
Walton le Dale	2	210¾
Preſton	1½	212¼
Cadley Moor	2	214¼
Broughton Bridge	1½	215¾
Barton	2	217¾
Maſkay Bridge	1½	219¼
Brock Bridge	¾	220
Baugrave	2¼	222¼
Garſtang	¾	223
Ellel	5	228
Golgate Bridge	1¼	229¼
Burrow	1	230¼
Scotforth	1½	231¾
Lancaſter	1½	233¼

Slyne	2½	235¾
Bolton	1½	237¼
Carnford	2½	239¾
Dare Bridge	2	241¾
Burton, Westm.	3	244¾
Holme	1½	246¼
Milthorpe	3	249¼
Heversham	1	250¼
Syzergh	3¼	253½
Kendal	4	257½
Or,		
From *Burton*, above, to Moor End	5½	250¼
Barrow Green	2½	252¾
Kendal	3	255¾
Hause Foot	9	264¾
Shap	6½	271¼
Thrimby	3½	274¾
Clifton	4½	279¼
Eamont Bridge	1½	280¾
Penrith,* Cumb.	1	281¾
CARLISLE, p. 172.	18	299¾

Carlisle by Appleby p. 172.

* *Another Road to Penrith*, p 172.

At Trentham, Trentham-Hall, Marquis of Stafford.

At Lawton, Mr. Lawton.

On r. of Ordrode is Rode-Hall, formerly a Seat of a Family of that Name, now Rich. Wilbraham Bootle, Esq.

At Bruerton, 163, an old Seat, Sir Charles Holt.

Beyond Holmes Chapel is the Hermitage, Mr. Hall.

At 187, is Winwic, the richest Rectory in England, being near 3000l. a Year, in the Gift of the Earl of Derby.

Before Budworth, on l. is Marybury, R. Smith, Esq. a Mere two Miles long.

Beyond Budworth, is Belmont, John Smith Barry, Esq on the right.

On the left, 194, Worsley Hall, Seat of a Family of that Name.

On the r. from Wigan to Standish, is Haigh-Hall, a Seat of the Earl of Balcarras.

On the l. between Euxton and Cureden, is Shaw-Hall, the Seat of William Farrington, Esq.

On the l. near Walton le Dale, is Walton-Hall, Sir Henry Philip Hoghton, Bart.

In Preston, on the r. Earl of Derby.

To the l. of 221, is Myerscough-Hall, James Greenalgh, Esq. and Kirkland-Hall, Alexander Butler, Esq.

On the r. Claughton-Hall, Mr. Brockhole; and nearly opposite is Myerscough-House, Charles Gibson, Esq.

On the r. are the Ruins of Greenall Castle; to the l. Ellel Grange, Edmund Rigby, Esq. and Ashton Hall, Lord Archibald Hamilton.

Before Garstang, on the r. Mr. D. Tower.

Opposite is an Avenue which leads to Mr. Gibson's.

To the l. of 230 is Ellel-Hall, A. Rawlinson, Esq.

At Lancaster, see the Castle and its Improvements, and the New Bridge, which claim the Attention of the Traveller; also the Town-Hall, and the beautiful Stone, of which the principal Buildings are composed.

At ½ a Mile from Lancaster, on the Road over the Moor to Kirkby Lonsdale, is Halton-Hall, William B. Bradshaw, Esq.

Here the Church, the River Lune, and all its beautiful Appendages, form an enchanting Landscape.

At 239, a fine View over the Sands.

About 245, on the r. the Ruins of Borwic-Hall, the ancient Seat of the late Sir Robert Bindloss, Bart.

Entering Burton, on the right, a new House, Major Pearson's.

Near 251, is Dallam Tower, the beautiful Seat of Daniel Wilson, Esq.

A Mile beyond Haverham, Leven-Hall, Earl of Suffolk.

Beyond Syzergh, on the left, Charles Strickland, Esq.

Two Miles and a half beyond Trimby, on the l. New Village, and Lowther, Earl of Lonsdale.

LONDON to *Northwich.*

To *Newcastle*, p. 135.	—	148¾
Talk, *Staff.*	5	153¾
Lawton, *Chesh.*	2¼	156
Dean Hill	3½	159½
Sandbach	2	161½
Booth-Lane Head	1¾	163¼
Middlewich	3½	166¾
Lower Bostoc-Green	2¼	169
High Bostoc-Green	¾	169¾
Davenham	1¼	171
Northwich	1¾	172¾

To *Newcastle*, p. 135.	—	148¾
Keel	2½	151¼
Little Madeley	1¾	153
Betley	3¼	156¼
Gorsty Hill, *Chesh.*	1½	157¾
Namptwich	6	163¾

To Namptwich by Stafford, p. 121.

To *Warrington*, p. 136.	—	184
Prescot, Lanc.	11	195
Liverpool	8	203

Another Road to Liverpool, viz.

To CHESTER, p. 121.	—	181½
Eastham Boathouse	10¼	191¾
Liverpool, by Water	7	198¾

On the r. from Prescot, 2 Miles from the Road, is Knowsley, the ancient Seat of the Earls of Derby.

About the same Distance from the Road, on the l. but nearer to Liverpool, is Croxteth-Hall, a Seat of the Earl of Sefton.

To *Warrington*, p. 136.	—	184
Navigation to Leigh	9¼	193¼

To *Wigan*, p. 136.	—	196¼
Ormskirk	10¼	206½

At Ormskirk, the Church, and the Vault of the Stanley Family.

To *Wigan*, p. 136.	—	196¼
Eccleston	9¾	206

To *Preston*, p. 136.	—	212¼
Kirkham	8¼	220½
Poulton	7	227½
Blackpool	3	230½

Blackpool has a fine Beach, and is a noted Place for Bathing. Near it is Rossall, Bold Fleetwood Hesketh, Esq. and Lytham Hall, John Clifton, Esq.

LONDON to *Whitehaven.*

To *Lancaster* * p. 136.		—	233¼
Bolton		5¾	239
Carnford		2½	241½
Burton,	Westm.	5	246½
Cartmel,	*Lanc.*	14	260½
Hawkshead		13	273½
Warsdale		12½	286
Egremont,	*Cumb.*	13	299
Whitehaven		6	305

Another Road, viz.

To Hawkshead, *above*	—	273½
Warsdale Chapel,		
Cumberland	14½	288
Enerdale	9	297
Whitehaven	5	302

* *In going from Lancaster, if the Tide is out, you may keep to the left, and over the Sands to Cartmel, which is 8 Miles nearer than by Burton; this Road may be also taken in going to Ulverston, Ravenglass, Dalton, &c.*

At Cartmel, see the handsome Gothic Church; and at Haiker, about one Mile farther, is the Seat of Lord George Cavendish, where there are some fine Paintings.

About three Miles farther is Bigland-Hall, the Seat of George Bigland, Esq.

To *Lancaster,* p. 136.	—	233¼
Hornby	11¾	245

At the three-mile Stone, on the r. of the Road from Lancaster to Hornby, East Park-Hall, a Seat of Lord Clifford, which commands a noble Prospect of the Vale. The River Lune serpentizing through the rich Meadows of the Village of Cator, and hanging Woods, whilst Hornby Castle and Church, and the Mountains of Ingleborough rising in majestic Grandeur, form a noble back Ground to as fine a Landscape as the North can produce.

Hornby Castle was once the Seat of Lord Mounteagle, now of John Marsden, Esq.

To *Burton,* p. 137.		—	244¾
Cartmel,	*Lanc.*	15¾	260½
Ulverston		7	267½
Broughton		9½	277
Ravenglass,	*Cumb.*	7¼	284½

Another Road, viz.

To Ulverston, *above*		267½
Kirby		
Cross the Sand to		
Millum		
Bootle	3	
Ravenglass	8	

Near Ulverston, see Furness Abbey, founded in 1127.

At Kirby is a magnificent Seat of the Family of that Name.

To Ulverston, *above*	—	267½
Dalton	5½	273

To *Kendal,* p. 137.	—	257½
Tebay	11½	269
Orton	2½	271½
Hough	7¾	279¼
Burrels	¾	279¾
Appleby	1¼	281

At Appleby the Castle.

Another Road. p. 172.

To *Kendal*, p. 137.	—	257½
Killath	15	272½
Cold Beck	4	276½
Kirby Stephen	5	281½
Brough Sowerby	3½	285
Brough	1¼	286¼
Or,		
To *Kendal*, p. 137.	—	257½
Lincoln's Inn Bridge	8½	266
Sedberg	2¼	268¼
Kirby Stephen	14¾	283

Near Kirby Stephen is Hartley Castle, Sir Philip Musgrave, Bart.

LONDON to *Cockermouth*.

To *Kendal*, p. 137.	—	257½
l. to Stavely	5	262½
Winander Mere	7½	270
Ambleside	1	271
Through Ridal Park to Ridal	2	273
Dunmail Raisestones, *Cumberland*.	4½	277½
Wynthburn Chapel	1½	279
Thurlipot	3	282
Smathod's Bridge	2¼	284¼
Cust	1¾	286
Keswic	1¼	287¼
Braithwait	2¾	290
Lawton	5	295
Cockermouth	4	299
Little Cliffton	5	304
Great Cliffton	1	305
Stainburn	1	306
Workington	1	307

On Winander Lake is Belle Isle, the Seat of John C. Curwen, Esq.

At 273, is Ridal-Hall, Sir Michael Le Fleming, Bart. Here are two fine Cascades, of which the smaller one, from the Summer-house, is truly beautiful.

At Calgarth, near Ambleside, is a Seat of the Bishop of Llandaff; and near the Inn, at Ambleside, a fine Cascade.

To *Penrith*, p. 137.	—	281¾
Hutton	7¼	289
Sebergham Bridge	7½	296½
Rosley	3	299½
Wigton	5	304½
Ware Bridge	2	306½
Holm	4	310½

To *Keswic*, p. 143.	—	287¼
Little Crostwaite	4	291¼
High Side	2	293¼
Orthwaite	2½	295¾
Uldale	2	297¾
Ireby	1½	299¼

To *Penrith*, p. 137.	—	281¾
Salkeld Dyke	7¼	289
Lazonby	1½	290½
Kirk Oswald	1½	292

To *Penrith*, p. 137.	—	281¾
Alston Moor	21¼	303
Haltwesel, *Northumb.*	11¾	314¾

To CARLISLE, p. 137	—	299¾
Brampton	11¾	311½

LONDON to *Manchester* and *Preston*.

To Hockliff, p. 119.	—	37¾
r. to Wooburn	4¼	42
Wavenden, *Buck.*	4	46

Broughton	2¾	48¾
Newport Pagnel	2¼	51
Stoke Golding	4½	55½
Hackleton	4½	60
*Northampton**	6	66
Kingsthorp	1½	67½
r. to Brixworth	5	72½
Lamport	2	74½
Maidwell	2	76½
Kelmarsh	1½	78
Oxendon	2¾	80¾
Harborough, Leic.	2¾	83½
Kibworth	5½	89
Great Glen	2½	91½
Oadby	3	94½
Leicester †	3½	98
Belgrave	1½	99½
Mountsorrel	5½	105
Quarndon, or Quorn	1½	106½
Loughborough	2½	109
Dishley	1¾	110¾
Hathern	1	111¾
r. to Kegworth	3¼	115
Cavendish Bridge	3¾	118¾
Shardlow, *Derb.*	1	119¾
Elvaston	3¼	123
Derby	3	126
Mackworth	2¾	128¾
Langley	1¾	130½
Brailsford	2½	133
Ashbourn	6¼	139¼
Bentley	2¾	142
New Inn	3	145
Newhaven	3½	148½
Hurdlow House	4¾	153¼
Over Street	1	154¼
Buxton	5¼	159½
Whitehall	2¾	162¼
Shaw Cross	2¾	165
Whaley Bridge, *Chesh.*	¾	165¾
Disley-Inn	3¼	169
Hesselgrave	2½	171½
Stocport	4¼	175½
Heaton, *Lanc.*	1½	177
Grimlow	3	180
Manchester ‡	2	182
Bolton	12	194
Chorley	12	206
Preston	10	216

Another Road to Preston, p. 136.

* *Another Road to Northampton,* p. 150.

† *Another Road to Leicester,* p. 151

‡ *Another Road to Manchester,* p. 131.

On the right of Wooburn, Wooburn Abbey, Duke of Bedford.

Beyond Newport Pagnel, on r. Mr. Praed, late Mr. Backwell. At Gayhurst, on the left, Mr. Wright.

At 59, is Horton, late Earl of Halifax, now Sir Robert Gunning.

Between 61 and 62, on the left, is Preston, Mr. Newman.

At 63½, on l. see Sir W. Wake's.

At 64½, on the r. is Queen's Cross, erected by Edward I. to the Memory of Eleanor his Queen; and adjoining thereto is the Seat of Mr. Bouverie.

Beyond 69 is Boughton, on the r. late Earl of Stafford.

At Brixswerth, on l. Mr. Raynsford.

At Lamport, Sir Justinian Isham.

At Maidwell, on r. formerly Sir Wm. Haslewood, late Lord Wm. Russell, whose Daughter married Mr. Seawen, Father of the present Owner.

At Kelmarsh, Mr. Hanbury.

At Hasselbee, George Ashby, Esq.

At 87, on the right, Langton-Hall, Mr. James.

At 89½, on left, Sir Charles Harford.
On the r. Sir George Robinſon, Bart.
A little beyond, at Stretton Parva, Benj. Kidney, Eſq.
At 102, on r. Wanlip, late Mr. Palmer, now Mr. Hudſon.
At 103, on l. Temple Rothely, Mr. Babbington.
At Quorn, Mr. Meynell.
Before Loughborough, on the l. Mr. Tate's, a white Houſe.
Beyond Loughborough, at Diſhley, the late Mr. Bakewell, celebrated for his Improvements in the Breed of Cattle.
On the r. at a Diſtance, Stamford, Mr. Daſhwood; an Obeliſk near the Road is in Grendon Park, Sir Wm. Gordon's, late Wm. Phillips, Eſq.
Near Cavendiſh Bridge is Dunnington Park, Earl of Huntingdon; ſome ſmall Remains of the Caſtle in the Village.
At Sharlow, Mr. Foſbrook.
At Elvaſton, E. of Harrington.
At Macworth, the Seat of Js. Mundy, Eſq.
At Marton, on the right, the Seat of F. N. C. Mundy, Eſq.
At Langley, on the right, Robert Cheney, Eſq.
Three Miles beyond Aſhbourn, to the l. are Oakover, Ilam, and Dovedale; the Road is lately turned to the r. being nearer and leſs hilly, and goes near the ancient Seat of Sir Wm. Fitzherbert, the old Road to Buxton continues, and meets the new one at New Inn Turnpike. At Oakover is the moſt capital Picture known of Raphael; and the romantic Scenes of Ilam and Dovedale lie in the Way to Buxton.
At Buxton, a celebrated Bath.
Beyond Diſley, on the l. Tho. Legh, Eſq. of Lyme-Hall.

At 101, Ardwic Green, a Seat of S. Birch, Eſq. and others.
At Chorley, on the l. Chorley-Hall, formerly a Family of that Name, now Mr. Crompton.

Between Chorley and Preſton, about a Mile diſtant from the latter, is the Seat of Sir Henry Philip Houghton, Bart.

LONDON to *Tamworth*.

To *Northampton*, p. 145		66
Kingſthorpe	1½	67½
l. to Chapel Brampton	3	70½
Creaton	3½	74
Thornby	3	77
Welford	3½	80½
North Kilworth, *Leic.*	3	83½
Miſterton	3	86½
Lutterworth	2	88½
Bitteſwell	1	89½
Clayceſter, *vulgo* } Claybrook	3	92½
High Croſs on Watling-Street	2	94½
At 1¼ farther go off Watling-Street, on right, to		
Burbage	3	97½
Hincley	2	99½
Witherley	6	105½
Atherſton*, Warw.	1½	107
Hall End	4	111
Wilnecote	1½	112½
r. to *Tamworth*	2½	115

At 72½, ſee on a Hill, a Mile to the left, Holmby-Houſe, where King Charles I. was impriſoned by the Parliament Forces.
At 73, on left, Teeton Houſe, Mr. Langton.

At 75, on right, Sir Wm. Langham.
At Misterton, Mr. Franks.
At Claybrook, Mr. Dicey.
Two Miles beyond Hincley, on r. Linely, Mr. Abney.
On l. of Witherley, Oldbury, Mr. Okeover, and Mancester, a Roman Station.

* *From Atherston, another Road to Tamworth*, viz.

To Grendon	—	110
Polesworth	2	112
Glascot	$2\frac{1}{2}$	$114\frac{1}{2}$
Tamworth	$1\frac{1}{2}$	116

At Grendon, the Seat of Lord R. Bertie.
Colesworth is famous in History for its Nunnery; and a Mile to the r. of it is Brancote, Sir Robert Burdett's.
At Tamworth, an ancient Castle belonging to the Earl of Leicester.

LONDON to *Buxton*, by *Brassington*.

To *Derby*, p. 145.	—	126
Keddleston Inn	$3\frac{1}{4}$	$129\frac{1}{4}$
Thro' Keddleston Park to		
Weston Underwood	$2\frac{1}{2}$	$131\frac{3}{4}$
Hognaston	$6\frac{3}{4}$	$138\frac{1}{2}$
Brassington	$2\frac{3}{4}$	$141\frac{1}{4}$
Hurdlow House	$10\frac{1}{4}$	$151\frac{1}{2}$
Buxton	$6\frac{1}{4}$	$157\frac{3}{4}$

To Buxton, by Asbbourn, p. 145.

Keddleston Park, a Seat of Lord Scarsdale; and near it is a medicinal Spring.

To *Northampton*, p. 145.	—	66
Harlestone	4	70
East Haddon	$3\frac{1}{2}$	$73\frac{1}{2}$
West Haddon	$3\frac{1}{2}$	77
Crick	$2\frac{1}{2}$	$79\frac{1}{2}$
Hillmorton, *Warw.*	3	$82\frac{1}{2}$
Rugby	$2\frac{1}{2}$	85
Newbold	2	87
Brinklow	$3\frac{1}{2}$	$90\frac{1}{2}$
Ansty	$3\frac{1}{2}$	94
Nuneaton	5	99
Hincley, Leic.	5	104

Another Road, p. 148.

At $67\frac{1}{2}$, on r. Dallington, Mr. Wright.
At 70, on l. Harleston, Mr. Andrew.
At 71, Althorpe Park, Earl Spencer; and about a Mile to the r. of that is Holmby-House, where King Charles I. was imprisoned by the Parliament Forces.
At Newbold, late Sir T. Skipwith, Bart.

To *Hinckley*, p. 148.	—	$99\frac{1}{2}$
Stapleton	3	$102\frac{1}{2}$
Cadeby	$2\frac{1}{2}$	105
Bosworth (Market)	$1\frac{1}{2}$	$106\frac{1}{2}$

LONDON to *Northampton*, by *Stoney Stratford*.

To *Stoney Stratford*, p. 119.	—	52
r. to Yardley Gobion	3	55
King's Grafton	1	56
Stoke Park	1	57
Queen's Cross	$6\frac{1}{2}$	$63\frac{1}{2}$
Northampton	$1\frac{1}{2}$	65

Another Road p. 145.

On the r. beyond Stoney Stratford, is Cosgrove, Col. Mansell; and the Priory, George Biggin, Esq.

On the r. is Stoke Park, Lady Harriet Vernon.

On the r. of King's Grafton is Grafton House, a Seat of the Duke of Grafton.

At Queen's Cross is the Seat of Mr. Bouverie.

LONDON to *Leicester*, a nearer Way than by *Harborough*, viz.

To *Welford*, p. 148.		—	80½
Husbands Bosworth,	*Leic.*	2½	83
Wigston		10	93
Leicester		3½	96½

A Mile before Leicester, on the left, see Branston-Hall, Mr. Winstanley, and Marfield Windmill, far off, in Charnwood Forest.

To Great Glen, p. 145.		—	91½
Billesden,	*Leicest.*	5	96½

To *Ashbourn*, p. 145.	—	139¼
New Inn	5¾	145
Pike-Hall	4	149
Winster	3	152

To *Manchester*, p. 146.	—	182
Middleton	7½	189½
Rochdale	5½	195

At 185 is Heaton, the Seat of Lord Grey de Wilton, newly built, and is said to have cost 30,000l.

At 188 is Alkerington, late Sir Ashton Lever's, the late Proprietor of the Museum in Leicester Fields.

At 192 is Edw. Gregg Hopwood, Esq

To *Manchester*, p. 146.		—	182
Bury		9	191
Haslingdon		8½	199½
Whalley		8½	208
Clithero		4½	212½
Sawley,	*York.*	2	214½
Gisburn		4	218½
West Marton		5	223½
Church Marton		1	224½
Broughton		2½	227
Skipton		3	230

Other Roads, p. 154, 157.

At Sawley, the Abbey; at Gisburn, Thomas Lister, Esq,

At West Marton, Marton-Hall, Mr. Heber; and Gledstone, Rev. Mr. Roundell.

At Broughton, Broughton-Hall, Mr. Tempest.

Beyond Broughton, on l. Thornton, John Kaye, Esq.

To Haslingdon, *above*	—	199½
Blackburn	7	206½

To Haslingdon, *above*	—	199½
Burnley	12	211½
Colne	6¼	217¾

LONDON to *Leeds* and *Rippon*, continued to *Thirsk*.

To *Loughborough*, p. 145.		—	109
Cotes		1	110
Hoton		1½	111½
Rempston,	*Notting.*	1	112½
Costal		1	113½
Bunny		2½	116
Bradmore		1	117
Ruddington		1	118

Trent Bridge	4	122
Nottingham	1	123
Red Hill	4¼	127¼
Mansfield	9¾	137
Pleasley, *Derb.*	3	140
Glapwell	2	142
Heath	2	144
*Chesterfield**	5	149
Whittington	3	152
Dronfield	3	155
Coal Aston	½	155½
Little Norton	1½	157
Heeley, *Yorksh.*	2	159
Little Sheffield	1	160
Sheffield	1	161
Chapel Town	5¾	166¾
r. to Worsborough	4¾	171½
Barnsley	2½	174
Staincross	3½	177½
Newmillerdam	3½	181
Sandal	1½	182½
Wakefield	1½	184
Newton	¾	184¾
Lofthouse	2¾	187½
Hunslet	4	191½
Leeds	1	192½
Chapel Allerton	2	194½
Moor Town	1	195½
Blackmoor (End of the Borough and Parish of Leeds)	1	196½
Alwoodly Gate	1	197½
Harewood	3	200½
Dun Keswic	1½	202
Spacey House	3	205
Harrowgate	3	208
Killinghall	2	210
Ripley	1	211
South Stainley	2½	213½
Rippon	5	218½

Cross the Leeming Road	4	222½
Baldersby	1½	224
Skipton Bridge	1	225
Cross the North Road to Bushley Stoop	1½	226½
Carleton Miniot	1½	228
Thirsk	2½	230½

* *Another Road to Chesterfield,* p. 155.

At Cotes, an old House, on the left; Mr. Pack's, who lives farther on, on the right.

Beyond Hoton, on the left, Stamford, Mr. Dashwood.

Bunny, Sir Tho. Parkyns; from the Hills beyond, see Wollaton, Lord Middleton, on the left; and, on the left of Bradmore, see Woods of Sir Gervase Clifton, of Clifton.

At Nottingham, the Castle, the Duke of Newcastle.

At Red Hill, enter the Forest of Sherwood; and five Miles farther, on left, is Newstead Abbey, Lord Byron.

A few Miles from Mansfield, Welbec, D. of Portland; Worksop, D. of Norfolk; Clumber, Duke of Newcastle; Thoresby, late D. of Kingston, now Mr. Evelyn Pierrepoint.

At Little Norton, Sam. Shore, Esq.

At Worsborough, on l. Mr. Edmunds.

Beyond Barnsley, on l Mr. Prince of Woolley.

Two Miles beyond Staincross, on the left, Woolley-Park, Godfrey Wentworth, Esq.

At Sandel, Remains of a Castle, where the Father of Ed. IV. was killed.

At Wakefield, a Chapel on the Bridge built by Ed. IV. to his Father's Memory.

At 188, on left, Mr. Proctor.

A Mile farther, on the right, see Methley, Earl of Mexborough.
Before Leeds, on the right, see Temple Newsham, Lady Irvine.
On the r. Gledhow, John Dixon, Esq.
At Harewood, on left, late Lord Harewood.
Gawthorp-Hall, the Remains of a Castle.
At Ripley, on l. Sir John Ingleby.
Beyond Ripley, on the left, a new House, Mr. Maffinger; Mr. Wood, on the right.
See Mr. Weddell's, at Newby, on r.
Near Rippon, Studley Park and Hacfall, Seats of the late Mr. Aillable.

LONDON to *Chesterfield*, *another Road*, viz.

To *Derby*, p. 145.	—	126
Entering Duffield	4¼	130¼
Right to the Bridge over Derwent River	¼	130½
Heage	5½	136
Oakerthorpe	3¼	139¼
Higham	2½	141¾
Stretton	1¼	143
Clay Cross	1¼	144¼
Tupton	1½	145¾
Chesterfield	3¾	149½

To Oakerthorpe, *above*	—	139¼
Alfreton	2	141¼

LONDON to *Manchester*, through *Matloc*, *Bakewell*, and *Chapel in Frith*.

To *Derby*, p. 145.	—	126
Duffield	4½	130½
Belper Lane End	4	134½
Sandy Ford	1½	136
Cromford	4½	140½
l. to Matloc Bath	1	141½
Over Matloc Bridge to *Matloc*	2	143½
Or,		
From Cromford	—	140½
R. cross Dervent River to *Matloc*	2	142½
Hackney Lane	2	144½
Darley	1¼	145¾
Rowsley	2¼	148
Bakewell	3¼	151¼
Ashford	¾	152
Warlow	3½	155½
New Dam	5½	161
Sparrow Pitt	2	163
Chapel in Frith	2	165
Whaley Bridge	3½	168½
Manchester, p. 146.	16¼	184¾

A mile beyond Derby, on r. Darley-Hall, Mr. Holden.
At Cromford, the Seat of Sir Richard Arkwright.
1½ Mile beyond Rowsley, on the r. is Haddon-Hall, Duke of Rutland.
About two Miles from Bakewell, to r. of the Road, is Chatsworth-Park, a magnificent Seat of the Duke of Devonshire.
1½ Mile beyond Wardlow Turnpike turn off on the right, by a decayed Wall, to Castleton, where is the Devil's Arse a Peake, and Mam Tor.

To *Derby*, p. 145.	—	126
Sandy Ford, above	10	136
Wirksworth	3	139

To *Warlow*, *above*	—	155½
Tideswell	2½	158

To Harrowgate, p. 153	—	208
Knaresborough	3	211
Ferensby	2½	213½
Minskip	3	216½
Borough Bridge	1	217½

Between Harrowgate and Knaresborough, on the left, is Bilton-Hall, John Watson, Esq.
On the right, crossing Knaresborough Bridge, is Coghill-Hall, Sir John Coghill, Bart.
At Knaresborough, the Castle and Dropping Well.
On the l. 1 Mile from Knaresborough, Scriven-Hall, Sir T. Turner Slingsby, Bart.

LONDON to *Bedford*, *Nottingham*, and *Skipton*, continued to *Kendal*.

To *Barnet*, p. 119.	—	11
The Obelisk, *Midd.*	¾	11¾
r. to Potter's Bar	3	14¾
Bell Bar, *Herts*	2	16¾
Hatfield	2¾	19½
Welwyn	5½	25
l. to Codicote	1½	26½
Langley	3	29½
Hitchin	4½	34
Shefford, *Bedf.*	7	41
Cotton End	5¼	46¼
Bedford	3¾	50
Clapham	2	52
Milton Erness	3	55
Bletsoe	1	56
Fox Ale-House, * *Northamp.*	4	60
Rushden	4	64
Higham Ferrers	1½	65½
Cross River Nine to		
Irthlingborough	1½	67
Burton Lattimer	4½	71½
Barton Seagrave	2	73½
Kettering	1½	75
Oakley New-Inn	5	80
Rockingham Forest	1	81
Rockingham	3	84
Cross Weyland River to		
Caldecot, *Rutl.*	1½	85½
Uppingham	4½	90
Preston	2½	92½
Manton	1½	94
Oakham †	2	96
Estrop, *Leicest.*	6½	102½
Burton Lazars	2	104½
Melton Mowbray	2	106½
Abkettleby	3¼	109¾
Nether Broughton	2¾	112½
Normanton, *Notting.*	7¼	119¾
Trent Bridge	5¼	125
Nottingham ‡	1	126
Red Hill	4¼	130¼
Mansfield	9¾	140
Pleasley, *Derb.*	3	143
Houghton	1	144
Clown	6	150
Aughton, *Yorksh.*	6	156
Whiston	2	158
Rotherham	2	160
Greasborough	1¾	161¾
Nether Hough	1	162¾
Wentworth	2½	165¼
Wortborough	4¾	170
Barnsley	2½	172½
Darton	3	175½
Bretton	3½	179
Midgley	1	180
Flockton	2½	182½
Highgate Lane	2½	185
Almondbury	2	187
Huddersfield	2	189
Fixby Hall	2	191

Ealand	3	194
Salter Hebble Bridge	$1\frac{1}{4}$	$195\frac{1}{4}$
Halifax	$1\frac{3}{4}$	197
Illingworth	$2\frac{1}{2}$	$199\frac{1}{2}$
Denholm Gate	3	$202\frac{1}{2}$
Thro' Denham Park to		
Cullingworth	3	$205\frac{1}{2}$
Keighley	$3\frac{1}{2}$	209
Steeton	3	212
Cross Hills	2	214
Kildwic	$\frac{3}{4}$	$214\frac{3}{4}$
Bradley ||	$1\frac{1}{2}$	$216\frac{1}{4}$
Shipton in Craven §	$2\frac{3}{4}$	219
Sturton	$1\frac{1}{2}$	$220\frac{1}{2}$
Gargrave	3	$223\frac{1}{2}$
Coniston	2	$225\frac{1}{2}$
Hellifield Cochins	3	$228\frac{1}{2}$
Long Preston	2	$230\frac{1}{2}$
Settle	$4\frac{1}{2}$	235
Giggleswic	1	236
Clapham	6	242
Ingleton	4	246
Thornton	1	247
Hebermount, *Westm.*	3	250
Kirby Lonsdale	3	253
Kearswic	1	254
Chapel House	7	261
Kendal	4	265

* *From the Fox Ale-House there is another Road, over Ditchford Bridge, through Findon, two Miles nearer.*

† *Other Roads,* p. 162, *and* 178.

‡ *Another Road,* p. 153.

|| *From Kildwic the Road is changed, and goes on the Side of the Canal, leaving out Bradley.*

§ *Other Roads to Skipton,* p. 152 *and* 154.

Beyond Potter's Bar, on left, Gibbons, and next Bib Brechman Park, Dr. Sibthorpe.

Beyond Obelisk, on l. Mr. Byng.

At Hatfield, Hatfield House, Marquis of Salisbury.

At 21, on l. Brocket Hall, Lord Melbourn.

At Welwyn, late Mr. Young.

On the right of 28, Knebworth Place, late Mrs. Lytton.

At Hitchin, Sir C. H. Ratcliff, Bart.

Beyond Hitchin, on l. see Lady Salisbury (late Sir Tho.) in a Wood.

Beyond Shefford, on left, Hawn Place, Lord Carteret.

At Cotton End, Mr. Nesbitt.

At Milton Ernefs, the Vicarage was endowed, and Alms-houses built by Sir Edmund Turnor, Knt. in 1695.

At Bletfoe, fome Remains of the Castle, Lord St. John.

Two Miles beyond Bletfoe, on l. is a new brick House at Sharnbrook, Mr. Gibberd; and a little beyond that, a white House, Colworth, Mr. Lee.

On the l. of Rushden, is Knufton-Hall, the Seat of the late Benjamin Kidney, Esq.

At Higham Ferrers, the Remains of a College.

At Irthlingborough, Mr. Taylor.

Half a Mile to the left of 69 is Findon, Sir Wm. Dolben, Bart.

At Burton Lattimer, Mr. Harper.

Barton Seagrave, a Seat of the late Dr. Wilcocks, Bishop of Rochester, now of his Son Jof. Wilcocks, Esq.

Rockingham Castle, a Seat of Lord Sondes.

At Ayton, near Uppingham, Mr. Brudenell.

On r. of Okeham is Burleigh on the Hill, a Seat of the Earl of Winchelsea; and on the right of 102

is Wiffendine, a Seat of the Earl
of Harborough.
Two Miles beyond Melton Mowbray, on the left, in a Seat be-
longing to the Family of Bennet.
A Mile beyond Nottingham, on l.
fee Wollaton-Hall, Lord Middle-
ton; the Approach to it is in the
Road between Nottingham and
Derby, two Miles from Notting-
ham; and more to the r. beyond
it, the late Sir Charles Sedley.
Near Mansfield, are Clumber Park
the D. of Newcastle's; Thorelby,
the late Duke of Kingston's, now
Mr. Pierrepoint; Welbec, and
Bolfover Caftle, D. of Portland;
Workfop, Duke of Norfolk; and
Rufford, late Sir Geo. Saville.
Four Miles beyond Nottingham, on
left, is Belkwood Park.
At 9, on the left, Newftead Abbey,
the Seat of Lord Byron.
Beyond Nether Hough, on the left.
is Wentworth Houfe and Park,
Earl Fitzwilliam.
A Mile beyond Worfborough, you
have a fine View of Wentworth
Caftle and Park, the Seat of the
late Earl of Strafford.
At Bretton on l. is the Seat of Sir
Tho. Blackett, Bart. late Went-
worth.
A Mile on this Side Almoudbury,
is Woodfom-Hall, Earl of Dart-
mouth.
Fixby-Hall, T. Thornhill, Efq.
A Mile beyond Kildwic is Ham
blethorpe-Hall and Park.
At Skipton, the Caftle, E. of Tha-
net.
A Mile to r. of Gargrave, Efhton
Hall, Matt. Wilfon, Efq.
On left of Hellifield, Hellifield-Peel,
Mr. Hammerton.
Between Hellifield and Long Pref-
ton, a Mile on left, over the River,
Halton Place, Tho. Yorke, Efq.

At Settle, between Town and Bridg
on right, Marfhfield, John Parker
Efq.   Near Settle, Ingleborough
Mountain.
At Gigglefwic, the ebbing and
flowing Well, and Bell Hill, Tho-
mas Lifter, Efq.
At Clapham, Chriftopher Clapham,
Efq.

LONDON to *Bedford*, by *Luton*.

To St. Albans, p. 119.	—	$21\frac{1}{2}$
Harpenden	$4\frac{1}{7}$	$25\frac{3}{4}$
Luton	$5\frac{3}{4}$	$31\frac{1}{5}$
Barton Clay	$6\frac{1}{4}$	$37\frac{3}{4}$
Silfoe	3	$40\frac{1}{4}$
Clophill	$1\frac{1}{4}$	42
Wilfhamfted	5	47
Elveftow	$2\frac{1}{4}$	$49\frac{1}{4}$
Bedford	$1\frac{3}{4}$	51

Bedford, by *Hitchin*, p. 157.

At 30, on the right, is Luton Hoo,
the Seat of the Earl of Bute.
On the r. near Silfoe, is Wreft Park,
a Seat of the Marchionefs Grey.
Three Miles beyond Clophill, a little to the Eaftward of the Road
is Hawne Place, late Earl Granville, now Lord Catteret.

LONDON to *Oakham*, by *Wellingborough*.

To *Newport Pagnel*, p. 145.		51
to Sherrington	2	53
Emberton	2	55
Olney	1	56
Warrington	$1\frac{1}{2}$	$57\frac{1}{2}$
Bofeat, Northamp-	$3\frac{1}{2}$	61
Wollafton	3	64
Crofs River Nine	3	67

Wellingborough	1	68
Great Harrowden	$1\frac{1}{2}$	$69\frac{1}{2}$
Ifham	2	$71\frac{1}{2}$
Kettering	$3\frac{1}{2}$	75
Oakham, p. 158.	21	96

To Kettering and Oakham, by Bedford, p. 158.

To the left of Bozeat is Eafton, Seat of the Earl of Suffex.

At Wollafton, Francis Dickins, Efq.

Entering Wellingborough, on the left, Earl Brooke.

At Great Harrowden, a Seat of the late Marquis of Rockingham.

LONDON to *Skipton* by *Leeds.*

To *Leeds*, p. 153.	—	$192\frac{1}{2}$
Headingley	2	$194\frac{1}{2}$
Cookridge	$3\frac{1}{2}$	198
Ot'ey	$4\frac{1}{2}$	$202\frac{1}{2}$
Burley	2	$204\frac{1}{2}$
Ilkley	4	$2c8\frac{1}{2}$
Addingham	3	$211\frac{1}{2}$
Skipton in Craven	6	$217\frac{1}{2}$

Other Roads, p. 152 and 157.

At Cookridge, on the r. Sir Charles Sheffield, Bart.

Before Otley, on the right, fee Farn-ley-Hall, Walter Fawkes, Efq.

From Otley Hill a large Profpect; and fee Wefton, Mr. Vavafour, to the right of Burley.

Four Miles beyond Otley, on the right, Denton-Hall, Sir James Ibbetfon.

On the left of Ilkley are two remarkable cold Baths, near the top of the Mountain much frequented for above 50 Years.

On the r. of Ilkley is Middleton,

---

the very ancient Seat of the Middletons, in whofe Poffeffion it has been 500 Years. They now refide at Stockhill Park, near Wetherby.

At Skipton, the Caftle, E. of Thanet.

To *Bedford*, p. 157.	—	50
Clapham	2	52
Oakley	2	54
Petenham	2	56
r. to Chellington	2	58
Harold	1	59

At Oakley is a neat Seat of the Duke of Bedford.

A Mile to the r. of Harold is Odell Caftle, Sir Willoughby Afton, Bart.

To *Higham Ferrers*, p. 157.	—	$65\frac{1}{2}$
Thrapfton	$9\frac{1}{2}$	75
Oundle	8	83
Cliff	5	88
Stamford	8	96

LONDON to *Harborough* by *Kettering.*

To *Kettering*, p. 158.	—	75
Rothwell	4	79
Defborough	$1\frac{1}{2}$	$80\frac{1}{2}$
Hermitage	2	$82\frac{1}{2}$
Little Bowden	3	$85\frac{1}{2}$
Harborough	$\frac{1}{2}$	86

At Rothwell, (or Rowell) Serjeant Hill.

| To *Kettering*, p. 158. | — | 75 |
| Oakley New Inn | 5 | 80 |

r. to Corby	2½	82½	Biggleswade	3	45
Weldon	1½	84	Nether Caldecot	1½	46½
			Beeston Cross	1¼	47¾
To *Harboro'*, p. 145.	—	83½	Girtford		48
Great Bowden	1	84½	Tempsford	1¼	49¾
Whelham	3	87½	Wiboston	3½	53¼
Slawston	1½	89	Barton Seagon	1½	54½
Hallaton	1	90	Cross Hall	1½	56¼
			Doddington, *Hunt.*	3¼	59¾
To Burton Lazars,			Or,		
p. 158.	—	104½	From Tempsford to		
Thorp Arnold	2½	107	Little Barford	2¾	53½
Waltham	3½	110½	St. *Neot's*, Hunt.	2	55½
			Re-enter the North Road		
			at 57		
To *Nottingham*, p. 158	—	126	Doddington	4	59½
Southwell	13½	139½	*Bugden*, or *Buckden*	1½	61
			Alconbury	5	66
To *Mansfield*, p. 158.	—	140	Weston	¾	66¾
Pleafley, *Derb.*	3	143	Wheatfheaf Inn	1	67¾
Stoney Houghton	1	144	*Stilton**	7	74¼
Bolfover	3½	147½	Norman Crofs	1	75¾
			Water Newton		81
Bolfover Caftle is a Seat of the Duke			Wanſford, *North.*	2½	83½
of Portland.			*Stamford,* Linc.	5½	89
			Cafterton, *Rutl.*	2	91
			Witham Com. *Linc.*	9	100
LONDON to EDINBURGH,			Coltfworth	2	102
by *Coldftream.*			*l.* to Gr. Ponton	4	106
To *Barnet*, p. 119.	—	11	Spittle Gate	3	109
The Obelifk, *Midd.*	¾	11¾	*Grantham*	1	110
r. to Potter's Bar.	3	14½	Gunnerby	1½	111½
Bell Bar, *Hertf.*	2	16¾	Fofton	4	115½
Hatfield	2¾	19½	Long Billington	2	117½
Welwyn	5½	25	Balderton, *Nott.*	4½	122
Woolmer Green	1½	26½	*Newark*	2	124
Broadwater	1½	28	South Mufcomb	2½	126½
Stevenage	3	31	North Mufcomb	1	127½
Graveley	2	33	Crumwell	2	129½
Baldoc	4	37	Carlton upon Trent	1¾	131¼
Bleak Hall	5	42			

M 2

Sutton	2	133¼
Weston	½	133½
Scarthing Moor	1½	135
Tuxford	2¼	137¼
Retford	7	144¼
Barnby Moor	3¾	148
Tarworth	1¼	149¼
Scroby	2½	151¾
Bawtry, Yorksh.	1¼	153
Roffington Bridge	4¾	157¾
Doncaster	4¼	162
Robin Hood's Well	7	169
Wentbridge	3¼	172¼
Darington	1¼	173½
Ferry Bridge	3½	177
Brotherton	1	178
Fairburn	2	180
Micklefield	4	184
Aberford	2	186
Bramham	4	190
Weatherby	3½	193½
Walfhford Bridge	3	196½
Thornvil Royal	3½	200
Boroughbridge	3	203
Ditchforth	6	209
Topcliffe	3	212
Bufhby Stoop	4	216
Sand Hutton	1	217
South Ottrington	3½	220½
Northallerton	4½	225
Lovefome Hill	4	229
Little Smeton	2	231
Great Smeton	1	232
Dalton	4¼	236¼
Croft	1½	237¾
Darlington, Durh.	3	240¾
Cotton-mund Hill	3¼	244
Ayecliffe	2	246
Woodham	3	249
Ferry Hill	3	252
Sunderland Bridge	4	256
DURHAM	3	259
Durham Moor	2	261
Plawfworth	2	263
Chefter-le-ftreet	2	265
Pelaw	1	266
Birtley	2	268
Gatefhead	5	273
Newcaftle, Northum.	½	273½
Gosford	3½	277
Stannington	6	283
Shotten Edge	5	288
Morpeth	1	289
Longhorfley	7	296
Wallingbridge	2	298
Framlington	2	300
Wittingham	8	308
Wooler Hough-head	10¾	318¾
Wooler	1½	320¼
Cornhill	12¾	333
Crofs the Tweed and enter Scotland		
Coldftream, *Berw.*	1½	334½
Greenlaw	10	344½
Tibby's Inn	3	347½
Tirlefton	6½	354
Norton Inn	2	356
Channel kirk Inn	5½	361½
Black Shields Inn at Falla, *Edinb.*	5	366½
Path Head	3½	370
Dalkeith	4½	374½
EDINBURGH	6	380½

Edinburgh by Berwic, p. 173; *by Carlifle*, p. 172; *by York*, p. 174; *by Kelfo*, p. 175.

* *Another Road to Stilton*, p. 192.

On l. a little beyond the Obelifk, is a Houfe built by the late Admiral Byng, now G. Byng, Efq.

A Mile beyond Potter's Bar, on the l. is Gubbins, a Seat of Mr. Hunter; and near Bell Bar is the Houfe of Sir Charles Cox.

On r. of Hatfield is a Seat of the Marquis of Salifbury. It formerly belonged to King James I. who exchanged it for Theobalds.

On the left of 22 is Brocket Hall, the Seat of Vifcount Melbourn.

On the l. of 29, Knebworth-Place, late of Mrs. Lytton.

At Stevenage, a remarkably-built Barn, the ridge of it broad enough to contain a Coffin, which it now does, and is to be feen with the Body of Henry Trigg, a Shopkeeper of that Town, who built it for that Purpofe, and, by Will, ordered his Body to be laid there.

At Bugden is the Bp. of Lincoln's Palace.

From Stilton to Grantham, at every Mile, are Blocks made of the famous Ketton Stone, with 3 Steps, which were placed there by Mr. Boulter, for the eafy mounting of his Horfe, he being a very corpulent Man, and travelled that Road every Week for many Years; each Stone engraved E. B. 1708.

A Mile from Stamford, on the r. is Burleigh-Houfe, the magnificent Seat of the Earl of Exeter, formerly the Refidence of Treafurer Burleigh, in the Reign of Queen Elizabeth. Here is a beautiful Canal; alfo an extenfive Park, which, with the Lordfhip round it, is fuppofed to contain more Game, Hares in particular, than any other Park in the Kingdom. Since the Houghton Collection of Pictures left this Kingdom, the Paintings in this Houfe are reckoned the moft valuable of any.

On the l. is Worthorp, a Seat in Ruins, alfo belonging to the E.

of Exeter. Here is an excellent and plentiful Spring of Water, from which the Town of Stamford is fupplied.

Upon the Hill, from Cafterton, on the l. is the Seat of John Wingfield, Efq.

At Woolfthorpe, a Hamlet to Coltfworth, is the Houfe in which Sir Ifaac Newton was born, whofe Manor and Eftates are now the Property of Edm. Turnor, Efq.

Beyond Grantham, on the right, is Belton, Lord Brownlow's; and a little beyond it, on a Hill, Sifon-Hall, Sir John Thorold, Bart.

From Gunnerby Hill, a great Profpect; Lincoln Minfter on the r. Belvoir Caftle on the left.

Crofs the Trent from Newark, on the r. Wintorp-Hall, Mr. Pocklington.

On the l. Kelham-Hall, Lord George Sutton; and on the Side of the Hill, above it, is Averham Park, another Seat of his Lordfhip's feen from Gunnerby-Hill.

At Carlton, on the r. another Mr. Pocklington.

At Bawtry, on the left, late Mr. Leifter's, now Peter Drummond's, Efq. Brother to Lord Kinnoul.

About two Miles on the right of Doncafter is Wheatley, Sir George Cooke, Bart.

Beyond Doncafter, on the l. on the Top of a Hill, is Cufworth, the fine Seat of Wm. Wrightfon, Efq.

At 3 Miles on right, Mrs. Yarborough's Wood's at Campfmount; and Campfal, the Seat of Bacon Frank, Efq.

About 7 Miles to the left, in a Bottom, is Shelbrook, a Seat of Baron Penryn, and Robin Hood's Well.

At Darrington, Wm. Sotherton, Efq.

On the right of 174½, is Grove-Hall,

Countess Dowager of Mexborough.

On the l. beyond Fairburn, is Ledston Hall and Park, an ancient Seat of the E. of Huntingdon. The Lodge in the Park, which is plainly seen on the Road, commands a fine and very extensive Prospect.

Bramham-Park, to the l. of Bramham, is the Seat of Mr. Fox, late Lord Bingley.

Allerton Park, late Duke of York, now Colonel Thornton, who purchased it of His Royal Highness for £.110,000.

At 13, on the r. Greave Hall, Mrs. Atkinson.

Beyond Topcliffe, on the l. Newby, Lord Grantham.

At 17 Miles from Boroughbridge, on the left, see Hornby Castle, the late Earl of Holderness.

On the right of Chester-le-street, is Lumley-Castle, E. of Scarborough.

Beyond Shotton Edge, on the l Blagdon, Sir M. W. Ridley, Bart.

At Long Horsley, —— Riddell, Esq.

A Mile West of Whittingham, is Ellington Park, Ld. Ravensworth.

Beyond Coldstream, on the r. Hirsel, Ld. Home; on the l. Lees, late Sir John Pringle, Bart. M. D.

Two Miles before Greenlaw, to the right, Marchmont-House, Earl of Marchmont.

Beyond Path-Head, on the r. Preston-Hall, Lord Adam Gordon.

At Dalkeith, on the right, the Palace of Dalkeith, Duke of Buccleugh.

On the left, Jeanfield, —— Douglas, Esq. and Newbattle, Marquis of Lothian.

LONDON to EDINBURGH, by CARLISLE.

To Boroughbridge, p.167	—	203
Kirby Hill	1	204
Union Inn, or York Gate	6	210
Royal Oak Inn	5	215
Leeming	3½	218½
Catteric	6½	225
Catteric Bridge	1	226
Greta Bridge	13½	239½
Bowes	6	245½
Brough, Westm.	13	258½
Appleby	8	266½
Crackenthorpe	2¼	268¾
Kirkby Thore	2¼	271
Sowerby	2	273
Eamont Bridge, Cum.	6½	279½
Penrith	1	280½
High Hesketh	9½	290
Low Hesketh	1½	291½
Carlton	4½	296
Haraby	1	297
CARLISLE	1½	298½
Westlington	6	304½
Longtown	3	307½
Kirk Andrews	1½	309
Langholm, Dumf.	9	318
Redpath	4½	322½
Mosspaul Green, Rox.	5½	328
Binks	3½	331½
Allanmouth	5	336½
Hawic	4½	341
Ashkirk	6	347
Selkirk Selk.	5	352
Cross Tweed to		
Fernyhall	4	356
Crofslee	5	361
Stage Hall	3	364

Bankhouſe		3	367
Middleton	Edinb.	9	376
Leſwade		6½	382½
EDINBURGH		5½	388

To the right of Sowerby, Acorn Bank, Family of the Nortons.

At 4, on the r. from Acorn Bank, is Brougham Caſtle, a fine Ruin; and one Mile farther on the l. is Brougham-Hall, Henry Brougham, Eſq. anciently a Roman Station.

A little beyond Eamont Bridge, on the r. Carlton Hall, Thomas Wallace, Eſq.

To the right of Kirk Andrews, Netherby, Sir James Graham, Bart.

Beyond Langholm, on the left, Langholm Caſtle, Duke of Buccleugh.

Five Miles beyond Langholm, on the r. Dr. Elliot.

Two Miles beyond Middleton, on l. Arniſton, Robert Dundas, Eſq. the ancient Seat of that Family.

LONDON to EDINBURGH, by *Berwic*, viz.

To *Morpeth*, p. 168.	—	289
Caucot	7	296
Felton Bridge	1	297
Newton	2	299
Alnwic	6½	305½
Charlton	6	311½
Wainford	4	315½
Belford	4½	320
Buckton	5	325
Haggerſton	3	328
Tweedmouth	7¼	335¼
Croſs the Tweed to		
Berwic	¼	335½

At 3 Miles, leave Berwic Bounds, and enter Scotland.

Ayton,	*Berw.*	7½	343
Preſt Inn		4	347
Broxburn		13½	360½
Dunbar		1½	362
Belton Ford		2½	364½
Linton		3½	368
Haddington		5	373
Tranent		7	380
Muſſelburgh		4	384
EDINBURGH		5	389

At Alnwic, a Seat of the Duke of Northumberland.

At Broxburn on the r. Broxmouth, Duke of Roxborough.

Before Linton, on r. is Tyningham, a fine Seat of the Earl of Haddington.

Before Haddingham, on the l. Amiſfield, Hon. Mr. Charteris.

Two Miles before Muſſelburgh, on r. Preſton Grange, Earl of Hyndford.

At Muſſelburgh, on the r. Pinkie Houſe, Marquis of Tweedale; and, one Mile and a Half farther, New Hales, Lord Hales.

LONDON to EDINBURGH, by YORK.

To *Ferrybridge*, p. 167.	—	177
Milford	3	180
Sherburn	1¼	181¼
Barkſton	1½	182¾
Towton	2¼	185
Tadcaſter	3	188
Street Houſes	3	191
YORK	6	197
Clifton	1	198
Skelton	3	201

Shipton	2	203
Easingwald	7½	210½
Thormanby	4	214½
Thirsk	5½	220
Thornton in Street	2¾	222¾
Northallerton	9	231¾
Hence to Edinburgh by Coldstream, p. 167.	156	387¾

On the right, betwixt Barkston and Towton, is Scarthingwell-Hall and Park, a Seat of Lord Hawke.

At Towton a famous Battle was fought betwixt the Houses of Lancaster and York.

Beyond Towton, on the l. see Haslewood-Hall, the Seat of Sir Walter Vavasour, Bart. The Situation remarkably fine.

Three Miles beyond Thormanby, on right, is Thirkleby, Sir Thomas Frankland, Bart.

LONDON to EDINBURGH by *Kelso*.

To Wooler, p. 168.	—	318¾
Mindrum Mill	10½	329¼
Kelso, Roxb	9¼	338½
Smallholm	6	344½
Lauder	11	355½
Black Shields	12	367½
Dalkeith	7	374½
EDINBURGH	6	380½

A Mile beyond Kelso, on the left, Fleurs, Duke of Roxborough.

Two Miles beyond Smallholm, on the r. Melerston, the Hon. Geo. Baillie.

At Lauder, on the right, Thirlstone-Castle, Earl of Lauderdale.

LONDON to *Richmond*.

To Catteric Bridge, p. 172.	—	226
Richmond	4	230

Near Richmond is Aske, Sir Thomas Dundas, Bart.

LONDON to *Askrig*.

To *Boroughbridge*, p. 167.	—	203
Kirby Hill	1	204
Union Inn, or York Gate	6	210
At 2½ farther left, to Nosterfield	7	217
Masham	3½	220½
Ellington	2½	223
Jervoise Abbey	2½	225½
Eastwitton	2	227½
Cover Bridge	½	228
Spennythorne	2	230
Harnby	1	231
Leyburn	1	232
Wensley	1	233
Redmire	3½	236½
Carperby	2½	239
Askrig	4½	243½

Another Road, viz.

To *Settle*, p. 159.	—	235
Stainforth	2¼	237¼
Horton	3¼	240½
Old Ing	4½	244
Bainbridge	13½	257½
Askrig	1½	259

At Cover Bridge begins Wensley Dale.

At Spennythorne, William Chaytor, Esq.

Near Wensley is Bolton-Hall and Castle, Duke of Bolton.

At Aysgarth, near Carperby; at Askrig; and in Bishopsdale; are some remarkable Falls of Water.

At Bainbridge, a Roman Station.

Cover Bridge, p. 176.	—	228
l. to Middleham	1	229

At Middleham, the Castle.

To *Baldock*, p. 165.	—	37
Bleak Hall	5	42
Ht 44½ *r. to* Potton	6	48

To the r. of 47 is Sutton, and Sutton Park, a fine Seat of Sir Roger Burgoyne, Bart.

To *Eaton Socon*, p. 166	—	54¾
St. Neot's Hunt.	2¼	57

Another Road, p. 166.

To *Eaton Socon*, p. 166	—	54¾
Great Stoughton, *Huntingdonsh.*	3½	58¼
Higham Ferrers *Northamptonsh.*	12	70¼

Another Road, p. 157.

To *Eaton Socon*, p. 166	—	54¾
Kimbolton, *Hunt.*	8	62¾
Thrapston, *Northamp.*	11	73¾

Another Road, p. 164.

At Kimbolton is a Seat of the Duke of Manchester.

To *Eaton Socon*, p. 166	—	54¾
Great Catsworth, *Huntingdonsh.*	10	64¾
Oundle, *Northamp.*	10	74¾
Cliff	5	79¾

Another Road, p. 164.

To *Stilton*, p. 166.	—	74¾
r. to Yaxley	2¼	77

LONDON to *Oakham* by *Hatfield*.

To *Eaton Socon*, p. 166	—	54¾
l. to Great Stoughton, *Huntingdonsh.*	3½	58¼
Great Chatsworth	6½	64¾
Brynton	2	66¾
Clapton, *Northamp.*	3	69¾
Lyford	2¾	72½
Bennifield	4¼	76¾
Dean Thorpe	3¼	80
Dean	1½	81½
Harringworth	4	85½
Glaytson, *Rutlandsh.*	2½	88
Manton	3	91
Oakham	3¼	94¼

Another Road, p. 163.

At Clapton is the Seat of the late Sir William Dudley, Bart. now of Sir Booth Williams.

At Dean is a Seat of the late Duke of Montague; and on l. of Manton is Martinsthorpe, a Seat of the Earl of Denbigh.

To *Bawtry*, p. 167.	—	152
Hatfield, *Yorksh.*	10½	162½

Thorne	4	166½
Booth Ferry	11	177½
Howden	2	179½
Weighton	12	191½

To *Howden*, above	—	179½
Holm Hall, *Yorksh.*	7	186½
Pocklington	9½	196

To *Bawtry*, p. 167.	—	152
Hatfield, *Yorksh.*	10½	162½
Thorne	4	166½
Snaith	7½	174
Selby	8	182
Cawood	4	186

To Wentbridge, p.167	—	170¼
Pontefract, *Yorksh.*	4¾	175

At Pontefract, Remains of the Castle.

To *Weatherby*, p. 167.	—	191½
Knaresborough, *York*	8	199½
Ripley	4½	204

Another Road, p. 153.

At Knaresborough, the Castle and Dropping Well.

To *Boroughbridge*, p. 167.	—	203
Aldborough, *Yorksh.*	2	205

LONDON to *Leeds* (the new Coach Road.)

To *Newark*, p. 166.	—	124
Kelham, *Nott.*	2¼	126¼
Knesall	7	133¼

Wellow	2½	135¾
Ollerton	1¼	137
Budby	3	140
Worksop	6	146

Or,

From *Ollerton*, above	—	137
Palethorp	2½	139½
Through Thoresby and Clumber Park to		
Worksop	6½	146
Gateford	2	148
South Anston, *York.*	4	152
Todwic	2	154
Aston	1½	155½
Hansworth	4	159½
Darnal	2	161½
Attercliff	1	162½
Sheffield	1½	164
Hence to *Leeds*, p.153	31½	195½

At Kelham, on l. Lord Geo. Sutton.

At Wellow, Sir Wm. Molyneux.

About a Mile, to the left, is Rufford, late Sir George Saville.

Beyond Ollerton, on right, Thoresby Park, late Duke of Kingston, now Mr. Pierrepoint.

At 142, on r. Clumber Park, Duke of Newcastle; and on the l. Welbec-Abbey, Duke of Portland.

Before Worksop, on the l. Worksop Manor, Duke of Norfolk.

At Worksop, Remains of the Abbey.

Near South Anston is Keveton Park, Duke of Leeds.

To the r. of Todwic is Laughton, the Seat of John Hatfield, Esq. remarkable for its fine Spire.

At Aston, a Seat of the late Earl of Holderness, in the present Occupation of Henry Verelst, Esq.

LONDON to *Doncaster* through *Tickbill*.

To *Newark*, p. 167.		—	124
Worksop, p. 182.		22	146
Carlton		3	149
Goldthorp		3	152
Tickbill,	York.	3	155
Wadworth		3	158
Lovershall		1	159
Balby		2	161
Doncaster		1½	162½

To the left of Carlton is Walling Wells, Taylor White, Esq.
At 153, on the left, Sandbec Park, Earl of Scarborough.

To *Askrig*, p. 176.		—	243½
Brickdale		10	253½
Kirby Stephen,	West	8	261½

Another Road, p. 143.

To *Darlington*, p. 167		—	238¾
Cockerton,	*Durh.*	1	239¾
West Auckland		8½	248¼
Bishops Auckland		3	251¼

At Bishops Auckland is the Palace and Park of the Bishop of Durham.

LONDON to *Tinmouth*.

To *Newcastle*, p. 168.	—	271½
Useborn	1	272½
Biker	1	273½
Chirton	4½	278
North Shields	1	279
Tinmouth	1½	280½

Another Road, viz.

To DURHAM, p. 168.		—	257
East Raynton		5	262
Houghton		1¾	263¾
East Harrington		2½	266¼
Bishop Wearmouth		3	269¼
Sunderland		¾	270
Cross the River Wear to			
Monk Wearmouth		—	270
Fulwell		2	272
Cleadon		2	274
Harton		2	276
South Shields		2	278
Cross the River Tyne to			
North Shields,	Northumberl.	—	278
Tinmouth		1½	279½

To *Newcastle*, p. 168.		—	271½
Ponteland,	*Northum.*	7½	279
Camboc		13½	222½
Harwood-head		4½	297
Elsdon		3	300

To *Morpeth*, p. 168.	—	287
Rothbury	15	302

To Wooler, p. 168.		—	318¼
Learmouth,	*Northum.*	10¾	329

LONDON to *Billingham*.

Greta Bridge, p. 172.		—	239½
Barnard Castle,	Durh.	4	243½
West Pits		7	250½
Walsingham		9	259½
Mugglefwic		10	269½
Sleaton,	*Northum.*	9	278½
Hexham		5½	284
Cross the Picts Wall to			
Billingham		13½	297½

To *Boroughbridge*, p. 167.	—	203
Royal Oak Inn, p. 172	12	215

¼ a Mile farther, left to		
Burniston	1	216
Exilby	1½	217½
Bedale	2	219½

To *Walsingham*, p. 182.	—	259½
Frosterley, *Durh.*	3	262½
Stanhope	2	264½

Near Stanhope is Stanhope-Castle, a Seat of the Earl of Carlisle.

To *Hexham*, p. 182.	—	284
Heydon Bridge	6	290
Beltingham, *Northum.*	3½	293½

To *Catterick Bridge*, p. 172.	—	226
Black Bull Inn	2	228
Piercebridge, Durh.	8½	236½
Heighington	5¼	241¾
Eldon	3¾	245½
Merrington	3	248½
DURHAM	7¾	256¼

LONDON to *Whitby*.

To YORK, p. 174.	—	197
Spittle Beck	11	208
Whitwell	1¼	209¼
New Malton	5¾	215
l. to Old Malton	1	216
How Bridge	2½	218½
Pickering	5	223½
Lockton	4½	228
Saltergate	4	232
Sleights	7½	239½
Whitby	4	243½

LONDON to *Hartlepool*.

To *Northallerton*, p. 167	—	223
Great Smeaton	7	230
One Mile farther right to		
Piersburgh	7	237
Yarm	3	240
Stockton	4	244
Hartlepool	10	254

LONDON to *Guisborough*.

To *Thirsk*, p. 175.	—	220
South Kilvington	1	221
North Kilvington	1	222
Kayton	2	224
Borrowby	1	225
Arncliff	7½	232½
Swainby	2	234½
Stokesley	5	239½
Ayton	2½	242
Newton	1¾	243¾
Pinchinthorp	1	244¾
Guisborough	2¾	247½

LONDON to *Hemesley*.

To YORK, p. 174.	—	197
Sutton on the Forest	8	205
Stillington	3	208
Gilling	7	215
Oswaldkirk	1	216
Sproxton	2½	218½
Helmesley	1½	220

At Stillington, Stephen Croft, Esq.

Near Helmesley, on left, Duncomb Park, Charles Slingsby Duncomb, Esq.

To *Hemesley*, above	—	220
Kirby Moorside	5½	225½

LONDON to *Scarborough*, by YORK.

To YORK, p. 174.	—	197
Spittle Beck	11	208
Whitwell	1¼	209¼
New Malton	5¾	215
Cross Derwent River to		
Norton	½	215½
Scagglethorp	2½	218
Rillington	1½	219½
Yeddingham Bridge	4½	224
Snainton	3½	227½
Brumpton	1½	229
Wykeham	1½	230½
Hutton Bushel	½	231
East Ayton	1	232
Fulsgrave	4	236
Scarborough	1	237

A Mile beyond Whitwell, and about two to the left of the Road, is Castle Howard, a magnificent Seat of the Earl of Carlisle.

A Mile beyond Rillington, on the l. Scampston, Sir Wm. St. Quintin; and a little farther, on r. Knapton, Ralph Lutton, Esq.

At Brumpton, Sir Geo. Cayley, Bart.

LONDON to LINCOLN and *Scarborough*, by *Hull*.

To *Stilton*, p. 166.	—	74¾
Norman Cross, *Hunt.*	1	75¾
PETERBOROUGH	5½	81¼
Walton	3	84¼
Werrington	¾	85
Glimpton	2	87
Norborough	1	88
Market Deeping, Linc.	1½	89½
Langtoft	2½	92
Baston	1	93
River Glen	1	94
Thurlby	1	95
Bourn	2	97
Cawthorp	2	99
Morton	1	100
At 101 left to		
Aslackby	4	104
Folkingham	2	106
Osbournby	3	109
Aswarby	1¼	110¼
Willoughby	2¾	113
Sleaford	2½	115½
l. to Lincoln Heath	7½	123
Green Man	2	125
LINCOLN*	8	133
Midge Inn	5½	138½
Spital	6	144½
Redbourn	6½	151
Hibalstow	1½	152½
Glanford Bridge	3½	156
Elsham	4	160
Barton	6	166
Cross the Humber to		
Hull, Yorksh.	7	173
Newlands	2	175
Beverley	7	182
Leckinfield	2¾	184¾
Scorborough	1½	186¼
Beswic	2¼	188½
Watton	1¼	189¾
Cranswic	1¼	191
Driffield	4	195
Scarborough	13	208

To Scarborough by York, p. 185.

**To Lincoln by Stamford*, p. 189.

At Peterborough, Rogers Parker, Esq.

At Aswarby, Sir Christopher Whichcote, Bart.

At Leafingham, ——— York, Efq. and Mifs Manners.
To the r. of 129 is Bloxholm, the Seat of Lord Robert Manners.
At 4 beyond Lincoln, on the l. is Sudbrooke Holme, Richard Ellifon, Efq.
At 9 beyond Lincoln, on l. Sommers Caftle, Sir Cecil Wray, Bart. and a little farther to the l. is Glenworth, lately a Seat of this ancient Family.
At Spital, on the r. Norton Place, John Harrifon, Efq.
At Elfham Rob. Thompfon, Efq.
Adjoining to Beverley are the Seats of Sir James Pennyman, Bart. and J. Courtney, Efq. and 5 Miles from it, on the York Road, is South Dalton, the Seat of Sir Charles Hotham, K. B.
At Watton, the Seat of J. Bethell, Efq.

To PETERBOROUGH, p. 185.	—	81¼
Newark	1½	83
Eye, Camb.	1½	84½
Thorney	3	87½

To LINCOLN, p. 186.	—	133
Langworth Bridge	6	139
Bollington	2	141
Wragby	3	144
Weft Barkwith	2	146
Eaft Barkwith	1	147
Hainton	2	149

At 4 Miles South of Eaft Barkwith is Panton Houfe, the Seat of Edmund Turnor, Efq.

At Hainton, the Seat of Geo. Henage, Efq.

To Spital, p. 186.	—	144½
Kirton Lindfey	6½	151

To Spital, p. 186.	—	144½
Broughton	11	155½
Burton Strather	9	164½

To Glinton, p. 185.	—	87
r. to Peakirk	1	88
r. to Dunbeer	3	91
Crowland, Linc.	2	93

At Crowland, the Abbey in Ruins.

LONDON to Flamborough Head.

To Driffield, p. 186.	—	195
Kilham	5	200
Bridlington	8	208
Sewerby	1½	209½
Flamborough	2	211½
Flamborough Head	2	213½

To Driffield, p. 186.	—	195
Kilham	5	200
Hunmanby	9	209

To Hull, p. 186.	—	173
Bilton	4	177
Prefton	3	180
Haydon	1	181
Keyingham	5½	186½
Ottringham	1	187½
Winettead	2	189½
Pattrington	1½	191

To Hull, p. 186.	—	173
Hornfea, Yorkfh.	15	188

To *Beverley*, p. 186.	—	182
Leaven	7	189
Bransburton	1½	190½
Brodingham	4	194½

LONDON to LINCOLN and *Grimsby* by *Stamford*.

To Coltsworth, p. 166	—	102
r. to Cold Harbour	8	110
Ancaster	5	115
Baynard's Leap	3	118
Green Man	9	127
LINCOLN	8	135
Walton	6¾	141¾
Snarford Park	3¼	145
Market Rasin	6½	151½
Walesby	2	153½
Stanton-le-hole	3½	157
Thurgaaby	3½	160½
Radal	2½	163
Briggesley	1½	164½
Waltham	1¾	166¼
Grimsby	3¾	170

Another Road to Lincoln, p. 185.

Near Market Raisin is W. A. Boucherett, Esq.

At Stanton-le-hole, Col. Maddison.

To *Market Raisin*, above	—	151¼
Caistoor, *Linc*	7½	159

To Stanton-le-hole, *above*	—	157
Binbrook, *Linc.*	4	161

At Binbrook, Mr. Genefs.

One Mile West of ditto is Kirmond, Edm. Turnor. Esq.

LONDON to *Gainsborough* and *Crowle*.

To LINCOLN, p. 186.	—	133
Saxilby	6	139
Fenton	3½	142½
Torksey	1½	144
Marton	2	146
Knaith	2	148
Lea	1	149
Gainsborough	2	151
Stockworth	4	155
Owston	4	159
Epworth	3	162
Belton	2	164
Crowle	5	169

A Mile beyond Saxilby, to the l. is Thorney, George Neville, Esq.
Before Fenton, on l. Kettlethorpe, Ch. Amcotts, Esq.
At Knaith, H. Dalton, Esq.
At Lea, Sir Edmund Anderson, Bart.
To the r. of Belton is Temple Bell Wood, Allen Johnston, Esq. and 2 Miles beyond it, on left, is Hirst, Cornelius Stovin, Esq.

LONDON to *Boston* and *Alford*.

To Norborough, p. 185.	—	88
At ½ a Mile farther, r. to James Deeping, *Linc.*	1½	89½
Spalding	10½	100
Pinchbec	2	102
Surfleet	2	104
Gosberton	3	107
Sotherton	3	110
Kirton	2	112
Boston	3	115
Sibsey	5	120
Stickney	5	125

Stickford	2½	127½	To *Boston*, p. 190.	—	115
East Keal	3	130½	Wrangle	8	123
Spilsby	1½	132	Wainfleet	7	130
Partney	1½	133½	Croft	1	131
Alford	5	138½	Burgh	2	133

Left of Partney is Langton, the Seat of Bennet Langton, Esq.

Near Alford is Well, Samuel Dashwood, Esq.

To Stickford, p. 191. — 127½
West Keal — 2 129½
Bolingbroke — 1½ 131

To *Spalding*, p. 190.	—	100	To Stickford, p. 191.	—	127½
Weston	4	104	West Keal	2	129½
Whaplode	2¾	106¾	Bolingbroke	1½	131
Holbeach	1¼	108½			

LONDON to *Louth* and *Saltfleet*.

To *Gosberton*, p. 190.	—	107	To *Sleaford*, p. 186.	—	115½
Quadring	1½	108½	Tattershall	12	127½
Donnington	2	110½	Haltham	4	131½
			Horncastle	4½	136
			West Ashby	2	138
			Calkwell	4	142
			Louth	6	148
			Saltfleet	10	158

VII.

GREAT AND DIRECT ROADS

Measured from SHOREDITCH CHURCH.

With the ROADS branching from them to Market and Sea-Port Towns.

LONDON to *Stilton*, by *Ware*.			Tottenham H. Cross	1	4½
To Kingsland, *Midd.*	—	1¼	Edmonton	2½	7
Newington Town	1¼	2½	Ponder's End	1½	8½
Stamford Hill	1	3½	*Enfield Highway*	1	9½
			Enfield Wash	½	10

Waltham Cross, *Herts.*	1¼	11¼
Theobalds	¾	12
Cheshunt Street	1	13
Cheshunt Wash	1	14
Wormley	1	15
Broxbourn	1	16
Hoddesdon	1	17
Amwell	2¾	19¾
Ware	1¼	21
Wade's Mill	1¾	22¾
Collier's End	2	24¾
Puckeridge	1¾	26½
l. to Buntingford	4½	31
New Chipping	1	32
Buckland	2	34
Royston	3	37
Kneesworth, *Camb.*	2¾	39¾
Arrington	4	43¾
Cungrave	1½	45¼
Caxton	3¾	49
Papworth Everard	2	51
Godmanchester, *Huntingdonsh.*	7	58
*Huntingdon**	1	59
Great Stukeley	2½	61½
Little Stukeley	¾	62¼
Wheatsheaf Inn	2¼	64½
St. Andrew's Chapel	3½	68
Stilton	3¼	71¼

Another Road to Stilton, p. 166.

* *Another Road to Huntingdon*, p. 194.

At 3, on the r. Mr. Hoare, Banker; a Piece of Water below the House

Before 5, on l. Hornsey-Hill-House, Mr. Gray, Linen-draper.

At Bush Hill, Mr. Mellish and Mr. Blackburn.

On the left of 5 is Bruce Castle, the Seat of the late Alderman Townsend, now Mr. Ayton, Banker.

On the r. of 9 is Durance, the Property of Sands Chapman, Esq.

On the left of 12 was Theobald's Palace, where King James I. died, afterwards the Property of the late Duke of Portland, who sold it to George Prescott, Esq. who pulled down the Palace, and built a handsome Seat, now the Residence of his Family.

On right of 14 is Cheshunt Nunnery, the Seat of the late Col. Blackwood, now his Widow's.

Near 15, on the l. is Wormly Bury, Sir Abraham Hume, Bart.

On the l. of Broxbourn is Broxbourn Bury, late Lord Monson, now Mr. Bosanquet.

Rear Puckeridge, on the l. is Hamels, the Seat of the late Dr. Freeman, now of the Earl of Hardwicke.

Near 45, on the r. is Wimpole Hall, a most beautiful Seat of the Earl of Hardwicke; and, opposite, Baldon House, Christopher Willoughby, Esq.

At Godmanchester is the Seat of General Clarke.

Near Huntingdon is Hinchinbrook, a Seat of the E. of Sandwich.

LONDON to *Huntingdon* by *Hatfield*.

To *Bugden*, p. 166.		61
Brampton	2	63
Nun's Bridge	1	64
Huntingdon	1	65

Another Road, p. 193.

Near Brampton, on the left, is Grafham, the Seat of the late Sir Robert Bernard, Bart.

Beyond Nun's Bridge, on l. Hinchingbrook House, E. of Sandwich.

To Edmonton, p. 192	—	7	Barkway	4	34½
Enfield	3	10	Barley	2	36½
			Fowlmere, *Camb*	5½	42
To Waltham Croſs,			Trumpington	6½	48½
p. 193.	—	11¼	Cambridge *	2½	51
Waltham Abbey	1	12¼	Milton	4	55
			Stretham Bridge	7	62
			Stretham	1¾	63¾
To Hoddeſdon, p.193.	—	17	ELY	4¼	68
Hertford	4	21	Littleport.	5	73
Before Hertford, on l. Balls, Earl of			Southery, *Norf.*	6½	79½
Leiceſter.			Downham	6½	86
At Hertford, the Caſtle.			South Runcton	3½	89½
			Setchey, or Seeching	3½	93
To *Ware*, p. 193.	—	21	North Runcton	2	95
Standon, *Herts.*	6	27	Hardwic	1½	96½
			Lynn Croſs †	1½	98
To *Caxton*, p. 193.	—	49	Gaywood Toll-Gate	2	100
Hilton	6½	55½	South Wootton	1	101
St. *Ives*, Hunt.	3½	59	Caſtle Riſing, Ch.	2	103
Somerſham	6	65	Sandringham Lodge	3	106
Chatteris Ferry	5	70	Derſingham	1	107
Chatteris, Camb.	1	71	Ingoldiſthorpe	1	108
Doddington	3½	74½	Mount Amelia	1	109
March	4½	79	New Bridge	1	110
Gay-Hall Ferry	4	83	*Snettiſham*	1	111
Wiſbech	6	89	Heacham	2	113
St. John's	7	96	Hunſtanton	2	115
St. Germain's	5	101	Hunſtanton Cliff	1	116
Lynn Regis	5	106			

* Another Road to Cambridge,
p. 201.

To *Huntingdon*, p. 193.	—	59	
Ripton Regis	3½	62½	† *Another Road to Lynn,*
Ramſay	6¼	68¾	p. 197.
Whittleſea	8¼	77	

At Trumpington are the Family-Seats of Chriſtopher Auſtry, Eſq. and the Rev. J. Pemberton.

LONDON to ELY and *Lynn,* continued to *Hunſtanton Cliff.*

To Puckeridge, p.193	—	26½
r. to Hare Street	4	30½

At Milton, on the r. is the Seat of Samuel Knight, Eſq.

Two Miles beyond Downham, on

right, Stowe Hall, late Sir Thomas Hare, Bart. now Lady Harris.

The Castle at Castle Rising belongs to the Earl of Suffolk.

Sandringham, late Major Hoste, now Mrs. Henley.

Mount Amelia, Major Gardener.

At Newbridge are the beautiful Plantations of Mrs. Styleman.

At Snettisham, the Seat of Nicolas Styleman, Esq.

At Heacham, Edmond Rolfe, Esq.

At Hunstanton are the Seats of Sir Edward Astley, Bart. and Nicolas Styleman, Esq.

Near the Cliff is a Bathing-Seat of the Earl of Mountrath.

VIII.

GREAT AND DIRECT ROADS

Measured from WHITECHAPEL CHURCH.

With the ROADS branching from them to Market and Sea-Port TOWNS.

LONDON to *Newmarket* and *Lynn.*						
To Mile-End,	*Mid.*	—	1	*Stanstead,*	*Essex*	2¾	32¾
Bow		1½	2½	Quendon		3¼	36
Stratford,	*Essex*	1	3½	Newport		2¾	38¾
l. to Layton Stone		2	5½	Littlebury		3½	42¼
Snaresbrook		1¼	6¾	Chesterford		2½	44¾
Woodford		¾	7½	*Bournbridge,*	*Camb.*	4	48¾
Woodford Wells		1½	9	Devil's Ditch		10	58¾
Bald Stag		1	10	*Newmarket*		1¾	60½
Epping		6½	16½	*l.* to Red House, *Suff.*		5¼	65¾
Potter's Street		4½	21	*Barton Mills*		3¾	69½
Harlow		2	23	*l.* to Hobb's Cross		3¼	72¾
Sawbridgeworth, *Herts*		3	26	A Lodge on the right		1¼	74
Hockeril, Or,				Heath on both Sides		1	75
Bishops Stortford,				Between Wangford Church *left*, and a			
	Herts	4	30	Farm House *right*		3	78
				Brandon		½	78½

Methwold,	*Norf.*	8	86½
Stoke Ferry		2	88½
Wareham		1½	90
Seeching		8	98
West Winch		1¼	99¼
Hardwic		1¼	100½
Lynn		1½	102

Another Road to Lynn, p. 195.

To the right of Layton-Stone is Wanstead-House, a magnificent Seat of the late Earl Tilney, now Sir James Tilney Long, Bart.

To the left of 14 is Copt-Hall, John Conyers, Esq. and near it is Warley's, Miss Carter.

On the left of Potter's Street is Mark-Hall, Mr. Lushington, an Avenue of Trees leading to it.

At Harlow, on the right, is the Seat of Mr. Gardiner.

Beyond Harlow, on r. in a Bottom, Pishiobury, Mrs. Mills.

Right of Sawbridgeworth is Hyde-Hall, late Sir Joa. Conyers, now Earl of Ruthin.

Left of Hockeril, Thornley-Hall, —— Raper, Esq.

To the right of Stanstead is Stanstead-Hall, Wm. Heath, Esq.

At 36½, on the left, Quendon Flats, Henry Cranmer, Esq.

At 39½, on the right, is Shortgrove, a Seat of the Earl of Egremont, occupied by his Brother, the Hon. —— Wyndham.

At 41, on the right, Audley-End, Lord Howard.

Chesterford is an ancient Roman Station.

To the right of Bournbridge is Horse-Heath, the Seat of Ld. Mountfort.

On the left of Newmarket-Heath are Gogmagog Hills, on which the late Lord Godolphin had a Seat, who left it to his Godson, Lord George William Frederic Osborne, now

Marquis of Carmarthen, eldest Son of the Duke of Leeds, who is a Minor. It is now inhabited by the Bishop of Elphin.

LONDON to *Chipping-Ongar* and *Dunmow*.

To Layton-Stone, p. 197.	—	5½
At the Obelisk, right to Woodford-Bridge	3½	9
Chigwell	1½	10½
Abridge	3	13½
Hare-Street	5	18½
Chipping-Ongar	2½	21
Moulton End	3½	24½
Machin Green	2½	27
Hatfield-Heath	3	30
Hatfield	2	32
Dunmow	8	40

Another Road to Dunmow, viz.

To *Harlow*, p. 197	—	23
Hatfield Heath	4	27
Hatfield	2	29
Dunmow	8	37

Another Road, viz.

To *Ongar*, above	—	21
Leaden Roding	8½	29½
High Roding	2½	32
Dunmow	4	36

N. B. *This last is only a By-Road through the Rodings.*

At Woodford Bridge, on the left, Ray House, Sir James Wright, Bart. and on r. Cladbury, Edward Harvey, Esq.

Beyond Chigwell, on the r. Rolls, Eliab. Harvey, Esq. and a little farther, on the left, Woolston, late George Scott, Esq.

At 16, to the right, is Albyns, Sir William Abdy, Bart.

To the right of Hare-Street, is Navestoc-Hall, Earl Waldegrave.

To the right of 20, Kelvedon Hall, John Wright, Esq. and Myles, late John Luther, Esq. now Mr. Fane.

Near Ongar is Greenstead-Hall, John Redman, Esq. and Blake-Hall, Sir Narborough Daeth.

At Hatfield, Mr. Barrington.

LONDON to *Cambridge,* by *Epping.*

To Chesterford, p.198	—	44¾
Cambridge	11	55¾

Another Road, p. 196.

To *Harlow,* p. 197.	—	23
Sherring Street	3	26
Hatfield Heath	1½	27½
Hatfield Broad Oak	2	29½

Adjoining to Hatfield is now Barrington Hall, John Shales Barrington, Esq.

To Newport, p. 198.	—	38¾
Saffron Walden, Essex	3¾	42½
Little Waldon	2	44½
Hadstoc	2½	47
Linton, *Camb.*	1½	48½

Before Waldon is Audley End, Lord Howard.

To *Newmarket,* p. 198	—	60½
Soham, *Camb.*	10	70½

To *Newmarket,* p. 198.	—	60½
Chippenham	3½	64

At Chippenham is the Seat formerly of Admiral Russell, Earl of Orford, since of Crisp Molyneaux, Esq. built by Inigo Jones, now modernized by Mr. Drummond Smith.

To Red House, p. 198	—	65¾
Milden Hall, *Suff.*	3¾	69½

At Milden-Hall are the Seats of Sir Charles Bunbury and —— Rushbrook, Esq.

LONDON to *Wells* in *Norfolk.*

To Brandon, p. 198.	—	78½
Mumford Br. *Nor.*	5¼	83¾
Longford Bridge	2¼	86
Hilborough	1½	87½
Swaffham	6½	94
Newton	4½	98½
Tittleshall	6	104½
Fakenham	6	110½
Houghton	4¼	115
Walsingham	1½	116½
l. to *Wells*	4½	121

Within 5 Miles of Swaffham, to the left, is Narford-Hall, the Seat of Brigg Fountaine, Esq.

One Mile farther is Narborough-Hall, Henry Peyton, Esq.

On the right of Swaffham, 3 Miles, is Necton, Wm. Mason, Esq.

Within a Mile of Newton, to the left, are the Ruins of Castle-Acre Abbey, late Earl of Leicester, now Thomas William Coke, Esq.

Near Newton, to the right, is Lexham, Colonel Wodehouse.

At Tittleshall is Godwic-Hall, an ancient Seat of Lord Chief Justice Coke, now of Wenman Coke, Esq.

On the left of 108 is Raynham-Hall, the Seat of Marquis Townshend; and a few Miles to the left of Raynham is Houghton-Hall, a Seat of the Earl of Orford.

At Walsingham is the Seat of Lee Warner, Esq. formerly an Abbey.

Within two Miles to the l. of Wells is Holkham-Hall, the Seat of the late Earl of Leicester, now of Tho. William Coke, Esq.

To *Walsingham*, p. 202		—	$116\frac{1}{2}$
Burham,	*Nor.*	$9\frac{3}{4}$	$126\frac{1}{4}$

Within five miles of Burnham, to the left, is Docking, the Seat of Mrs. Henley, enriched with beautiful Plantations.

Within 3 Miles is Brancaster, formerly a Roman Camp, (Brandolunum,) remarkable now for a Malt-House built of Stone, supposed to be the largest in the Kingdom.

LONDON to *Cromer*.

To Brandon, p. 198.		—	$78\frac{1}{2}$
r. to Ickborough Street,	*Norf.*	$5\frac{1}{2}$	84
Watton		$6\frac{1}{4}$	$90\frac{1}{4}$
Turtle-Green Cross		$5\frac{1}{2}$	$95\frac{3}{4}$
Dereham		$4\frac{1}{2}$	$100\frac{1}{4}$
Hoolcundellington		$3\frac{1}{2}$	$103\frac{3}{4}$
Bawdswell		$4\frac{3}{4}$	$108\frac{1}{2}$
Reapham		$\frac{3}{4}$	$109\frac{1}{4}$
Sall		$2\frac{1}{4}$	$111\frac{3}{4}$
Saxthorpe		$4\frac{1}{4}$	116
Gresham Street		$6\frac{1}{2}$	$122\frac{1}{2}$
Cromer		$4\frac{3}{4}$	$127\frac{1}{4}$

Within a Mile of Watton is Merton, Colonel de Grey.

Near Reapham, Heydon-Hall, Wm. Wiaget Bulwer, Esq.

At Sall is the Seat of Edward Hase, Esq.

Near Saxthorpe is Blickling, a Seat of the Earl of Buckinghamshire; Wolterton, the Seat of Lord Walpole of Wolterton; and a few Miles to the left is Melton Constable, a Seat of Sir Edward Astley, Bart.

Near Cromer is Felbrig, the Seat of the Right Hon. William Wyndham.

To *Watton*, p. 203.		—	$90\frac{1}{4}$
Higham,	*Norf.*	7	$97\frac{1}{4}$
Wynham		6	$103\frac{1}{4}$

To *Dereham*, p. 203.		—	$100\frac{1}{4}$
Foulsham,	*Norf.*	$10\frac{3}{4}$	111
Holt		11	122
Cley		3	125

To *Reapham*, p. 203.	—	$109\frac{1}{4}$
Cawston	$3\frac{1}{4}$	$112\frac{1}{2}$

LONDON to NORWICH.

To *Newmarket*, p. 198.		—	$60\frac{1}{2}$
l. to Red House,	*Suff.*	$5\frac{1}{4}$	$65\frac{3}{4}$
Barton Mills		$3\frac{3}{4}$	$69\frac{1}{2}$
Cross a Brook straight over the Heath between two Lodges		1	$70\frac{1}{2}$
Thetford,	Norf.	$9\frac{1}{2}$	80
r. a Windmill to the *l.*		1	81
A Stone Cross to the *l.*		$3\frac{1}{2}$	$84\frac{1}{2}$
Larlingford		3	$87\frac{1}{2}$
Frettle Bridge		4	$91\frac{1}{2}$

Attleborough	2	93½
Wyndham	6¼	99¾
Hetherset	3¾	103½
Cringleford	2½	106
NORWICH	3	109
And thence to		
Alyesham	12	121

Another Road to Norwich, p. 211.

On the r. of Thetford is Euston-Hall, a Seat of the Duke of Grafton.

One Mile from Wyndham, on the l. is Kimberley-Hall, the Seat of Sir John Wodehouse, Bart.

Within two Miles of Hetherset, to the r. is Hethel, Sir Thomas Beevor, Bart.

Three Miles from Norwich is Bixley-Hall, a Seat of the Earl of Rolebery.

Three Miles and ½ beyond Norwich is Pixworth-Hall, Major Longe.

The Mile-Stones from Thetford to Norwich are well adapted for Travellers in Carriages, having two Sides towards the Road, not square but flaunted, so as the Number may be seen at a great Distance.

To *Thetford*, p. 204.	—	80
E. Harling, *Norf.*	8	88

To NORWICH, above	—	109
Wurstead, *Norf.*	11½	120½
N. Walsham	2½	123

Sir Miles and a half beyond Norwich is Rackheath-Hall, late Sir Horatio Pettus, Bart.

Three Miles beyond North Walsham is Gunton, Lord Suffield.

Three Miles from North Walsham is Westwic, the beautiful Seat of John Berney Petre, Esq.

LONDON to *Yarmouth*.

To Mile End, *Midd.*	—	1
Bow	1½	2½
Stratford *Essex.*	1	3½
r. to Ilford	3¼	6¾
Chadwell Street	2¼	9
The Whalebone	1	10
Rumford	1¾	11¾
Hare Street	1	12¾
Brook Street	3¾	16½
Brentwood	1½	18
Shenfield	1	19
Mountnessing Street	2	21
Ingatestone	2	23
Margaretting Street	2	25
Stisted	1½	26½
Widford	1	27½
Moulsham	1	28½
Chelmsford	¼	28¾
Right in the Middle of the Town to		
Springfield	1¼	30
Boreham Street	3	33
Hatfield Peverell	1¾	34¾
Witham	2¾	37½
Riven-Hall End	1½	39
Kelvedon	2	41
Gore Pitt	1	42
Stanway	5	47
Colchester	2¼	49¼
Lexdon	1¾	51
Stratford Street, *Suff.*	6	57
Brantham	1¼	58¼
Copdoc	5¾	64
Ipswich	5	69
Kesgrave	3¼	72¼
Martlesham	1¾	74
Woodbridge	2½	76½
Melton Street	1	77½
Ufford Street	1¼	79¾

Wickham Market	2	81¼
Glemham	3	84¼
Stratford St. Andrew	1¾	86
Saxmundham	3	89
Kelsale	1	90
Yoxford	3	93
Hinton Street	3	96
Blyborough	2	98
Henham Park on r.	2	100
Tooley, or St. Olave's Bridge	7¾	107¾
Beccles	¼	108
Gillingham	1	109
Hadsko Dam, *Norf.*	5	114
Fritton	2¼	116¼
Gorleston	4¼	120½
Little Yarmouth	1½	122
Yarmouth	1	123

One Mile and a Half to the left of Yoxford is Sibton-Park, the Seat of John Clayton, Esq.

A new Road has been made to Yarmouth, as follows:

To *Blyborough*, above	—	98
Blyborough Bridge	1	99
Leave the Beccles Road, turn on the r. keeping Henham Park on l. to		
Wagford	2	101
l. to Frostenden Church	2	103
Wrentham	1½	104½
Benacre Turnpike	1½	106
Kesingland	1½	107½
Pakefield	3	110½
l. to Kirklee Church	½	111
Lowestoft	1	112
Yarmouth	9	121

Another Road to Yarmouth, viz.

To *Bury St. Edmund's*, p. 212.	—	72
Bungay	38½	101½
Gillingham		
Hadsko		
Fritton		
Gorleston		
Little Yarmouth		121

The Mile-stones on this Road have the same Convenience as those from Thetford to Norwich, p. 205.

For three Miles on to Ilford Bridge, on the r. see Shooter's Hill, with the Tower built by Commodore James's Widow to his Memory.

At 6, on the l. is Aldersbrook, late Edward Hulse, Esq. now Sir James Tilney Long, Bart. and farther to the l. is Wanstead, a magnificent Seat of the late Lord Tilney, now of the above Sir James Tilney Long.

To the left of Ilford is Valentines, Wm. Webber, Esq. Highlands, Wm. Raikes, Esq. and Cranbrook, late Andrew Moffatt, Esq.

A little beyond Rumford, on the left, is Gidea Hall, Richard Benyon, Esq.

Beyond Mr. Benyon's Park, on l. on the Common, is a white House, built to see the Races from, on the Common, when there were Races; more to the l. a red brick House, Mr. Eaton.

At 13, on right, is Hare Hall, J. Wallinger Esq.

To the left of 15 is Dagnam Park, Sir Richard Neave, Bart. a white House.

To the left of 16 is Weald-Hall, Christ. Tower, Esq.

At 18, on r. is Thorndon-Hall, a new built Seat of Lord Petre; and on the l. is Shenfield Place, Mr. Heatley's.

At 20, on the left, Tooby-Hall, on a Hill, late Mr. Blencow, now Mr. Monro's; and near it Fitchwater, Mr. Wright's.

At 23, on l. of Ingateſtone, is Writtle-Park, another Seat of Lord Petre's.

At 23½, on the left, the Hide, Tho. Brand Hollis, Eſq.

To the left of 25 is Coptford-Hall, Mrs. Holden.

At 25, on r. a new brick Houſe, Mr. Sydney.

At 26¼, on the left, Hylands, J. R. Comyns, Eſq.

At 28, on the right, Moulſham-Hall, Lady Mildmay.

At 30, on the l. Springfield Place, Mr. Brograve; and on r. Lady Waltham.

On r. of 31 is New Houſe, the Seat of the late Rich. Hoare, Eſq. ſince Sir Elijah Impey's, now Mr. Walford's; and on the left is New Hall, late the Seat of Lord Waltham, now of Luttrell Olmius, Eſq. who married his Siſter.

To the l. of Hatfield Peverell is Terling Place, the Seat of John Strutt, Eſq.

At 34, on r. Mr. Shane.

At 34½, on r. a new white Houſe, Capt. Tyrrell.

At 36, on the right, Hatfield Priory, Mr. Wright, Coach-maker in Long-Acre.

In the Town of Witham, on the r. is the Seat of the late Lord Abercorn, now Thomas Kynaſton, Eſq. Here the Queen was lodged and entertained by his Lordſhip on her arrival in England from Mecklenburgh.

To the right of 39 is Braxted Lodge, late Peter Du Cane, Eſq.

To the left of Kelvedon is Fœlix Hall, late Daniel Matthews, Eſq. now Sam. Tyſon, Eſq.

Before Colcheſter, on l. ſee a new white Houſe on a Hill; the Parſonage-Houſe at Mile-end.

At Copdoc was a remarkable large Elm, which being blown down, has furniſhed a Sign called the Copdoc Elm.

A little before Ipſwich, on r. Sir Robert Harland is building a new Houſe (1793).

Entering Yoxford, on l. Mr. Davis.

Going out of Yoxford, on l. Cookfield-Hall, a white Houſe in the Meadows, Sir John Blois.

Near Yoxford is Heveningham, Sir Joſhua Vanneck.

At 96, on l. Thorington-Hall, Mr. Golden. Five Oaks.

At Blyborough, the Church to be ſeen.

At 99, on l. Henham Park, Sir John Rous.

At 106, on l. Weſton, Mr. Sawbridge.

At 108½, on r. Gillingham, Mrs. Schutz.

At 116, on r. of Fritton, ſee Herringfleet-Hall; in the ſame Wood, above a Piece of Water, M. Leeſe.

At Ipſwich is the Seat of the Rev. William Fonnereau; and a few Miles to the right is Nacton, late the Earl of Shipbrooke, now John Vernon, Eſq. and alſo of Philip Bowes Broke, Eſq.

On the oppoſite Side of the River, at Nacton, is Woolverton Park, the Seat of William Berners, Eſq.

At Woodbridge, the Priory, an ancient brick Houſe, ſouth of the Church, belonging to the Rev. Thomas Carthew.

At Milton, on the r. leaving the Town, a good Brick Houſe, ——

P

Brooke, of Ufford, Esq. left to him by Mr. Negus, who built it.

At Ufford, the Seat of the said —— Brooke, Esq.

Near Wick Market, on the r. is Loudham, the Seat of Jacob Whitbread, Esq. and near it the Remains of Campsey Nunnery.

At Glenham is the Seat of Dudley North, Esq.

At Saxmundham is the Seat of Charles Long, Esq.

At Heveningham, near Yoxford, is the Seat of the late Sir Gerard Vanneck, now Sir Joshua Vanneck.

To *Dunmow*, p. 200.	—	37
Great Easton	2¼	39¼
Thaxstead	4	43¼

LONDON to NORWICH, the Coach Road.

To *Chemlsford*, p. 206	—	28¾
R, at the Town's End to		
Broomfield	2½	31¼
Little Waltham	1¾	33
Blackwater St. Anne's	3	36
Young's End	2	38
Braintree	2½	40½
Bocking Street	½	41
High Garret	2¼	43¼
Halstead	3½	46¾
Sudbury *, Suff.	9¼	56
By Rodbridge Street to		
Long Melford	3½	59½
By Shipling, Thorn, and Cockfield to		
Bradfield	5½	65
Bury St. Edmund's †	7	72
Ixworth	6¾	78¾
Botesdale	8¾	87½
Schole Inn, *Norf.*	7½	95
Stratton	10	105
NORWICH	10	115

To Norwich by Newmarket, p. 204.

* *Another Road to Sudbury*, p. 214.

† *Another Road to Bury*, p. 213.

Before Waltham, on right, a Seat of John Jolliffe Tufnel, Esq.

Between Sudbury and Long Melford, on the l. is Listen Hall, William Campbell, Esq.

At one Mile from Long Melford, on the r. is Acton Place, William Jennings, Esq.

On the l. 2 Miles before Halsted, is a neat House of the late Capt. Manisten, and a distant View of Earl Nugent's Seat at Gosfield.

On the l. of Halsted, a new House, built by —— Edwards, Esq.

Before Sudbury is Bulmer Hill, from which is a very fine View over the Town.

At 7 Miles from Sudbury, on the l. near the Road, is Shrimplingthorn, Mr. Fiske; and at 65 on the r. Bradfield-Hall, Arthur Young, Esq. Secretary to the Board of Agriculture.

At Long Melford is a noble old Seat, called Melford-Hall, Sir Harry Parker, Bart. also Kentwell-Hall, Mr. Moore;—and at the South End of the Village is an old Seat of Sir Mordaunt Martin, Bt.

At 69, on the r. is Rushbrook, Sir Charles Davers, Bart.

LONDON to *Bury St. Edmund's* by *Newmarket*.

To *Newmarket*, p. 198	—	60½
Kenford Bridge	4½	65

Saxham	5½	70½
Bury St. Edmund's	4½	75

Another Road, p. 197.

To the right of Saxham is the Seat of Mr. Muire; and Ickworth, a Seat of the Earl of Bristol.

LONDON to *Clay* by *Bury St. Edmund's*.

To *Bury*, p. 211.	—	72
Thetford, *Norf.*	12	84
Watton	12	96
Shipdam	5	101
Dereham	5	106
Holt	18	124
Clay	3	127

LONDON to *Haverill.*

To *Braintree*, p. 211.	—	40¼
High Garret	2¾	43¼
Gosfield	1¾	45
Swan Street	2½	47½
Sible Hedingham	½	48
Great Yelham	3	51
Redgwell	2½	53½
Baythorn End	2	55½
Sturmer	2	57½
Haverill Suff.	1½	59

At Gosfield, on the left, Gosfield-Hall, late Earl Nugent, now Marquis of Buckingham, who married his Sister.

At 55, on the right, Baythorn Park, John Pike, Esq.

At Sturner, by the Church, Mr. Todd.

To Swan Street, *above*	—	47½
Castle Hedingham	1½	49
The Compasses	2¼	51¼
Sudbury	4¾	56

At Castle Hedingham is the Seat of Lewis Majendie, Esq.

To Yeldham, p. 213.	—	51
Clare, *Suff.*	5	56

To Kelvedon, p. 206.	—	41
Coggeshall	3	44

To *Sudbury*, p. 211.	—	56
Chilton Park	2	58
Lavenham	3	61
Bildeston	6¼	67¼
Stow Market	8¼	75½
Mendlesham	6½	82
Diss, *Norf.*	9¾	91¾
Or,		
To Botesdale, p. 211.	—	87½
Diss, *Norf.*	5	92½

At Lavenham, vulgarly pronounced *Lanham*, is a Church well worthy the Attention of a Traveller.

To *Sudbury*, p. 211.	—	56
Lavenham	7	63
To the right, at the 65 Mile-stone to		
Cockfield	7	70
Felsham	4	74
Guddings	½	74½
Drinkstone	2½	77

To Botesdale, p. 211.	—	87½
Buckenham	9	96½

To Copdoc, p. 206.	—	64
Bramford, *Suff.*	3	67
Needham	6	73

To *Ipswich*, p. 206.	—	69
Claydon, *Suff.*	4½	73½
Coddenham	2¾	76¼
Thwaite Street	9¼	85½
Yaxley Street	3¾	89¼
Osmondston	3¾	93
Harleston	7	100
Bungay	7	107
Loddon, *Norf.*	6½	113½

At Loddon is Langley-Hall, the Seat of Sir Tho. Beauchamp Proctor.

To *Ipswich*, p. 206.	—	69
Claydon	4½	73½
Debenham	10	83½
Eye	7	90½

To *Blyborough*, p. 207.	—	98
Lowestoff, Suff.	19	117

To *Blyborough*, p. 207.	—	98
Southwould, *Suff.*	5¾	103¾

To Yoxford, p. 207.	—	93
Halesworth, *Suff.*	8½	101½

To *Woodbridge*, p. 206.	—	76½
Tunstal, *Suff.*	8	84½
Leiston	8½	93
Dunwich	6	99

At Leiston, the Abbey.

To *Wickham*, p. 207.	—	81¼
Framlingham	6	87¼

To *Woodbridge*, p. 206.	—	76½
Rendlesham	5	81½
Tunstal	3	84½
Aldborough	9	93½

On the l. about a Mile beyond Rendlesham Church and Rectory, is Naunton-Hall, once the Residence and Court of Redward, King of the East Angles; now the Seat of Sir G. Wombwell, Bart.

To *Woodbridge*, p. 206.	—	76½
Orford, *Suff.*	11½	88

In passing Butley, between Woodbridge and Orford, on the r. are the fine Remains of that Abbey, the Property of Lord Archibald Hamilton.

On the r. about a Mile short of Orford, is Sudburn-Hall, formerly the Seat of the Earls of Hereford; now of the Marquis of Hereford.

Stratford Street, p. 206	—	57
Hadleigh, *Suff.*	6½	63½

LONDON to *Harwich*.

To *Colchester*, p. 206.	—	49¼
r. to Ardley	6½	55¾
l. to Wignel Street	2½	58¼
Mistley Thorn	2½	60¾
Bradfield	2¼	63
Ramsey Street	4¾	67¾
Ramsey	½	68¼
Dover Court	1¼	69½
Harwich	2	71½

Before Mistley Thorn, on the right, is Mistley-Hall, a Seat of the late Right Hon. Richard Rigby, now General Rigby.

Mistley Thorn takes its Name from a large Thorn now destroyed.

At Ramsey, on l. Michaelstow-Hall, Lewis Peak Garland, Esq.

Another Road, viz.

Wignel Street, p. 216.	—	58¼
Manningtree	1¼	60
Mistley Thorn	¾	60¾
Harwich. p. 216.	10¾	71½

To *Colchester*, p. 206.	—	49¼
Greenstead	2¾	52
Elmstead Market	3	55
Frating	2	57
St. Osyth	5	62

At St. Osyth, the Priory, Earl of Rochford.

To *Colchester*, p. 206.	—	49¼
Greenstead	2¾	52
Wivenhoe Heath	1	53
Wivenhoe Cross	1	54
Wivenhoe	1	55

On r. entering the Heath, is the Seat of J. M. Rebow, Esq.

To *Colchester*, p. 206.	—	49¼
Dedham	8¾	58

To *Colchester*, p. 206.	—	49¼
Mile End	2¾	52
The Causeway	2½	54½
Great Horsley	½	55
Nayland, *Suff.*	2	57

At Mile-End, the Parsonage.

LONDON to *Maldon*.

Margaretting, p. 206.	—	25
r. to Gallywood Common	2	27
Great Baddow	2¼	29¼
Danbury	3½	32¾
Runsells	1	33¾
Maldon	3¼	37

Or,

To *Chelmsford*, p. 206.	—	28¾
Great Baddow	1½	30¼
To *Maldon*	8¼	38½

Near Danbury, on the right, Danbury Place, Lewis Disney Ffytche, Esq.

To *Maldon*, above.	—	37
Snoreham	5	42
Southminster	5	47

To *Maldon*, above.	—	37
Snoreham	5	42
Althorn	3	45
Burnham	3½	48½

To *Maldon*, above.	—	37
Snoreham	5	42
Steple	4	46
Bradwell	5½	51½

Near Bradwell is Bradwell-Lodge, a Seat lately built by the Rev. H. Bate Dudley. This House is so remarkable at Sea, that it is considered by the Coasting Traders as a Sea-Mark; and is almost as conspicuous as the Roman Temple, now called St. Peter's Chapel, which stands about a Mile and a Half from it. The Buildings, and Laying-out of the Pleasure-Grounds of Bradwell Lodge, cost 15,000.

To Steple, p. 218.	—	46
St. Lawrence	2½	48½
Tillingham	2	50½

LONDON to *Rochford* and *Wakering*.

To *Brentwood*, p. 206.	—	18
Shenfield	1	19
r. to Billericay.	4¼	23¼
Wicford	5¾	29
Raleigh	5	34
l. to Hockley	2	36
Rochford	3¾	39¾
Sutton	1¼	41
South Church	3¼	44¼
Great Wakering	3¼	47½

Near this is South End, a new Bathing Place.

A new Turnpike Road to South End.

To the Whalebone, p. 206.	—	10
r. to Dagenham	2½	12½
Raynham	2½	15
Wennington	1½	16½
Aveley	2	18½
Stifford	2½	21
Baker Street	2	23
Orsett	1	24
Horndon	2	26
Vange	4	30
Bowers	3	33
Hadley	4	37
South End	5	42

At 18, Gate to Lady Dacre.

At 19, see on l. Lady Dacre.

At 20, on l. Ford Place, Mr. Hogarth.

Near 21, on r. see Zach. Batton, Esq.

Beyond 21, on l. John Batton, Esq. red brick House.

At Orsett, on l. Mr. Baker, a white House.

To *Raleigh*, p. 219.	—	34
r. to Swan's Green	1¼	35¼
Hadley	1½	36¾
Adam's Elm	2	38¾
Milton Hall	2¼	41
South Church	1½	42½

Adam's Elm, *above*	—	38¾
Lee	½	39¼

Adam's Elm, *above*	—	38¾
Prittlewell	2¼	41

LONDON to *Tilbury Fort*.

To *Rumford*, p. 206.	—	11¾
r. in the Middle of the Town to		
Hornchurch	2¼	14
Upminster	1½	15½
r. to Corbet's Tie	1	16½
South Okendon	3¼	19¾
Stifford	2¼	22
Grey's Thurroc	2¼	24¼
Tilbury Fort	4	28¼

A nearer Way to Tilbury is by Gravesend, whence you have only to cross the Thames to the Fort.

At Upminster, New-Place, Mr. Esdaile; and a Mile beyond it Cranham-Hall, late General Oglethorpe, now Sir Thomas Apprecce, Bart.			

To the right of 16, Hackton Hill, late Edward Braund, Esq.

At 17½, on the left, Stubbers, John Ruffel, Esq.

To the right of 20, is Bell House, Lady Dacre.

To Stratford, p. 206.			3½
West Ham		½	4
East Ham		2	6
Barking		1	7

Beyond West Ham, on the left, Ham House, late Dr. Fothergill.

At Barking, Bifrons, Bamber Gascoyne, Esq.

CROSS ROADS.

ANDOVER to *Newbury.*

Inham		—	2½
Up. Hufborn		5	7½
Highcleer		4½	12
Newbury		4	16

At Inham, Mr. Dewer.
At Highcleer, Earl of Carnarvon.

APPLEBY to DURHAM.

To *Brough,*	Westm.	—	8
Bowes,	*Yorksh.*	13	21
Barnard Castle,	Durh.	4	25
Staindrop		6	31
Raby		1	32
West Aucland		5	37
Bishops Aucland		3	40
DURHAM		10	50

At 7, on the left, is Streatlam Castle, a Seat of the late Earl of Strathmore; and at Raby

is Raby Castle and Park, belonging to the Earl of Darlington. At Bishops Aucland are the Palace and Park of the Bishop of Durham.

ARUNDEL to CHICHESTER.

To Almsford Hill		—	3
Mackerel's Bridge		¾	3¾
Croker Hill		2¼	6
Maudling		2	8
CHICHESTER		2	10

At Arundel is Arundel Castle, Duke of Norfolk. *See the Remarks on this Castle,* p. 22.

Beyond Croker Hill to r. is Boxgrave Priory, and the Remains of Halnaker House, late Lady Derby, now Duke of Richmond.

At 4, to the right, is Slindon, Earl of Newburgh.

About 4, on the l. see Walberton House, the Seat of Mr. Nash.

To the r. of Maulding is Good-Wood, Duke of Richmond.

At Hampnet, near Chichester, on the l. is Hampnet Place, Mr. Steele.

Ashbourn to *Mansfield*.

To Kniveton		—	3
Carlington		3¾	6¾
Wirksworth		2½	9¼
Wigwell		1½	10¾
Hotstandel Bridge		2	12¾
Critch		1½	14¼
Wingfield		2	16¼
Alfreton		2¾	19
Sutton,	*Not.*	5½	24½
Mansfield		3½	28

Ashbourn to *Manchester*.

To Bottom House		—	10
Leek,	Staff.	4½	14½
Bosley,	*Chesh.*	7	21½
Macclesfield		5½	27
Poynton		7	34
Norbury		1	35
Stocport		4	39
Manchester,	Lanc.	7	46

Ashbourn to *Namptwich*.

Okeover,	*Staff.*	—	3
Colton-Hall		4	7
Cheadle		5	12
Lane End		6	18
Stoke		2	20
Newcastle		2	22
Audley		4	26
The Dumbles		2	28
Namptwich,	Chesh.	10	38

At 2, on the l. Middle Mayfield, Thomas Ley, Esq.

At 3, Okeover-Hall, Edward Walhouse Okeover, Esq.

At 7, on the r. Colton-Hall, Thomas Gilbert, Esq.

At 11, on the r. Hales-Hall, Edward Grosvenor, Esq.

At 14, on the r. Blake-Hall, Simon Mountford, Esq.

At 16, on the r. Coverswall Castle, Visc. Vane.

At 17, on the r. Park-Hall, Thomas Parker, Esq.

At 18, on the l. Longton-Hall, Sir John Heathcote, Knt.

At 20, on the r. Little Fenton, Thomas Broad, Esq.

At 28, Thomas Fletcher, Esq.

At 29, on the l. Balterley-Hall, John Crewe, Esq.

Ashbourn to *Sheffield*.

To Bentley	—	2¾
New Inn	3	5¾
Newhaven	3½	9¼
r. to Conskbury	4½	13¾
Bakewell	1½	15¼
Hassop	3	18¼
Calver	1¾	20
Grindleford Bridge	2	22
Over long & high Moorsto		
Little Sheffield, *Yorksh.*	9	31
Sheffield	1	32

2½ Miles beyond Ashbourn is Dovedale, and Ilam, Mr. Porte.

At Hassop, the Seat and Plantations of Mr. Eyre.

Ashbourn to *Chesterfield*.

To Kniveton	—	3
Carsington	3¾	6¾
Cromford	7¾	14½
Matlock Bath	1	15½

Matloc	2	17½
Kelstedge	3¼	20¾
Walton	4¼	25
Chesterfield	2	27

AUST FERRY to WORCESTER.

To Beachley, *Gloc.*	—	3½
Sudbury	2	5½
Strode	2½	8
Avington	2½	10½
Alberton	1½	12
Lidney	1	13
Selloe	1¾	14¾
Little Michel	6	20¾
Michel Dean	3½	24¼
Chilcot	5½	29¾
Newent	1¼	31
Catesford	3	34
Ledbury, *Heref.*	5½	39½
Little Malvern	4½	44
Malvern, *Worc.*	4½	48½
Powic	5½	54
WORCESTER	2¼	56¼

Near Ledbury, on the Colwall Road to Great Malvern, is Hope-End, the Seat of Sir Henry Tempest, Bart. The Views from this Seat are extensive and picturseque.

At Great Malvern, curious painted Glass in the Priory-Church. From the Hill, a most rich and beautiful View of the Vale of Evesham.

At Powic, on r. Mr. Lygon's Plantations are seen, but not the House.

BANBURY to *Leicester* and *Melton Mowbray*.

To Wardington, *Northamp.*	—	4½
Chipping Warden	1½	6
Byfield	3¼	9¼
Charwelton	2	11¼
Badby	2¾	14
Daventry	2½	16½
Ashby Ledgers	4	20½
Kilsby	3	23½
Dove Bridge	5	28½
Shawell, *Leic.*	1½	30
Lutterworth	2½	32½
Dog and Gun	5¾	38¼
Blaby	2½	40¾
Aylestone	1¾	42½
Leicester	2½	45
Thurmaston	3	48
Syston	2	50
Rearsby	2	52
Brooksby	2	54
Frisby	2	56
Melton Mowbray	4	60

To the right of 5 is Egdcott, W. H. Chauncy, Esq. and Dunsmore, a Roman Station.

At 6, on the left, Arberry Banks, a Roman Station.

At 13, on right, Fawsley Park, late Lucy Knightley, Esq.

To the r. of Daventry, Burrow Hill, a Roman Station.

At 49, on the r. Barkby, Mr. Pochin,

On the left, Wanlip, Mr. Hudson.

Two Miles to the right of 52, Gaddesby, Mr. Ayre.

At 54, on the left, Mr. Whitbread.

At 55, on the l. Rotherby, Mrs. Tombes.

BANBURY continued to *Grantham* and *Lincoln*.

To *Melton Mowbray*, above	—	60
Walthan on the Wolds	5	65

Grantham, Linc.	10	75
Ancaster	8	83
Lincoln	20	103

BATH to *Birmingham* and *Derby*.

To the Monument on Lansdown		4
Toll-Down House	5	9
Cross Hands Inn	3	12
Petty France, Gloc.	$2\frac{1}{2}$	$14\frac{1}{2}$
Cold Harbour	$7\frac{1}{2}$	22
Nympsfield	4	26
Frocefter	$1\frac{1}{2}$	$27\frac{1}{2}$
Whitminster	$3\frac{1}{2}$	31
Quedgeley	5	36
GLOCESTER*	$2\frac{1}{2}$	$38\frac{1}{2}$
Longford	2	$40\frac{1}{2}$
Twigworth	1	$41\frac{1}{2}$
Tewksbury	8	$49\frac{1}{2}$
Shire Stone and Br.	$3\frac{1}{4}$	$52\frac{3}{4}$
Ripple, Worc.	$\frac{3}{4}$	$53\frac{1}{2}$
Severnstoke	4	$57\frac{1}{2}$
Kemsey	3	$60\frac{1}{2}$
WORCESTER	4	$64\frac{1}{2}$
Droitwich	7	$71\frac{1}{2}$
Broomsgrove	6	$77\frac{1}{2}$
Birmingham, Warw.	14	$91\frac{1}{2}$
LICHFIELD, Staff.	16	$107\frac{1}{2}$
Burton on Trent	12	$119\frac{1}{2}$
Derby.	12	$131\frac{1}{2}$

From Glocester to Worcester, another Road, viz.

To Maizemore		$2\frac{3}{4}$
Longdon	$9\frac{3}{4}$	$12\frac{1}{2}$
Upton	$3\frac{1}{2}$	16
Powic	7	23
WORCESTER	$3\frac{1}{4}$	$26\frac{1}{4}$

In 1784, a new Cut was opened, by which the Steepness of Frocester-Hill was much lessened.

At $4\frac{1}{2}$, on r. Thomas Whitington, Esq.

At 7, on l. Durham, Mr. Brathwaite.

At 10, on l. Doddington Park, Sir Wm. Codrington.

At 14, on r. Badmington Park, Duke of Beaufort.

At 22, on r. Kingscote, the Seat of Robert Kingscote, Esq.

At 16, on r. Spring Park, Lord Ducie.

Near Severnstroke is Crome, a Seat of the Earl of Coventry.

BATH to *Taunton, Exeter*, and *Falmouth*.

Dunkerton		4
Badstoc	3	7
Chilcompton	5	12
Old Down Inn	$1\frac{1}{2}$	$13\frac{1}{2}$
Emboro'	2	$15\frac{1}{2}$
WELLS	$3\frac{1}{2}$	19
Coxley	2	21
Polsham	1	22
Glastonbury	$2\frac{1}{2}$	$24\frac{1}{2}$
Northover	1	$25\frac{1}{2}$
Street	1	$26\frac{1}{2}$
Pipers Inn	3	$29\frac{1}{2}$
Ashcott	$\frac{1}{2}$	30
Knowle	$7\frac{1}{2}$	$37\frac{1}{2}$
Bridgewater	$2\frac{1}{2}$	40
North Petherton	$2\frac{1}{2}$	$42\frac{1}{2}$
West Monkton	5	$47\frac{1}{2}$
Taunton	$3\frac{1}{2}$	51
Bishops Hull	2	53
Wellington	5	58
Rockwell Green	$1\frac{1}{2}$	$59\frac{1}{2}$
Sampford Arundel	$1\frac{1}{2}$	61
Red Ball	$1\frac{1}{2}$	$62\frac{1}{2}$

Maiden Down	½	63
South Appledore	2	65
Cullumpton	5	70
Bradnich	3	73
EXETER	9	82
To *Truro*, p. 33.	84	170
Penryn	9	179
Falmouth	2	181

This is nearer thro' Tiverton, and most frequented.

At 5, on l. Combe-Hay, T. Smith, Esq.

* *Another Road from Bath to Taunton*, p. 231.

In the Road from Bath to Wells, on the l. is Comb-Hay, the elegant Seat of John Smith, Esq.

On the same Road, beyond Redstoc, on the l. is Ammerdown, Thomas Jolliffe, Esq. built by Mr. Wyatt.

On the l. of the 11 Mile-stone is Downside-House, Capt. Fooks, of the Navy.

At Chilcompton, Major Tucker.

At Glastonbury, the Abbey.

On l. of Durston is the Seat of Lord Hawley.

Beyond Ashcott, at a distance, the Obelisk; at Burton Pynsent, Countess Dowager of Chatham's.

On 2, Shipwic, G. Templar, Esq.

Near West Moncton, Walford, H. W. Sandford, Esq.

Half a Mile farther, Court House, M. Brickdale, Esq.

Forty-nine, on r. Hestercombe, T Tyndale Warre, Esq.

Fifty-five, on r. Heatherton Park, Sir T. Gunston.

BATH to BRISTOL, the Lower Road.

To Twyverton,	*Som.*	—	2
Newton		1	3
Keynsham		4½	7½
Brislington		3	10½
BRISTOL		2½	13

On the l. of 3 is Newton St. Loo, the Seat of J. Smith Langton, Esq.

At 8, on r. —— Butcher, Esq.

At 9½, on r. —— Wier, Esq.

Before Brislington, on l. —— Ireland, Esq. and a little beyond, on left, —— Bryce, Esq.

At 11, on left, —— Tongue, Esq.

BATH to BRISTOL, the Upper Road.

To Kelston,	*Som.*	—	3¾
Bitton,	*Gloc.*	2½	6¼
Willsbridge		1	7¼
West Hannam		1¼	8½
St. George		2	10½
BRISTOL		2½	13

Before Kelston, on left, Sir Cæsar Hawkins.

At Willsbridge, Mr. Pearsall.

BATH to CHESTER.

To BRISTOL, *above*,	Som.	—	13
Wotton under Edge,	*Gloc.*	19¼	32¼
Glocester		18¼	50½
Tewkesbury		11¼	61¼
Worcester,	Worc.	15½	77¼
Kidderminster		14½	91¾
Bewdley		2	93¾
Bridgenorth,	Salop.	15½	109¼

Shrewsbury	20½	129¾
Whitchurch	20½	150¼
CHESTER	20½	170¾

BATH to St. DAVID's.

To BRISTOL, p. 230.	—	13
Westbury, *Glocef.*	3	16
Compton	4	20
Ayleverton	3½	23½
Auft Ferry	1½	25
Crofs the Severn to		
Beachley	3	28
Chepftow, Monm.	3	31
Ragland	15	46
Abergavenny	10	56
Thence to		
St. DAVID's, p. 84.	132	188

Near Chepftow is Piercefield, the beautiful Seat of —— Smith, Efq.

BATH to EXETER.

To WELLS, p. 228.	—	19
Polfham	3	22
Glaftonbury	2½	24½
Street	2	26½
Piper's Inn	3	29½
Aifhcott	½	30
Bridgewater	10	40
North Petherton	2½	42½
Weft Monkton	5	47½
Taunton	3½	51
Wellington	7	58
Tiverton	14	72
EXETER	14	86

Beyond Aifhcott, on l. Sedgmoor; and, at a Diftance, the Obelifk, built by Sir Rich. Pynfent, in Memory of the late Earl of Chatham.

On the r. of Shopwic, George Templer, Efq.
At Weft Monkton, on r. is Walford, Hen. W. Sandford, Efq. and, Half a Mile beyond, Court Houfe, Matt. Brickdale, Efq.

BATH to HEREFORD.

To GLOCESTER, p. 227	—	38½
Thence to		
HEREFORD, p. 94.	30	68½

BATH to *Nottingham*.

Petty France, p. 227.	—	14½
Didmarton, *Gloc.*	3	17½
Tetbury	6	23½
Crofs Way	8	31½
*Cirencefter**	2½	34
Barnefley	4	38
Bibury	3	41
Aldfworth	3½	44½
Shireborne	3	47½
Stowe	7½	55
Morton	4¼	59¼
Halford Bridge, War.	10¼	69½
Eatingdon	2½	72
Wellfburne	4½	76½
Barford	3¼	79¾
Longbridge	1¼	81
Warwic	1¼	82¼
Guy's Cliff	1¼	83½
Wooton	1¼	84¾
Kenilworth	2½	87¼
COVENTRY	5	92¼
Folefhill	2	94¼
Longford	1	95¼
Bedworth	2	97¼
Collicroft	¾	98
Griff	½	98½

Coton	1	99½
Nuneaton	1	100½
Hincley, Leic.	5	105½
Earls Shilton	3	108½
Leicester	11	119½
Belgrave	1½	121
Mountsorrel	4½	125½
Quarendon, or Quon	1	126½
Loughborough	4	130½
Nottingham, p. 153.	14	144½

On r. of Petty France, Badmington Park, Duke of Beaufort.

At Cirencester, the Seat and fine Woods of Earl Bathurst.

At Barnesley, on l. Barnesley Park, James Musgrave, Esq.

At Bibury, Mr. Cresswell.

At Shireborn, Lord Sherborn.

At Guy's Cliff, a Seat of Mr. Greathead.

At Kenilworth, the noble Remains of the Castle belonging to the Earl of Clarendon.

Stonely, Lord Leigh, lies two Miles to the right of Kenilworth ; the old Road went by it.

Plantations on the Heath by Mr. Gregory.

Half a Mile beyond Coventry, on the l. see Newhouse, Mr. Clarke's.

Before and after Bedworth, see Sir Roger Newdigate's House, amongst the Woods on the left.

A Mile on the left of Earls Shilton is Kirkby, Lord Wentworth; and beyond it, on left, Tooley Park, Mr. Dodd, late Mr. Boothby's.

Two Miles before Leicester, on r. Branston-Hall, Mr. Winstanley.

For the rest, see p. 147.

* From Cirencester to Stowe, another Road, along the Foss Way, viz.

To New House	—	3
Fos Cross	3	6
Northleach	4	10
Stowe	8½	18½

At 8½, on left, Stowel, Lord Chedworth.

BATH to OXFORD.

To Aldsworth, p. 232.	—	44½
Burford, Oxf.	6½	51
Witney	7	58
Eynsham	5	63
OXFORD	5	68

At Barnesley, on left, Barnesley Park, James Musgrave, Esq.

At Bibury, Mr. Cresswell.

Beyond Aldsworth, on left, see Sherborn Lodge.

Another Road, viz.

To Chippenham, p. 64.	—	13½
Marlborough, p. 64.	19	32½
Aldborn	7	39½
Lamborn, Berks	6	45½
Wantage	6	51½
OXFORD	13	64½

Another new Road from Bath to Oxford.

To Chippenham, p. 64.	—	13
Malmsbury	10	23
Charlton	2	25
Criclade	10	35
Highworth	8	43
Coleshill	2	45
Farringdon	4	49
Kingston Inn	8	57
Fifield	1½	58½
Tubney Warren	1½	60

Beſſiſleigh	2	62
Cumner Hill	3	65
OXFORD	2	67

At Malmſbury, the Abbey.

At Charlton, Earl of Suffolk.

Beyond Highworth, on r. Hannington, Rev. Mr. Freke.

At Coleſhill, Hon. Mr. Bouverie.

Before Coleſhill, on r. Buſcot Park, Mr. Loveden.

At Kingſton Inn, on l. A.W. Blandy, Eſq.

Another Road, viz.

To Croſs Hands Inn	—	12
Petty France	3	15
Didmarton	2	17
Tetbury	6	23
Cirenceſter	10	33
Fairford	7	40
Lechdale	3	43
Farringdon	6	49
Kingſton Inn	8	57
OXFORD	10	67

At 7, on the l. is Durham, a fine Seat of Mr. Braithwaite.

On the r. of Petty France is Badmington Park, a beautiful Seat of the Duke of Beaufort.

A Mile l. of the Duke of Beaufort's is a fine Roman Encampment, very perfect.

At Cirenceſter are the fine Seat and Woods of Earl Bathurſt

BATH to *Plymouth*.

To EXETER, p. 229.	—	82
Thence to *Plymouth*, p. 38.	39½	121

BATH to *Southampton*.

To Midford	—	3
Hinton	2	5
Phillips Norton	2	7
Beckington	3	10
Warminſter, Wilts	6	16
Heytſbury	3	19
Knook	1	20
Codford	3	23
Deptford Inn	3	26
Steeple Longford	3	29
Stapleford	2	31
South Newton	2	33
Foulſton	2½	35½
SALISBURY	2½	38
Alderbury	4	42
White Pariſh	4	46
Romſey	8¾	54¾
Upton	3¼	58
Half-Way Oak	1¼	59¼
Southampton	3¾	63

Near Midford is Prior Park, a Seat built by the late Ralph Allen, Eſq

BATH to *Portſmouth*.

To SALISBURY, *above*	—	38
The Hut	7	45
Stocbridge	8	53
WINCHESTER	8½	61½
Waltham	10	71½
Wickham	5¼	76¾
Southwic	4	80¾
Portſmouth	7¾	88½

Another Road, viz.

To *Romſey*, above	—	54¾
WINCHESTER	11	65¾
Waltham	10	75¾
Wickham	5¼	81

Fareham	4	85
Cosham	4¾	89¾
Portsmouth	4¼	94

BATH to *Brighthelmstone.*

To Southwic, p. 236.	—	80¾
Havant	7¼	88
CHICHESTER	9	97
Arundel, p. 222.	10	107
Findon	8	115
Bramber	5	120
Brighthelmstone	9	129

Another Road, viz.

To Wickham by Stocbridge, p. 236.	—	76¾
Fareham	4	80¾
Cosham	4¾	85½
Havant	4½	90
Brighthelmstone, above	41	131

BATH to *Stourton.*

To Beckington, p. 236	—	10
Froome	3	13
Long Leat	4	17
Maiden Bradley	3	20
Stourton	4	24

At Long Leat is an ancient Seat of the Marquis of Bath; at Maiden Bradley, that of the Duke of Somerset; and at Stourton is the Seat and beautiful Gardens of Sir Rich. Colt Hoare, Bart.

BATH to *Taunton* and *Exeter* by *Bridgewater.*

To WELLS, p. 228.	—	19
Polsham	3	22
Glastonbury	2½	24½
Northover	1	25½

Street	1	26½
Piper's Inn	3	29½
Ashcot	½	30
Bridgewater	10	40
North Petherton	2½	42½
Taunton	8½	51

Another Road, p. 228.

Beyond Ashcot, on L. see Sedgmoor, and at a Distance the Obelisk, at the Countess Dowager of Chatham's, built by Sir Richard Pynsent, in Memory of Mr. Pitt.
On r. is a Seat of George Templar, Esq.
At two Miles from North Petherton, on the r. is —— Sandford, Esq. and Half a Mile farther is West Monkton, before which is a white House, Matthew Brickdale, Esq.

BATH to *Blandford.*

To *Warminster*, p. 236.	—	16
Blandford	27	43

BATH to *Weymouth.*

To *Old Down*	—	13
Shepton	5	18
Connard's Grave Inn	1	19
Ansford Inn	12	31
Sherborn	12	43
Long Burton	3	46
Middle Marsh	4	50
Dorchester	11	61
Melcomb Regis	7½	68½
Weymouth	½	69

At Sherborn, the Seat and beautiful Park of the Earl of Digby.
To r. of Long Burton is Leweston House, Sir F. Nash; and to the l. West Hall, Rev. Mr. King.

4

At Middle Marsh, on l. the Gránge, Mr. Sturt; near which is Castle Hill, a Seat of Mr. Foy; and to r. Mintern, a Seat of Adm. Digby.
At 50, on r. of the Road, is Ceine Abbey, to the right of which is Sydling, Sir John Smith, Bart.

BATH to *Weymouth* through *Blandford*.

To *Warminster*, p. 236.	—	16
Shaftsbury	15	31
Blandford	12	43
Dorchester	16	59
Weymouth	8	67

BATTEL to *Lewes*.

To Boreham-Street	—	8
Gardner's Street	2	10
Horse-Bridge	4	14
Ringmer	9	23
Lewes	3	26

Between Boreham-Street and Gardner's Street, Windmill-Hill, Mr. Conyers.
Laughton Pound, 6 Miles from Horse-Bridge

BAKEWELL to *Chesterfield*.

To Rowsley	—	3¼
Leading Gate	5	8¼
Walton	3	11¼
Chesterfield	2	13¼

At 2, on l. Haddon-Hall, Duke of Rutland

BANBURY to *Campden*.

North Newton, *Oxf.*	—	2½
Shutford	2½	5
Brailes, *Warw.*	5½	10½

Shipston,	Worcest.	3½	14
Ebbrington Mill		4¾	18¾
Campden,	Gloucest.	2¼	21

On r. of 19 is Ebbrington, late Sir Wm. Keyte, Bart. which he set on Fire and burnt, with himself in it.

BARNSTAPLE to *Launceston*.

To Roundshill, *Dev.*	—	3
St. John's Chapel	1	4
Newton Tracy	2	6
Torrington	5½	11½
Little Torrington	1	12½
Petrocstow	5½	18
Hatherleigh	4	22
Five Oaks	5	27
Bridistow	6½	33½
Lyston	9	42½
Launceston	4	46½

BAWTRY to *Sheffield*.

To *Tickhill*	—	4
Maltby	4	8
Wickersley	3	11
Cankley Mill	4	15
Tinstey	1½	16½
Attercliff	2	18½
Sheffield	1½	20

BAWTRY to *Rotherham*.

To Wickersley, *above*	—	11
Rotherham	4	15

BEDFORD to *Northampton*.

To Bromham Bridge	—	3
Turvey	5	8
Brayfield, *Bucks*	¾	8¾
Lavendon	1¼	10
Yardley, *N.amp.*	4	14
Denton	2	16

Brayfield	1	17
Little Houghton	1½	18½
Northampton	3½	22

At Bromham, the Seat of Lord Trevor.
At Brayfield, the Seat of William Farrer, Esq.
Before Denton, on r. Castle Ashby, E. of Northampton; and on left, Yardley Chase.

BEDFORD to *Woburn*.

Houghton-Conquest Turnpike	—	6½
Between Houghton and Ampthill Parks to		
Ampthill	1½	8
Liddington Turnpike	3	11
Ridgemount	2	13
Through Woburn-Park to Woburn	2	15

At Ridgemount, on l. Mr. Potter.

BEVERLEY to *New Malton*.

To Lund	—	7
Bainton	3	10
Wharram le Street	11½	21½
North Grimston	2	23½
Norton	4½	28
New Malton	½	28½

BIRMINGHAM to *Manchester*.

To Soho, *Stafford.*	—	2
Sandwell Park	2	4
Wednesbury	4	8
Neachill Hill	4	12
Wolverhampton	1	13
Pendeford Hall	4	17
Penkridge	6	23
Stafford	6	29

Alston Hall	5	34
Stone	2	36
Newcastle	9	45
Manchester	36	81

The Soho, an extensive Manufactory of Mathew Boulton, Esq.
At 4, on the right, Earl of Dartmouth.
At 12, on the r. Neachill Hall, John Inman, Esq.
At 14, on the r. Golbrook-Hall, Mr. Jones.
At 17, on the l. Thomas Fowler, Esq.
At 20, on the l. Somerford-Hall, Hon. Edward Monckton.
At 24, on the r. Tiddesley-Hall, Sir Edward Lytelton. Bart.
At 34, on the r. Aston-Hall, John Wheild, Esq.
At 37, on the l. Darlaston-Hall, John Jervis, Esq.
At 41, on the l. Trentham-Hall, Marq. of Stafford.

BIRMINGHAM to *Shrewsbury*.

To Hamstead, *Staff.*	—	3
Walsall	5	8
Wolverhampton	6	14
Tettenhall	2	16
Wrottesley Lodge	3	19
Shrewsbury	25	44

BIRMINGHAM to *Ludlow*.

To *Kidderminster*	—	18
Cleobury Mortimer	11	29
Ludlow	11	40

Near Cleobury is Morley, the Seat of Sir Walter Blount.

BIRMINGHAM to *Warwic*.

To Knowle	—	10
Hatton	6	16
Warwic	4	20

BLANDFORD to *Trowbridge* and *Bradford*.

To Shroton, *Dorfet*.	—	6
Ewerne Minſter	1	7
Sutton Waldron	1	8
Funtmill	1	9
Shaftsbury	3	12
Eaſt Knoyle, *Wilts.*	5	17
Deverell	7	24
Crokerton	1½	25½
Sambourn	1	26½
Warminſter	½	27
Weſtbury Leigh	3	30
Weſtbury	1	31
Heywood Common	1	32
Trowbridge	3½	35½
Bradford	3	38½

N. B. *You may go to Bradford without going through* Trowbridge, *which lies a little to the right of the Road.*

At Heywood Common is Heywood Houſe, Thomas Phipps, Eſq.

BLANDFORD to *Poole*.

To Wimborn Minſter	—	10
Poole	6	16

Near Wimborn, on the r. Kingſton-Hall, Mr. Bankes.
On the l. High Hall, Mr. Fitch.
Two Miles beyond Wimborn, on the r. Merley-Houſe, the Seat of Ralph Willett, Eſq.

Another Road.

To Blandford St. Mary	—	1
Charlton Marſhall	1	2

Spetiſbury	1	3
Corſe Mullen	4	7
Poole	8	15

At Spetiſbury, on the l. Mr. Jekyll; and on the r. beyond, the Seat and fine Park of R. E. D. Groſvenor, Eſq.
On the r. near Corſe, late Tho. Fred. Wentworth, Eſq. now Earl of Strafford.
A little farther, on the r. Henbury, Mr. Churchill.

BLANDFORD to *Sherborne*.

To Dunweſton	—	2½
Shillingſtone	2½	5
Sturminſter-Newton	5	10
Stalbridge	4	14
Sherborne	6	20

A Mile from Blandford is Brianſtone-Houſe, newly built, with pleaſant Walks through the Plantations, called Brianſton Cliff, to Blandford Bridge, the Seat of H. W. Portman, Eſq.
On the r. of Shillingſtone are two high Hills, called Hodd and Hambleton, where are the Remains of an ancient Roman Encampment.

BOSTON to *Sleaford*.

To Kirton Holme	—	4¼
Swinſhead, North End	1¼	6
Garric	4	10
Heckington	2	12
Kirkby Laythorp	3	15
Sleaford	2	17

BOSTON to *Lynn*.

To Kirton	—	3½
l. to Fofs-Dyke Waſh *	6	9½

* See p. 246.

Saracen's Head	3	12½
Fleet	4½	17
Gedney	1	18
Sutton	2	20
Crofs Keys Wafh*	3½	23½
Crofs Keys, *Norf.*	1½	25
Weft Lynn	5	30
Ferry over to		
Lynn Regis	¼	30¼

BOURN to *Coltfworth.*

To Endenham, *Linc.*	—	3¼
Grimfthorpe	2	5¼
Swinftead	1	6¼
Corby	2	8¼
Coltfworth	5	13¼

At Grimfthorpe, the Caftle and Park, a Seat of the Duke of Ancafter.

BRAINTREE to *Maldon.*

To Black Notley	—	1
White Notley	2½	3½
Falkbourn	1½	5
Cheping Hill	1½	6½
Witham	½	7
Wickham	3	10
Langford	1½	11½
Heybridge	1	12½
Maldon	¾	13¼

At Falkborn, John Bullock, Efq.

Near Cheping Hill, Witham Place, late Lord Stourton, now Mr. Talbot.

At Wickham Bridge, Mr. Burton.

At 11½, on the r. is a Seat of Nicolas Weftcomb, Efq.

* *A Table for paffing over* Crofs-Keys *and* Fofs-Dyke *Wafhes, in the County of Lincoln.*

Moon's Age.		Full Sea	Begin to pafs over Fofs-Dyke Wafh.	Begin to pafs over Crofs Keys Wafh.	End paffing over Fofs-Dyke Wafh.	End paffing over Crofs Keys Wafh.
		H. M.	H. M.	H. M.	H. M.	H. M.
1	16	7— 0	10— 0	10—30	4—15	3—35
2	17	7—48	10—48	11—18	5—53	4—23
3	18	8—36	11—36	12— 6	6—21	5—11
4	19	9—24	12—24	12—54	7— 9	5—59
5	20	10—12	1—12	1—42	7—57	6—47
6	21	11— 0	2— 0	2—30	8—45	7—35
7	22	11—48	2—48	3—18	9—33	8—23
8	23	12—26	3—26	3—36	10—21	9—11
9	24	1—24	4—24	4—54	11— 9	9—59
10	25	2—12	5—12	5—42	11—57	10—47
11	26	3— 0	6— 0	6—30	12—45	11—35
12	27	3—48	6—48	7—18	1—33	12—23
13	28	4—36	7—36	8— 6	2—21	1—11
14	29	5—24	8—24	8—54	3— 9	1—59
15	30	6—12	9—12	9—42	3—57	2—47

BRIDPORT to EXETER, by *Lime*.

To Chidioc,	*Dorf.*	—	3
Charmouth		3½	6½
Lime		2	8½
Cullyford,	*Devon*	6½	15
Sidford		7½	22½
Newton Popler		2½	25
Bishops Clyst		7½	32½
Heavy Tree		3½	36
EXETER		1	37

Another Road by Axminster, p. 32.

BRISTOL to *Banbury*.

To Stapleton,	*Gloc.*	—	3
Hanborough		2	5
Wiblet		4	9
Yate		1	10
Chipping Sodbury		1	11
Petty France		5	16
Didmerton		3	19
Tetbury		6	25
Cross Way		8	33
Cirencester		2½	35½
Barnesley		4	39½
Bibury		3	42½
Aldsworth		3½	46
Burford,	Oxf.	6½	52½
Shipton Underwood		4	56½
Chipping Norton		6½	63
South Newton		7	70
Bloxham		2	72
Banbury		3½	75½

To the right of Petty France is Badmington Park, a Seat of the Duke of Beaufort.

Before Cirencester, on left, the Seat and Park of Earl Bathurst.

At Barnesley the Park, J. Musgrave, Esq.

At Bibury, Mr. Cresswell.

Beyond Aldsworth, on left, see Sherborn Lodge.

BRISTOL to *Bridgewater*.

Bedminster	—	1½
Langford	10½	12
Cross	5	17
East Brent	5	22
South Brent	1	23
High Bridge	2½	25½
Huntspill	1	26½
Bridgewater	6½	33

BRISTOL to CHESTER.

To Westbury,	*Gloc.*	—	3
Henbury		2	5
Compton		2	7
Ayleverton		3½	10½
Aust Ferry		1½	12
Cross the Severn to			
Beachley		3	15
Chepstow,	Monm.	3	18
Trelagh Grainge		5½	23½
Trelagh		2½	26
Goghekes		2½	28½
Lediard		1	29½
Monmouth		3¼	32¾
Lady Well,	*Heref.*	3½	36¼
Garron Bridge		2¾	39
Wormeloy Stump		5	44
Red Hill		5½	49½
HEREFORD		1¼	50¾
Morton		4¼	55
Wellington Bridge		1	56
Dinmore Hill		3	59
Wharton		2¼	61¼
Evington Bridge		1¼	62½
Leominster		2½	65

Lyston		2½	67½
Richard's Castle		4	71½
Overton,	*Salop*	2½	74
Ludlow		2	76
Oniberry		4¾	80¾
Newton		2¾	83½
Little Stretton		6	89½
Church Stretton		1½	91
All Stretton		1½	92½
Lebotwood		2½	95
Dorrington		3½	98½
Stapleton		½	99
Pulley Common		3¼	102¼
Shrewsbury		2¾	105
Hadnal Chapel		5¼	110¼
Lea Bridge		4¾	115
Reese Heath		3½	118½
Rees		1½	120
Whitchurch		5½	125½
Thence to			
CHESTER, p. 128.		20	145½

On the right, a little from Bristol, is Redlands, the Seat of the late John Cousins, Esq and on the l. of Westbury is King's Weston, the Seat of Lord Clifford.

At Henbury, Blaize Castle, —— Farr, Esq.

Near Chepstow is Persefield, the beautiful Gardens of the late Valentine Morris, Esq. now Mr. Smith; and also the Ruins of an old Castle.

At 31, on the r. is Troy House, a Seat of the Duke of Beaufort.

On the left of Wormelow Stump, Meemd, the Seat of Sir Richard Symonds, Bart.

Between Hereford and Morton, on the l. Holmer, a House belonging to Mr. Caldecot.

Before you go over Dinmore Hill, pass on the l. Burghope, an ancient Mansion, formerly the Seat of Sir John Dineley Goodyere, Bart. who was murdered by his Brother, Capt. Samuel Goodyere. It now belongs to Lord Selsea.

On the r. a Mile short of Wharton, is Hampton Court, a Seat of the late Countess of Coningsby, now Lord Malden, built, as tradition goes, by Henry IV.

On the l. going to Ludlow, is Berrington, a fine House lately built by the Right Hon. Tho. Harley.

Near it, on the left, is Eye, Mr. Gorges; and see also, on the left, at a Distance, Shobden Court, Visc. Bateman.

On the l. a new-built Brick House, near the Road, not far from Ludlow, Mr. Green; and on the left also, before you pass Ludlow Bridge, is Ludford, where, near the Church, is the Seat of Sir Francis Charlton, Bart. who has here a large Park.

A little beyond Ludlow is a Bowling-Green, whence is a fine Prospect, and the Ruins of the Castle celebrated for being the Residence of the Lord Marches of Wales, the Death of Prince Arthur, &c.

On the l. is Oakley Park, late the Earl of Powis, now Lord Clive.

On the left of Newton is Stoke Castle.

At Church Stretton, on the left, is the large and fertile Hill of Longment; and, a little beyond it, the beautiful Seat and Park of Robert Corbett, Esq.

On the right all the Way between Church Stretton and Shrewsbury, see the Wrekyn, a very high Hill.

At Dorrington, on the r. is Condover, the Seat of N. O. S. Owen, Esq. and on the l. is Lyth Hill, which affords a most beautiful ride.

At 3, on the l. of Hadnall, is Hardwicke, a Seat of Sir Richard Hill, Bart.

At Lea Bridge, on the r. is Hawkstone House, and the beautiful Park of Sir Richard Hill; and at Rees, the Seat of his Brother, John Hill, Esq.

Bristol to *Crewkerne.*

From Bristol to		
Pensford	—	6¾
Clutton	3	9¾
Temple Cloud	1¼	11
Farrington	1½	12½
Chewton Mendip	2½	15
Wells	5½	20½
Polsham	3	23½
Glastonbury	2½	26
Street	2	28
l. to Compton	3	31
Littleton	1¾	32¾
Somerton	1¾	34½
Long Sutton	2½	37
Longlode	2	39
Martoc	2½	41½
West Chinnoc	4¼	45¾
Crewkerne	2¾	48½

Bristol to Haverfordwest.
The Mail-Coach Road.

Westbury, *Glouc.*	—	3
Compton	3	6
Chisel, or New Ferry	3½	9½
Cross the Severn at High Water to		
Black Rock	3	12½
Poltskewit	1¼	13¾
Crick	1	14¾
Caerwent	1	15¾
Rock and Fountain	3	18¾
Unicorn	2	20¾
Cats Ash	2	22¾
Christ Church	2	24¾
Newport, Monm.	2¼	27
Thence to		
Haverfordwest, p. 89.	103	130

At 13, on l. is Penhow Castle, —— Lloyd, Esq.

At 22, on l. is Llanovery, Robert Salusbury, Esq.

Bristol to Hereford.

To Black Rock, p. 251	—	12½
Postskewit Monin, *Mon*	1¼	13¾
Crick	1	14¾
Shirenewton	2	16¾
Davenden	4	20¾
Trelagh	4	24¾
Monmouth	5	29¾
Lady Well, *Heref.*	3½	33¼
Garron Bridge	2¾	36
Wormley Stump	5	41
Red Hill	5½	46½
Hereford	1¼	47¾

At 13, on r. St. Pietre Park, Tho. Lewis, Esq.

At 16, on r. Itton Court, John Curre, Esq.

At 24, John Rumsey, Esq.

Bristol to *Weymouth.*

To Pensford	—	7
Old Down	8	15
Weymouth, as in p. 238.	50	65

Bristol to Taunton.

To Crofs	—	16½
Bridgewater	16½	33
North Petherton	2½	35½
Taunton	8½	44

At 2 Miles from North Petherton, on the right, —— Sandford, Efq. and Half a Mile farther is Weft Monkton, before which is a white Houfe, Matthew Brickdale, Efq.

Bristol to Worcester.

To Horfield	—	2
Filton	1½	3½
Almonfbury	3	6½
Alliftone	3½	10
Farnhill	5	15
Stone	1¾	16¾
Neport	1¾	18
Cambridge	5¼	23¼
Or,		
Alliftone, *above*	—	10
Thornbury	1	11
Hill	4	15
Berkley	3	18
Cambridge	5¼	23¼
Whitminfter	3½	26¾
Putley	1½	28
Quodgeley	3¼	31¼
Glocester	2¾	34
Thence to		
Worcester, p. 225.	25½	59½

To l. of 6, is Knowle, Barnard Chefter, Efq.

To the l. of Newport, is Berkeley Caftle, Seat of the Earl of Berkeley.

At Thornby, the Caftle, Duke of Norfolk.

At Hill, Lady Fufh.

Bristol to *Durfley*.

To Stapleton, *Glocefl.*	—	2
Hambrook	3	5
Iron Acton	4	9
Woodend	6	15
Wotton-under-edge	5	20
Stinchcombe	4	24
Kingfhill	1	25
Durfley	1	26

At 3 Miles, on the l. Stoke-Gifford Lodge, Duchefs Dowager of Beaufort.

At 4, on the r. Frenchay, Edward Harford, Efq.

At 16, on the r. Tortworth Court, Lord Ducie.

At 19, on the l. Bradley Houfe, Thomas Nelmes, Efq.

At 24, on the l. Peer's Court, Edward Hofkins, Efq.

At 25, on the l. Thomas Purnell, Efq.

Bristol to Exeter.

To Barrow Court, *Somerfet.*	—	5
Churchill	7	12
Crofs	5	17
Eaft Brent	4	21
South Brent	2	23
Huntfpill	4	27
Bridgewater	6	33
Walford	8	41
Taunton	4	45
Wellington	7	52
Stampford Arundel	3	55
Collumpton	9	64
Exeter	12	76

At South Brent, Rev. Thomas Gould, B. D.

On the r. of Huntfpill, George Saunders, Efq.

A little farther, on the l. Thomas Greenwood, Efq.

At 41, on the r. Henry William Sandford, Efq.

At 42, on the r. Weſt Monkten, Matthew Brickdale, Efq.

At 43, on the r. Hefiercombe, Copleſton Warre Bampfylde, Efq.

At 49, on the r. Heatherton, Sir Thomas Gunfton, Knt.

Briſtol to *Tewkesbury.*

To Filton Hay, *Glocef.*		4
Alveſton	6	10
Stone	6	16
Newport	2	18
Cambridge	5	23
Whitminſter	4	27
Quedgeley	4	31
Glocefter	3	34
Twigworth	2	36
Wooton	5	41
Tewkesbury	3	44

One Mile from Briſtol, on the l. Redland Court, Slade Baker, Efq.

At 4, on the l. The Rodney, John Weeks, Efq.

At 6, on the l. Knowl Park, Mrs. Chefter.

At 11, on the l. Grovefend, Nathaniel Crowther, Efq.

At 14, on the r. Tortworth Park, Lord Ducie.

At 18, on the l. Berkeley Caſtle, Earl Berkeley.

At 22, on the l. Goffington-Hall, Henry Jones, Efq.

At 26, on the l. Fromebridge Wire-Mill.

At 33, on the l. Hempſtead Houfe, Daniel Lyfons, Efq.

Bromyard to *Moreton-in-the Marſh.*

To Gaines		5
Brodway	3	8
St. John's	5	13
Worcefter	1	14
Churchill	3	17
Wyre Piddle	6	23
Evefham	7	30
Broadway	6	36
Spring Hill	2	38
The Troopers	2	40
Burton-on the-Hill	2	42
Moreton-in-the-Marſh	2	44

One Mile on the l. of Bromyard, Rockhampton, Richard Barnaby, Efq.

At 6, on the r. Knighwick, Rev. Dr. Stillingfleet.

At 7, on the l. Whitborne Court, Richard Chambers. Efq.

At 10, on the r. Leigh Court, John Spooner, Efq.

At 18, on the l. White Lady Aſton, Rev. Richard Hurdman.

At 36, on the l. Broadway Hill, Sir John Cotterell, Bart.

At 38, on the r. Earl of Coventry.

Bromyard to *Stourbridge.*

To Upper Sapy, *Worcef.*		6
Hundred Houfe Inn	6	12
Dunley	4	16
Kidderminſter	6	22
Churchill	3	25
Stourbridge	4	29

At 7, on the r. Stanford Park, Edw. Winnington, Efq.

At 25, on the r. Francis Smith Stokes, Efq.

Bury to *Botesdale.*

	—	16
Scole	6	22
Harleston	8	30
Bungay	8	38
Gillingham	7	45
Haddiscoe	5	50
Fritton	2½	52½
Gorleston	4½	57
Yarmouth	2	59

Buxton to *Matloc.*

To Tideswell	—	7
Wardlow	2½	9½
Ashford	3½	13
Bakewell	1	14
Rowsley	3¼	17¼
Darley	2¼	19½
Matloc	3¼	22¾

Before Ashford is Monsal Dale; and at Ashford a Mill for sawing and polishing Marble.

At Bakewell, Dr. Bullock, and good Monuments in the Church for the Vernons.

Beyond Bakewell, Haddon-Hall, Duke of Rutland.

Buxton to *Worksop.*

To Fairfield	—	1
Tideswell	6	7
Stony Middleton	5¼	12¼
Calver	1¾	14
Brampton	6	20
Chesterfield	3	23
Brimington	2	25
Stavely	2	27
Barlborough	3½	30½
Whitwell	3½	34
Worksop	4	38

Before Worksop, on the r. Worksop Manor, Duke of Norfolk.

Buxton to *Warrington.*

Moss House, *Chesh.*	—	3
New Inn	2½	5½
Macclesfield	4½	10
Broken Cross	1½	11½
Chelford	5	16½
Ollerton Gates	3	19½
Knutsford	2½	22
Warrington, p. 136.	11	33

Cambridge to Coventry, (*the New Road.*)

To Fenny Stanton, *Hunting.*	—	10
Godmanchester	4	14
Huntingdon	1	15
l. to Brampton Pound	1¾	16¾
Ellington	3	19¾
Spaldwic	3½	23¼
Bythorn	4½	27¾
Thrapston, Northa.	4¼	32
Cranford	5	37
Barton Seagrave	2½	39½
Kettering	1½	41
Rowell, or *Rothwell*	4	45
Desborough	1½	46½
Hermitage House	2	48½
Little Bowden	3	51½
Harborough, Leic.	½	52
l. to Lubenham	2	54
Theddingworth	2½	56½
Husbands Bosworth	1½	58
North Kilworth	2	60
Walcote	3	63
Misterton	1	64
Lutterworth	1	65

Pailton	5	70
Streetaſton	1	71
Stretton	½	71½
Brinklow	1½	73
r. to Comb Abbey	2½	75½
Binley	1½	77
Stoke	1½	78½
COVENTRY	1½	80

Another Road, below.

At 5, on the r. Long Stanton, the Seat of Lady Hatton.

A little beyond Fenny Stanton, on the l. is another Seat of Lady Hatton, now inhabited by Parker Hammond, Eſq.

Beyond Huntingdon, on the right, Hinchinbrook Houſe, Earl of Sandwich.

Two Miles beyond Thrapſton, to the right, is Drayton, Viſe. Sackville; and to the l. Woodford, a Seat of Lady St. John.

At Cranford, a Seat of Sir George Robinſon, Bart.

At Barton Seagrave, Mr. Wilcock's; and, about 3 Miles to the right, Boughton Houſe, the late Duke of Montagu.

At Rowell, Serjeant Hill; and a Mile to the r. Ruſhton, Lord Cullen.

At Deiborough, Mr. Joyce.

A Mile on the right of Hermitage Houſe is Dingley, a Seat of the late Lord Howard of Walden, now of J. P. Hungerford, Eſq.

At Comb Abbey, a Seat of Lord Craven.

CAMBRIDGE to COVENTRY, (*the Old Road.*)

To Burn Leyes Com.	—	7
Eltiſley	4½	11½
St. *Neot's,* Hunt.	5½	17
Croſs the Ouſe to		

Eaton Ford	½	17½
r. to Stoughton Highway	5	22½
r. to Stonley	2	24½
Kimbolton	½	25
Tilbrook	1½	26½
Hargrave, N. ampt.	3	29½
Chelſton	3	32½
Higham Ferrers	2	34½
Or,		
From Stoughton Highway	—	22½
l. to Gr. Stoughton	½	23
Perton Hall, *Bedf.*	3	26
Yielden	5	31
Higham Ferrers	3½	34½
Wellingborough	4½	39
Wilby	2	41
Ecton	3	44
Billing	1½	45½
Weſton Favel	2	47½
Northampton	2½	50
Crick, p. 150.	13½	63½
Dunchurch, *Warw.*	7	70½
COVENTRY, 120.	11	81½
Or,		
From *Northampton*	—	50
to Daventry	11	61
Dunchurch	8	69
COVENTRY	11	80

Another Road, p. 258.

Three Miles from Cambridge, on the right, is Maddingley-Hall, the Seat of Sir John Hynde Cotton, Bart.

At Kimbolton, the Caſtle and Park, Duke of Mancheſter.

About a Mile before Yielden, to the left, is Melchborn Park, Lord St. John.

At Billing, Lord John Cavendish.
Four Miles on this Side Coventry is Comb Park and Abbey, a Seat of Lord Craven.

CAMBRIDGE to *Yarmouth*.

To Quy,	Camb.	—	5
Bottisham		2	7
Newmarket		6	13
Kentsford Bridge		4	17
Barrow Bottom		4½	21½
Saxham		1	22½
Bury		4½	27
Ixworth		7½	34½
Botesdale		9	43½
Osmonstone, or Scole Inn,	Norf.	8½	52
Harleston		7	59
Bungay,	Suff.	7	66
Beccles		5½	71½
Thence to			
Yarmouth, p. 207.		15	86½

Beyond Bury, on the right, John Symonds, Esq.
Three Miles beyond Bury, on the l. Sir Charles Banbury.
Beyond Botesdale, on the left, Thomas Holt, Esq.
On the r. a Mile before Bungay, see on the other side the Waveney, Flixton-Hall, a noble brick Mansion, —— Adair, Esq.

CAMBRIDGE to *Norwich*.

To Scole Inn, *above*	—	52
Long Stratton	10	62
Norwich	10	72

CARLISLE to *Egremont*.

To Dalston	—	4½
Hawkesdale	1½	6

Upper Welton	2½	8½
Thorney Stone	7	15½
Uldale	1½	17
Ouse Bridge	4½	21½
Cockermouth	5	26½
Little Clifton	5	31½
Distington	4½	36
Morresby	2½	38½
Whitehaven	2	40½
Hensingham	1½	42
Egremont	4½	46½

To the right of 7, Rose Castle, Bishop of Carlisle.

CARLISLE to *Keswic*.

Thorney Stone, *above*	—	15½
Langlands	1½	17
Orthwaite	1½	18½
High Side	2½	21
Little Crosthwaite	2	23
Keswic	4	27

CARLISLE to *Cockermouth*, by *Wigton*.

To Woodhouses	—	5½
Micklethwaite	3	8½
Wigton	2¼	10¾
Shaken Bridge	3	13¾
Newland's Row	2½	16¼
Kirkland Guards	2	18¼
Bothel	1	19¾
Cockermouth	7¾	27

CARLISLE to *Allonby*.

To *Wigton*, above	—	10¾
Waverton	2¼	13
West Newton	6	19
Allonby	3½	22½

S 2

CARLISLE to *Holm*.

To Moor Houfe	—	4½
Kirkbanton	1¾	6¼
Fingland	3¼	9½
Kirkbridge	1½	11
Long Newton	2½	13½
Mofs Side	2	15½
Holm	2	17½

CARLISLE to *Bownefs*.

To Kirkandrews	—	3
Burgh	2	5
Drumburgh	4½	9½
Bownefs	3½	13

In this Road you crofs and re-crofs the Picts Wall at 6¼, at 8, at 9¾, at 10½, and pafs the Weft End thereof at the Entrance of Bownefs, formerly a Roman Station, called *Blatum Bulgium*.

CANTERBURY to *Afhford*.

To Shamford Street	—	4½
Chilham	1¾	6¼
Godmerfham	1¾	8
Bilting	1½	9½
Kennington	3½	13
Afhford	1½	14½

At Chilham is Chilham Caftle and Park, the Seat of Tho. Heron, Efq.
At Godmerfham is Ford Park, the Seat of Thomas Knight, Efq.

CANTERBURY to *New Romney*.

To St. Laurence	—	½
r *to* Nackington	1	1½
Sheetend	1½	3

l. to Stone Street	1	4
The George	6	10
Stanford	4	14
Lymne Hill	3	17
Dymchurch	5	22
New Romney	4	26

At Nackington, the Seat of Richard Miller, Efq.
On the r. of 3 is Hippington, H. G. Fauffett, Efq. and on the l. —— Tillard, Efq.
On the r. of 8 is Evington, Sir John Honywood, Bart.
On the r. of 13, Mount Morris, Matthew Robinfon Morris, Efq. built, about the Beginning of the prefent Century, by Thomas Morris, Efq. one of King James the Second's Private Treafurers.

CAERMARTHEN to *Cardigan*.

To Llanelwith Ch.	—	3½
The County Stone	9¼	12¾
Kilrah Kilreaden, *Pemb.*	1¼	14
Velindra Mill	2½	16½
Bridel	6½	23
Cardigan	3	26

CHARD to *Bath*.

To *Ilminfter*, Som.	—	5
Hambridge	5	10
Langport	4	14
Somerton	5	19
Kenton Mandeville	6	25
Pylle	6	31
Shepton Mallet	4	35
Stratton	5	40
Radftoc	5	45
Dunkerton	2	47
Bath	5	52

On the r. of Ilminster is Dillington, Maurice Lloyd, Esq.

On the r. of Somerton, Will. Howe, Esq.

At Pylle, Henry William Portman, Esq.

On the l. of Stratton is Downside House, Capt. Fookes.

Beyond Dunkerton, on the r. is Combhay, John Smith, Esq.

BATH to *Taunton*, &c. through *Somerton* and *Langport*.

To Street, p. 228.	—	26½
l. to Compton Dunden	3	29½
Littleton	1¾	31¼
Somerton	1¾	33
Taunton	18	51

Before Somerton, Mr. Howe's.

BATH to EXETER, &c. through *Chard, Honiton,* and *Axminster*.

Somerton	—	33
Langport	5	38
Curry Rivel	2	40
Hambridge	2	42
Puckington	2½	44½
Ilford Bridges	½	45
Ilminster	2	47
Chard	5	52
Stockland	6	58
Honiton	6	64
EXETER, p. 33.	17	81
Or from Chard to		
Axminster	7	59
EXETER, p. 33.	26	85

Before 42, Earnshill, R. T. Combe, Esq.

Before Ilminster Dillington, T. Trent, Esq.

CHELMSFORD to CAMBRIDGE.

To Broomfield	—	2½
Great Waltham	2½	5
Black Chapel	4¼	9¼
Barnston	1½	10¾
Dunmow	2¼	13
Great Easton	2¼	15¼
Thaxted	4	19¼
Saffron Walden	7¼	26½
Chesterford	4¼	30¾
Bournbridge, *Camb*	2¾	33½
Cambridge	6	39½

At Waltham, on the right, is Langleys, J. Joliffe Tufnal, Esq.

A Mile beyond Dunmow, on the left, is Newton-Hall, the Seat of Sir John Henniker, Bart.

To the l. of Easton is Easton Lodge, Lord Maynard.

CHELMSFORD to *Raleigh*.

To Great Baddow	—	1½
Rettenden	6½	8
Battle Bridge	1	9
Raleigh	3¼	12¼

CHELMSFORD to *Gravesend*.

London Road	—	1¼
l. to Stock	4¼	5½
Billericay	3	8½
Noke's Bridge	2½	11
Horndon	5½	16½
West Tilbury	3½	20
Tilbury Fort	2	22
Cross the Thames to		
Gravesend, Kent	½	22½

At Horndon Hill, a most beautiful and extensive Prospect.

CHELMSFORD to *Bath*.

To Lackhampton	—	2
Birdlip	4	6
Cranham Wood	1	7
Prinaſh Park	2	9
Painſwic	3	12
Caincroſs	5	17
Rodborough	1	18
Inchborow	2	20
Nailſworth	1	21
Horſley	1	22
Tiltop's	1	23
Kingſcote	1	24
Laſborough	1	25
Boxwell Houſe	1	26
Badminton Park	3	29
Petty France	1	30
Croſs Hands	3	33
Doddington Park	1	34
Dirham Park	3	37
Hamſwell	2	39
BATH	5	44

At two Miles on the right is Lackhampton Court, the Seat of Henry Norwood, Eſq.

At ſix Miles enter Birdlip.

At ſeven Miles, Cranham Woods, three Miles over.

At nine Miles on the right is Prinaſh Park, the Seat of —— Howell, Eſq.

At eleven Miles on the right is Painſwic Houſe, the Seat of Benjamin Hyatt, Eſq.

At ſeventeen Miles on the right is Dudbridge, the Seat of John Hawker, Eſq.

At eighteen Miles on the left is Hill Houſe, the Seat of Sir George Oneſiphorus Paul, Bart. near which is Rodborough Fleece Inn.

At twenty Miles on the right is Pudhill Houſe, the Seat of John Wade, Eſq. and on the left is Dunkirk Houſe, the Seat of Samuel Peach, Eſq.

At twenty-two Miles on the right is the Seat of Edward Wilbraham, Eſq.

At twenty-three Miles on the left of Tiltop's is Chavenge Houſe, the Seat of Henry Stephen's Eſq.

At twenty-four Miles on the right is Kingſcote, the Seat of Robert Kingſcote, Eſq.

At twenty-ſix Miles on the right is Boxwell Houſe, the Seat of Richard Huntley, Eſq.

At twenty-nine Miles on the left is Badmiuton Park, the Duke of Beaufort.

At thirty-four Miles on the right, Doddington Park, the Seat of Sir Wm. Codrington, Bart.

At thirty-ſeven Miles on the right is Dirham Park, the Seat of Wm. Blathwaite, Eſq.

At thirty-nine on the right is Hamſwell, the Seat of Thomas Whittington, Eſq.

CHESPTOW to *Glocester*.

To Teddenham, *Gloceſt.*	—	3
Aylburton	5	8
Blakeney	5	13
Newnham	3	16
Minſterworth	8	24
Highnam	2	26
Gloceſter	2	28

CHESTER to *Cardiff*.

To Pulford		—	5
Merford,	*Flintſh.*	$2\frac{1}{2}$	$7\frac{1}{2}$
Wrexham,	Denb.	4	$11\frac{1}{4}$

Ruabon		5½	17
New Bridge,	*Salop*	2	19
Chirk		2	21
Ofweftry		5	26
Llanymynuc		5	31
Poole		10	41
Newtown,	Mont.	13½	54½
Clay Hill		1¾	56¼
Llanbader Vunneth		7¾	64
Llanbifter,	*Radn.*	3	67
Llandewy		3¾	70¾
Llanbedar Vaur		3¼	74
Ithon River		5	79
Builth,	Brec.	6	85
Llanthewy Coombe		1	86
Caple Cunoke		2	88
Llanyhangel Vechan		7	95
Llandivilog		2	97
Brecon		3	100
River Tavy		4	104
Bullavan Hills		1	105
Caple Tavechan		6	111
Pont Stucketh, *Glam.*		2	113
Ruins of Morleft Caftle		1	114
Beacon Hill		5	119
Caerphilly Caftle		12	131
Coal Works		1	132
Iron Works		1	133
Cardiff		6	139

On the l. before Wrexham, is Acton, the Seat of P. Yonge, Efq.

At Gresford, a good Church, which has fix Bells, called the Wonders of Wales, the largeft weighing 1300 cwt.

On the l. near Ruabon, is Winftay, the Seat of Sir Watkin Williams Wynn, Bart.

Two Miles beyond New Bridge is Chirk Caftle, the Seat of Richard Middleton, Efq.

One Mile beyond Pool, on the r. Powis Caftle, the Seat of Lord Powis.

At 5 Miles before Brecon, on the r. Caftle Madoc, Mr. Powell.

CHESTER to *Manchefter.*

To Tarvin		5
Kelfall	3	8
Vale Royal	7	15
Northwich	3	18
Mere Town	7	25
Dunham Park	4	29
Altringham	2	31
Crofs Street	3	34
Manchefter	6	40

At 15, on the r. Thomas Cholmondeley, Efq.

On the l. of Northwich, Winnington-Hall, Lord Penrhyn.

At 23, on the r. Tabley-Hall, Sir John Leicefter, Bart.

At 29, on the l. Earl of Stamford.

CHESTER to *Woore.*

To Tarvin, *Chef.*		5
Duddon	2	7
Torporley	3	10
Wardle Hall	5	15
Namptwich	5	20
Woore	9	29

CHESTER to *Worrington.*

Mickle Trafford		3
Dunham	3	6
Frodfham	5	11
Sutton	2	13
Prefton	2	15
Darefbury	1½	16½
High Walton	2	18½

6

Low Walton	½	19
Warrington, Lanc.	1½	20½

On the l. between Dupham and Frodsham, see an Arm of the Sea. Pass the Mersey, over a Bridge, on the Banks of which, to the r. Aston, a Seat of Harvey Aston, Esq.

Opposite to Frodsham, over the river, on the l. see Holton Castle, in the Parish of Runcorn.

On the l. nearer Warrington, is Hall Wood, Capt. Norton; and Norton Priory, Sir Rich. Brooke.

CHESTERFIELD to *Winster*.

To Walton	—	2
Leading Gate	3	5
At 6, right to		
Bridge Town	5½	10½
Winsley	1	11½
Winster	1½	13

Hence to Buxton and Manchester. See NOTTINGHAM to MANCHESTER.

CHIPPENHAM to GLOCESTER.

The Plough	—	2
Corston	5	7
Malmsbury	2¼	9¼
Tetbury, *Gloc.*	4¾	14
Minching Hampton	6	20
Stroud	3	23
Painswic	4	27
GLOCESTER	7	34

A Mile beyond Chippingham, on l. Harden Hewish, Miles Branthwaite, Esq.

Two Miles before Glocester, on l. Matson, late G. A. Selwyn, Esq. now Lord Sidney.

CIRENCESTER to BRISTOL.

To *Tetbury*, Glocest.	—	10
Weston Birt	3	13
Didmarton	3	16
Petty France	3	19
Cross Hands	3	22
Yate	3	25
Cleeve Hill	7	32
Stapleton House	2	34
Bristol	2	36

At Cirencester, on the left, Earl Bathurst.

On the l. of Tetbury, Eastcourt, Thomas Eastcourt, Esq.

At 13, on the l. Weston Birt, Peter Halford, Esq.

At 15, on the l. Pinkney House, Thomas Cresswell, Esq.

At 17, on the l. Badminton Park, Duke of Beaufort.

At 21, on the r. Little Sodbury, Winscombe Henry Hartley, Esq.

At 32, on the r. Mrs. Chester.

At 34, on the r. Isaac Elton, Esq.

COLCHESTER to *Bishop Stortford*.

To Lexden	—	1¾
l. to Stanway	2¼	4
Mark's Tey	1½	5½
Coggeshall	4	9½
Blackwater	2¾	12¼
Braintree	3	15¼
Rayne	1¾	17
Stebbing Ford	3½	20½
Dunmow	3	23½
Bonington Green	4	27½
Takeley Street	1	28½
Hockerill	3½	32
Bishop Stortford	½	32½

A Mile and a Half beyond Coggeſ-hall, on r. Great Coggeſhall, Mr. Hanbury.
At two Miles and Half, on right, ſee Stiſtead Village, and Mr. Onely's Seat.

COLCHESTER to *Merſey.*

To Abberton Green	—	4½
The Strode	2½	7
Enter Merſey Iſle, and keep the right to		
Weſt Merſey	2	9
Or the left to		
Eaſt Merſey	1	10

COLCHESTER to *Cambridge.*

To Lexden,	*Eſſex.* —	2
Ford Street	3	5
Wake's Coln	3	8
Earle's Coln	2	10
Stonebridge	1	11
Halſtead	2½	13½
Brook Street	2	15½
Swan Street	1½	17
Haverill, p. 213.	11	28
Withersfield,	*Camb.* 2	30
Horſeheath	5	35
Linton	3½	38½
Abington	3	41½
Croſ. the London Road to Newmarket; and by Gogmagog Hills to		
Cambridge	6½	48

At Earle's Coln, Mr. Hill, a white Houſe.
A little before Halſtead, Mr. Morley.
On Gogmagog Hills is the Seat of the late Lord Godolphin, now in-habited by the Biſhop of Elphin.

COVENTRY to *Mancheſter.*

To Canwell Gate,		
	Staff. —	21
Swinfen Ha	4	25
Lichfield	3	28
Rugeley	7	35
Colwich	3	38
Sandon Hall	6	44
Hilderſtone	4	48
Park Hall	6	54
Rownal Hall	4	58
Leek	6	64
Mancheſter	32	96

At 21, on the l. Sir Robert Lawley, Bart.
At 24, on the l. Shenſton Park, Lord Berwick.
At 31, on the l. Beaudeſert-Hall, Earl of Uxbridge.
At 37, on the r. Sir William Wolſe-ley, Bart.
At 44, on the r. Lord Harrowby.

CRANBROOK to *Lewes.*

To Hartley,	*Kent.* —	2
Tub's Lake	1	3
Hve Gate	2	5
Hawkhurſt	1	6
Cuper's Corner	2	8
l. to Hurſt Green	1	9
r. to Burwaſh	5	14
Lewes	19	33

At 6, on the left, are Elford, the Seat of Samuel Boys, Eſq. and a ſmall but ancient Building called the Hall Houſe.

CREWKHERNE to *Weymouth.*

South Perrot, *Dorset*	—	3¾
The Three Sisters	4	7¾
Maiden Newton	5¼	13
Frompton	2½	15½
Stepleton	4½	20
Melcomb Regis	6¾	26¾
Weymouth	½	27¼

At Frampton is the Seat of Francis John Browne, Esq. also a little to the left is Sydling, the Seat of Sir John Smith, Bart.

CRICKLADE to *Cirencester.*

To Latten	—	1
South Cerney, *Gloc.*	2	3
Cirencester	3¾	6¾

At Cirencester, Earl Bathurst.

CROYDON to *Guildford.*

To Beddington, *Surry*	—	2
Carshalton	1	3
Cheam	2¾	5¾
Ewell	2¼	8
Epsom	1½	9½
Leatherhead	3½	13
Fetcham	1	14
Great Bookham	1½	15½
Little Bookham	½	16
Effingham	1	17
East Horsley	1¾	18¾
West Horsley	1	19¾
East Clandon	1	20¾
West Clandon	1	21¾
Merroe	1	22¾
Guildford	2¼	25

At Beddington is the Seat of the ancient Family of Carew.

Beyond Leatherhead, on the r. in a Botton, is the Earl of Tyrconnel.

At Fetcham, rising the Hill from Leatherhead, Sir George Warren, who married Mr. Revel's Daughter and Heiress. See on right, Claremont, Earl of Tyrconnel; St. George's Hill near Cobham; the Tower and Buildings in the Garden of Pain's Hill, at Cobham; and Botleys, Sir Joseph Mawbey's, near Chertsey.

To the right of the Tower, see Mr. Paine's, at Weybridge; to the l. Mr. Sewell, late Sir Tho. Sewell's, by Cobham.

At Great Bookham, on the r. Eastwic Park, Earl of Effingham's, inhabited by Mr. Laurell; and on the l. a House built by the late Admiral Broderick, now Lady Downe.

At Little Bookham, on the right, a new Brick House, Mr. Pollens.

At Effingham, on l. white House, Col. de Lancey.

At East Horsley, on the right, Mr. Currie, late James Fox, Esq.

At West Horsley, on r. Henry Perkins Weston, Esq. formerly the Nicholas', inhabited by Mr. Wood.

At East Clandon, on the right, Mr. Sumner's, built by Admiral Boscawen, formerly the Heaths.

At West Clandon, Lord Onslow, Clandon Park.

Before Guildford, see Stoke, on the r. Mr. Aldersey.

About two Miles beyond Guildford, on l. is Losely, Miss Molyneux.

CUCKFIELD to *Hastings.*

To Chayley Inn	—	7
Newic	2	9
Maresfield	4	13
Buxted	1	14

Hadlow Down	4	18
By Cross-in-Hand Turnpike		
To Burwash	10	28
Hurst Green	4	32
Robertsbridge	2	34
Battel	6	40
Hastings	7	47

Beyond Hadley Down, on left, Gatehouse, Mr. Dalrymple.

Beyond Cross-in-Hand Turnpike, on r. Heathfield Park, heretofore Bailey Park, so changed in Honour of the late gallant Lord Heathfield, its late owner, now Francis Newbery, Esq.

At Battel, Battel Abbey, Sir Godfrey Webster, Bart.

Beyond Battel, on r. Crowhurst Park, Mr. Pelham's; on l. Beauport, General Murray's.

Another Road from Cuckfield to Hastings, from Cross-in-Hand Turnpike through Heathfield, which is very good in Summer, many Miles nearer, and a delightful Ride.

To Heathfield	—	2½
Dallington	4	6½
Wood's Corner	½	7
Battel	5½	12½
Hastings	7	19½

At Heathfield Park, the Seat of Francis Newbery, Esq. is a Tower built in Honour of the late Lord Heathfield, the gallant Defender of Gibratar; whence is a most rich, beautiful, and extensive, View, as well over the Sea as the surrounding Country.

At Darlington, on the r. is Herring's Place, the Seat of P. G. Crauford, Esq.

Beyond Wood's Corner, on the l. is Rose-Hill Park, John Fuller, Esq. and, on the r. Ashburnham-House and Park, the Residence of the Earl of Ashburnham.

DARTFORD to *Sevenoaks*.

To Hatley,	*Kent*	—	1
Darent		1	2
Sutton Street		1	3
Farningham		2½	5½
Aynesford		1	6¼
Shoreham		2¾	9
Otford		1¼	10¼
Sevenoaks		3	13¼

At Hatley, on l. Mr. Murphy.

In Farningham Church-Yard, see the Mausoleum, a Burying-Place of the Nash Family.

A little beyond Aynesford, on the r. is Lullingstone Place and Park, the Seat of Sir John Dixon Dyke, Bart.

At Sevenoaks, on the r. Sir Charles Farnaby Ratcliffe, Bart. On l Knowle Park, Duke of Dorset.

DERBY to *Nottingham* and LINCOLN.

To Chaddesden		—	2
Sponden		1	3
Shackle Cross		1	4
Risley		3½	7½
Sandy Acre		1½	9
Stappleford,	*Nott.*	1	10
Lenton		4	14
Nottingham		1½	15½
Radcliff		5½	21
Saxondale		2½	23½
Stoke		7¾	31¼
Newark		3¼	34½

At Chaddefden, Sir Robert Mead Wilmot, Bart.

At 6, Lady Lake, on left.

At Stappleford, Sir John Borlafe Warren.

Three Miles before Nottingham, on left, Wollaton Hall, Lord Middleton.

Two Miles beyond Nottingham, on l. Colwie, Mr. Mufters.

Three Miles on l. Holme Pierpoint, late Duke of Kingfton.

A little beyond Saxondale, the Road turns to the l. and keeps upon the Fofs Way, a Roman Road from Leicefter to Lincoln.

Or,

From Nottingham	—	$15\frac{1}{2}$
To Red Hill	4	$19\frac{1}{2}$
Oxton	$4\frac{3}{4}$	$24\frac{1}{4}$
Southwell	$4\frac{3}{4}$	29
Upton	2	31
Kelham	3	34
Newark	2	36
Wifby Wood	$8\frac{1}{2}$	$44\frac{1}{2}$
Brace Bridge	$7\frac{1}{4}$	$51\frac{3}{4}$
LINCOLN	$1\frac{3}{4}$	$53\frac{1}{2}$

At Kelham, Lord George Sutton.

DERBY to CHESTER.

To Mickle Over	—	$3\frac{1}{2}$
Etwall	$2\frac{3}{4}$	$6\frac{1}{4}$
Hilton	2	$8\frac{1}{4}$
Fofton	$3\frac{1}{2}$	$11\frac{3}{4}$
Afton	$1\frac{1}{4}$	13
Sudbury	$\frac{1}{2}$	$13\frac{1}{2}$
Doveridge	$3\frac{1}{2}$	17
Crofs Dove River to		
Uttoxeter, Staff.	2	19
Stramfhall	$1\frac{1}{2}$	$20\frac{1}{2}$

Beamhurft	$1\frac{3}{4}$	$22\frac{1}{4}$
Checkley	$2\frac{1}{4}$	$24\frac{1}{2}$
Upper Tean	$1\frac{3}{4}$	$26\frac{1}{4}$
Draycot	$1\frac{1}{4}$	28
Enter Meer Lane	2	30
Meer	$1\frac{1}{2}$	$31\frac{1}{2}$
Lane End	$1\frac{1}{2}$	33
Delph Lane	1	34
Stoke	$1\frac{1}{2}$	$35\frac{1}{2}$
Newcaftle under Line	$1\frac{1}{4}$	$36\frac{3}{4}$
Chefterton	$2\frac{3}{4}$	$39\frac{1}{2}$
Audley	$2\frac{1}{2}$	42
Gorfty Hill, Chefh.	$3\frac{1}{2}$	$45\frac{1}{2}$
The Hough	3	$48\frac{1}{2}$
Namptwich*	$3\frac{1}{2}$	52
CHESTER, p. 131.	$19\frac{1}{2}$	$71\frac{1}{2}$

*Another Road from Newcaftle to Namptwich, p. 139.

At Sudbury, a Park and Seat of Lord Vernon.

At Doveridge, Sir Henry Cavendifh.

DERBY to Mansfield.

To Morley, Derb.	—	$4\frac{1}{2}$
Smalley	2	$6\frac{1}{2}$
Heynor	$2\frac{1}{2}$	9
Eaftwood, Nott.	2	11
Annefley	$4\frac{1}{2}$	$15\frac{1}{2}$
Mansfield	$6\frac{1}{2}$	22

At Annefley, Wm. Chaworth, Efq.

DOLGELLY to Manchefter and Buxton.

To Bala	—	19
Corven	12	31
Llangollen	10	41

Wrexham	13	54
Barn Hill	12	66
Namptwich	14	80
Middlewich	10	90
Knutsford	9	99
Altringham	7	:06
Manchester	8	114
Buxton	22	136

DONCASTER to Sheffield.

To Balby	—	1½
Warmsworth	1¼	2¾
Conisbrough	2¼	5
Hooton Roberts	2½	7½
Thirburgh	1½	9
Rotherham	3	12
Tinsley	2½	14½
Car Brook	1	15½
Attercliff	1	16½
Sheffield	1½	18

DONCASTER to Manchester.

To Mar	—	4
Hickleton	2	6
Darfield	4	10
Ardsley*	3	13
Dodworth	4	17
Silkston	2	19
Hoyland Swayne	2½	21½
Thurlstone	2	23½
Salter's Brook	7	30½
Woodhead, Chesh.	2¾	33¼
Tintwistle	5	38¼
Mottram Longdale	2¼	40½
Stealey Bridge	4	44½
Asheton Underline	2	46½
Manchester	7	53½

From Ardsley it is but a little Way about to go by Barnsley, and thence to Silkston.

Another Road, by Rotherham, viz.

To Rotherham, p. 281.	—	12
Chapel Town	6	18
High Green	1	19
How Brook	1	20
Hunself	4	24
Paw Hill	4	28
Salter's Brook	5	33
Manchester, p. 281.	24	57

DONCASTER to Barnsley.

To Ardsley, p. 281.	—	13
Barnsley	2½	15½

DONCASTER to Keighly.

To Red House	—	5
l. to North Elmsal	4	9
Wragby	5	14
Wakefield	6	20
East Ardsley	4	24
Bruncliff	4½	28½
Adwalton	1	29½
Wisket Hall	1½	31
Bradford	3	34
Cottingley Bridge	4½	38½
Bingley	1	39½
Keighley	4½	44

At Wragby on the right, Nostel Park, Sir Rowland Wynn, Bart.

DONCASTER to Grimsly.

To Hatfield, Yorksh.	—	6½
Stewarth	2¾	9¼
Lovill	1¼	10½

Crowle,	*Linc.*	9¼	19¾
Burringham		1¼	21
Claxborough		4½	25½
Burton Stather		3	28½
Wintrington		4½	33
North Fereby		4½	37½
Barton		3¼	40¾
Barrow		3	43¾
Thornton		2¼	46
Kirmington		4½	50½
Kelby		4½	55
Laſeby		4½	59½
Grimſby		4½	64

Dorchester to *Yeovil.*

To Frampton	—	6
Maiden Newton	2	8
Sydling	2	10
Yeovil	6	16

At Frampton, P. Browne, Eſq.
At Sydling, Sir John Smith; and farther on, upon left, Melbury, Lady Ilcheſter.

Dover to *Ramſgate* and *Margate.*

To Kingſwold	—	6
Walmer	1½	7½
Deal	1½	9
Sandwich	5	14
Ebsfleet	2	16
Cliff's End	1¼	17¼
St. Lawrence	1½	18
Ramſgate	1½	19½
St. Peter's	3	22
Margate	3	25½

A little beyond Sandwich are a few ſmall Houſes, the only Remains of the ancient Town of Stonar, the *Lapis Tituli* of the Romans.

Ebsfleet is a Place of great Antiquity, famous for the landing of the Saxons under Hengiſt.

About two Miles on the right of St. Peter's is King's Gate, a delightful Seat of the late Lord Holland.

Dryton to *Buxton.*

To Oakley Hall,	*Staff.*	—	3
Broughton Hall		5	8
Eccleſhall		4	12
Stone		6	18
Rough Cloſe		4	22
Foſbrook		3	25
Cheadle		3	28
Ipſtones		4	32
Longonr		12	44
Buxton,	Derb.	4	48

One mile from Drayton, on the l. Tunſtall-Hall, Rev. Peter Broughton.
At 8, on the l. Broughton Hall, Rev. Sir Tho. Broughton, Bart.
At 10, on the r. Sugnall-Hall, John Turton, Eſq.
At 13, on the l. Hilcott-Hall, George Anſon, Eſq.
At 29, on the l. Booth-Hall, John Granville, Eſq.
At 32, on the l. Belmont-Hall, John Sneyd, Eſq.
At 33, on the l. Whitehough Hall, Sam. Frith Eſq.

Dunstable to *Bedford.*

Houghton Regis	—	1½
Chalgrave	2½	4
Tuddington	1	5
Weſtoning	3	8
Flitwic	1½	9½

Dennel End	1	10½
Ampthill	1½	12
Houghton Conquest	1½	13½
Bedford	6½	20

At Chalgrave, Lieutenant General Parslow.

At Flitwick, — - Fisher, Esq.

Beyond Ampthill, on the r. Houghton Conquest, late Marquis of Tavistoc; on the left, Ampthill Great Park, Earl of Offory.

ELY to *Bury St. Edmund's.*

To Dulbridge	—	3
Soham	2½	5½
Fordham Bridge, *Suff.*	3½	9
Grange Water	3¾	12¾
Barrow Bridge	5¾	18½
To Spittle	3½	22
Bury St. Edmund's	1	23

ELY to PETERBOROUGH.

To Witchford, *Camb.*	—	3
Witcham	2½	5½
Maypole	1½	7
Chatteris	4½	11½
Garter's Bridge, *Hunt.*	2	13½
North Bridge	5¼	18¾
Ponder's Bridge	3½	22¼
Horsey Bridge	4	26¼
Stangrave	2	28¼
PETERBOROUH, *North.*	1½	29¾

EVESHAM to *Birmingham.*

To Norton, *Wor.*	—	3
Dunnington, *Warw.*	4	7
Arrow	2	9
Aulcester	½	9½
Coughton	2	11½
Ipsley	4	15½
Bealy	2	17½
King's Norton	5½	23
Silly Oak	2	25
Birmingham	3	28

At Arrow, a Seat of the Marquis of Hertford.

EXETER to *Ilfracomb.*

To Syar Newton, *Dev.*	—	4½
Dunsum House	1¼	5¾
Crediton	1¾	7½
Druxford	2	9½
Marchut	4½	14
Huntsford	3½	17½
Chawley	2	19½
Chimleigh	1	20½
Chington House	4½	25
Chidingford	2¼	27¼
Beatford	2	29¼
Bathing	6¼	35½
Ronsom	1½	37
Barnstaple	1	38
Marwood	3	41
Ilfracoomb	6	47

EXETER to *Minehead.*

To Stoake, *Devon.*	—	3½
Rew	1	4½
Silverton	2½	7
Long Causeway	4½	11½
Tiverton	2¼	13¾
Bampton	6¾	20½
Gilberts	2½	23
Berry, *Som.*	1½	24½
Lime Kilns	9	33½
Embercum	1¾	35¼
Minehead	3	38¼

FERRYBRIDGE to *Huddersfield*.

To Pontefract	—	2
Purston Jackling	2	4
Wakefield	6½	10½
Horbury	2½	13
Over Shittlington	2½	15½
Grange Park	1½	17
Almondbury	4½	21½
Huddersfield	2½	24

Grange Park, John Lister Kaye, Esq.
Near Almondbury, Woodsham-Hall, Earl of Dartmouth.

FERRYBRIDGE to *Leeds*.

Brotherton	—	1
Fairburn	1½	2½
At 5¼ left to		
West Garforth	6½	9
Whitchurch	2	11
Halton	1	12
Leeds	3	15

To the left, before you turn off from the Great North Road, is Ledston Hall and Park, an old Seat of the Earl of Huntingdon, now John Scott, Esq. the Lodge in the Park commands a very extensive Prospect.
To the left of Whitchurch is Temple Newsham, Lady Irwin.

FLAMBOROUGH to *Scarborough*.

To Speeton, *Yorksh*	—	6
Richton	1½	7½
Hunmanby	2½	10
Seamor	6½	16½
Scarborough	4½	21

FROME to BRISTOL.

To Oakford, *Som.*	—	2
Woolverton	2	4
Midford	5	9
Bath	4	13
Newton Park	3	16
Keynsham	5	21
Bristol	5	26

At 3, on the r. Standerwic Court, Harry Edgell, Esq.
At 10, on the r. Midford Castle, —— Pew, Esq.
Newton Park, the Seat of Will. Gore Langton, Esq.
At 17, on the r. Kelweston House, Lady Hawkins.

FROME to *Chard*.

To Nunney, *Som*	—	3
South Hill	4	7
Bruton	5	12
Castle Cary	4	16
Sparkford	5	21
Yeovil	8	29
East Coker	3	32
Crewkherne	6	38
Crickett St. Thomas	5	43
Chard	3	46

On the l. of Bruton, the Earl of Ilchester.
On the r. of Yeovil, the Earl of Westmorland.
On the r. of Crewkherne, Earl Poulett.

FROME to *Porloc*.

To Stoney Lane, *Som.*	—	4
Doulting	6	10
Shepton Mallet	2	12
Westholme	3	15
Glastonbury	7	22
Piper's Inn	5	27
Bridgewater	10	37
Nether Stowey	9	46

Weſt Quantoxhead	6	52
Watchett	3	55
Dunſter	6	61
Porloc	10	11

Two Miles on the r. of Nether
Stowey is Woodlands, John Day,
Eſq.
On the r. of Weſt Quantoxhead, the
old Family Seat of John Fownes
Luttrell, Eſq.
At 53, on the l. St. André, Rob.
Everard Balch, Eſq.
At 68, on the l. Holnicote Houſe,
Sir Thomas Dyke Ackland, Bart.

FROME to *Sherborn.*

To Longleat,	*Som.*	3
Maiden Bradley	3	6
Stourhead	4	10
Wincanton	6	16
Maperton	3	19
Sherborn	7	26

At Longleat, Marquis of Bath.
On the l. of Maiden Bradley, the
Duke of Somerſet.
At 19, on the r. William Smith, Eſq.

GLOCESTER to *Bath.*

To Quedgeley,	*Gloc.*	3
Whitminſter	4	7
Frocefter	4	11
Kingſcote	5	16
Petty France	9	25
Doddington Park	4	29
Hamſwell	6	35
Bath	4	39

One Mile from Gloceſter, on the r.
Hempſtead Houſe, Daniel Lyſons,
Eſq.

At 3, on the r. Quedgeley Houſe,
—— Hayward, Eſq.
At 8, on the r. Fromebridge Wire-
mills
At 11, on the l. Richard Bigland,
Eſq.
At 15, on the r. Thomas Daunt, Eſq.
At 16, on the r. Robert Kingſcote,
Eſq.
At 23, on the r. Boxwell Houſe,
Richard Huntley, Eſq.
At 20, on the l. Badmington Park,
Duke of Beaufort.
At 29, on the r. Doddington Park,
Sir William Codrington, Bart.
At 32, on the r. Dirham Park, Will.
Blathwaite, Eſq.
At 35, on the r. Thomas Whitting-
ton, Eſq.

GLOCESTER to *Cirenceſter.*

To Barnwood,	*Gloc*	2
Whitcombe	3	5
Highgate	4	9
Duntſborne Abbots	2	11
Daglingworth	4	15
Cirenceſter	2	17

One Mile on the r. of Cirenceſter, is
Wooton, Rev. Mr. Bryant.
At 2, on the r. Barnwood Court,
Robert Morris, Eſq.
At 5, on the r. Whitcombe Park,
Howe Hick, Eſq.
At 10, on the l. Cotswold Houſe,
Samuel Wallbank, Eſq.
At 11, Duntſborne Abbots, Rev.
Mr. Chapman.
At 16, on the l. Stratton Houſe,
Rev. Mr. Daubeney.

GLOCESTER to COVENTRY.

To Heydon's Elm		6
Bedlam	2	8

Cheltenham	1½	9½
Prestbury	1¾	11¼
The Beacon	2¼	13½
Winchcomb	3	16½
Didbrook	3	19½
Snowshill	3½	23
Campden	5¼	28¼
Mickleton	2¾	31
Clifford	6½	37½
Stratford on Avon, Warw.	1¾	39¼
Clopton Park	4¾	44
Longbridge	2½	46½
Warwic	1½	48
COVENTRY, p. 232.	10	58

On the right of Winchcomb are the Ruins of Sudeley Castle; and four Miles beyond it is Tuddington, the Seat of Viscount Tracy.

At Clopton Park is a Seat of Mrs. Partridge.

GLOCESTER to *Kidderminster.*

To Corse Lawn	—	4
Longdon	8	12
Hanley	5	17
Madresfield	3	20
Brook House	3	23
WORCESTER	3	26
Hawford	3	29
Westwood Park	3	32
Waraseley House	3	35
Hartlebury Park	1	36
Kidderminster	4	40

At 16, on the r. Hanley, Edward Lechmere, Esq.

At 20, on the l. William Lygon, Esq.

At 31, on the l. Lord Sandys.

On the r. of Westwood Park, Sir Hebert Packington, Bart.

On the l. of Hartlebury Park, the Bishop of Worcester.

GLOCESTER to *Great Malvern.*

To Maizemore	—	2¾
Longdon	10	12¾
Little Malvern	9	21¾
The Wells	1	22¾
Great Malvern	2	24¾

GLOCESTER to *Tetbury.*

See Tetbury to GLOCESTER.

The Road to Malvern, over the Wytch, is not eligible for Carriages in general, particularly those not accustomed to the Country. But, from the Wytch, which is a Road cut through the Rock, on the Summit of the Malvern, the View is grand, extensive, and beautiful beyond description. On a clear Day, and with the naked Eye, fifteen Counties in England and Wales, four Cities, and the Shores of the Irish Channel besides innumerable Towns and Villages, and two beautiful Rivers, are clearly distinguishable.

Ledbury to *Great Malvern* and WORCESTER.

Rabbits Warren, *Worc.*	—	5
Little Malvern	1	6
Great Malvern	2	8
Powic	5	13
WORCESTER	3	16

At Great Malvern, the Church, an Ancient Priory, belonging to Mr.

Edward Foley, is adorned with
some curious old Paintings on
Glass; but now, with the Church
itself, for want of Repairs, is haf-
tening faft to Ruin.

HEREFORD to *Hay* by *Whitney Bridge*.

To Hanmer's Crofs	—	10
Letton	2	12
Willerfly	2	14
Winforton	$\frac{3}{4}$	$14\frac{3}{4}$
Whitney Bridge	3	$17\frac{3}{4}$
Clifford	$1\frac{1}{4}$	19
Hay, Breckn.	2	21

At 12, Letton Court, John Freeman,
Efq.
At $17\frac{1}{4}$, Whitney Court, Tomkins
Dew, Efq.

HEREFORD to *Leicefter*.

To Shecknall, *Heref.*	—	6
Lower Eagleton	3	9
Frome's Hill	4	13
Ridgeway Crofs	3	16
Sinton, *Worceft.*	$3\frac{1}{4}$	$19\frac{1}{4}$
Braunsford	$2\frac{1}{4}$	$21\frac{1}{2}$
Braunsford Bridge	1	$22\frac{1}{2}$
WORCESTER	$2\frac{1}{4}$	$24\frac{3}{4}$
Fennel Green	$2\frac{3}{4}$	$27\frac{1}{2}$
Droitwich	$3\frac{1}{2}$	31
Upton	3	34
Broomfgrove	$3\frac{1}{4}$	$37\frac{1}{4}$
Norton	$\frac{3}{4}$	38
The Lickey	2	40
Northfield	$4\frac{3}{4}$	$44\frac{3}{4}$
Edgbafton, *Warw.*	$3\frac{3}{4}$	$48\frac{1}{2}$
Birmingham	$1\frac{3}{4}$	$50\frac{1}{4}$
Saltley	$1\frac{1}{2}$	$51\frac{3}{4}$

Caftle Bromwich	$4\frac{1}{4}$	$56\frac{1}{4}$
Bacon's End	$1\frac{3}{4}$	58
Meriden	$6\frac{1}{2}$	$64\frac{1}{2}$
Allefley	4	$68\frac{1}{2}$
COVENTRY	2	$70\frac{1}{2}$
Leicefter, p. 233.	$24\frac{1}{2}$	95

On the left of 16 is Ombrefley, the
Seat of Lord Sandys.
At Caftle Bromwich, Sir Henry
Bridgeman.

HEREFORD to *Montgomery*.

To Prefteign, p. 99.	—	$23\frac{3}{4}$
Norton, *Radn.*	2	$25\frac{3}{4}$
Knighton	$2\frac{3}{4}$	28
Clunn, *Salop.*	5	33
Blynn	$2\frac{3}{4}$	$35\frac{3}{4}$
Redcourt, *Mont.*	$5\frac{1}{2}$	$41\frac{1}{4}$
Montgomery	$3\frac{3}{4}$	45

On the right, within a Mile of Montgomery, is a Seat of the Earl of
Powis.

HEREFORD by *Ledbury*, to WORCESTER.

To Tupfley	—	$1\frac{1}{2}$
Lugwardine	$1\frac{1}{2}$	3
Burteftree	$1\frac{1}{2}$	$4\frac{1}{2}$
Dormington	$1\frac{1}{2}$	6
Stoke Edith	$1\frac{1}{4}$	$7\frac{1}{4}$
Tarrington	$1\frac{1}{4}$	$8\frac{1}{2}$
The Trumpets	$3\frac{1}{2}$	12
Ledbury Mills	$2\frac{3}{4}$	$14\frac{3}{4}$
Ledbury	1	$15\frac{3}{4}$
Little Malvern, *Worc.*	5	$20\frac{3}{4}$
Great Malvern	$2\frac{3}{4}$	$22\frac{1}{2}$
Powic	$6\frac{1}{2}$	29
WORCESTER	2	31

One Mile to the r. of 4½ is Longworth, the Seat of James Walwyn, Esq. and 2 Miles to the r. is Suston Court, the Seat of Sir James Hereford, whose Family has possessed the same ever since 1223, the 7th of Henry the Third.

At Stoke Edith, the Seat of the Hon. Edward Foley.

Near Ledbury, Cottleditch, the Seat of Lord Sommers.

Hereford to Worcester, through *Bromyard.*

To Lugg Bridge	—	2
Ewe Withington	2	4
Bunley Gate	4	8
Stoke Lacy	2	10
Bromyard	4	14
Bromyard Heath	2	16
Bridge over the River Teme	2	18
Broadway	2½	20½
Worcester	7	27½

At 16 is Brockington, a Seat of Captain Barnaby.

Hereford to *Abergavenny.*

To Goose Pool	—	4
Willoc's Bridge	2	6
Wormbridge	3	9
Kenderchurch	2¼	11¼
Pontrilas	¾	12
Rowlston	1½	13½
Llanihangel	5½	19
Plantillo Pertholy	2½	21½
Abergavenny	2½	24

On the r. about four Miles from Hereford, near the Road, is Allensmoor, a new House lately built by Edward Letchmere Pattishull, Esq.

At Wormbridge, the Seat of the late Sir Edward Clive, a Baron of the Exchequer, now inhabited by his Widow.

At Pontrilas, the Seat of Henry Shiffner, Esq.

On the r. is Kentchurch, John Scudamore, Esq.

Hereford to *Aberystwith.*

Credon-Hill	—	4
Foxley	3	7
Norton	2	9
Ecles-Green	2	11
Woonton	3	14
Llyonshall	3	17
Kington	2	19
Stanner	2	21
New Radnor	6¼	27¼
Penybank	7	34¼
Nantmell	6	40¼
Rayder	4	44¼
Camystwith	16	60¼
Aberystwith	15	75¼

To the left of the 4 Mile-stone, is the Scite of Oriconium, a Roman station, near the Village of Kentchester; and on the left, near the Road, is Credon-Hill and Camp.

One Mile to the right of the 7th Mile-stone, is Foxley House, Woods, and the celebrated Scene of Ladylift, Mr. Price's.

Near the Road, at the 11th Mile-stone, to the right hand, is Sansfeld House, new built, Mr. W. Weston's.

One Mile to the left, Kennersky, late Sir John Morgan's, now Mr. Clutton's.

Two Miles to the left of the 14th Mile-done is Newport Houfe and Woods, Honorable Andrew Foley M. P. for Droitwich.

Two Miles to the right hand from Llyonfhall. is Haywood Houfe, Park. and Woods, Earl of Oxford

Three Miles from Kington, near the Road, Stanner Rock and Scenery

One Mile to the left of the 4 Mile ftone, on a Hill, the handfome Church of Old Radnor.

To the right haud, near the 7th Mile ftone, Downton, a handfome white Houfe of Mr. Percival Lewis ; to the left, a handfome old brick Houfe, called Harpton, Mr. John Lewis.

Two Miles from New Radnor, to the right hand, near Llanvihargel, Nantmellan Llanredo. a Miner Well ; and, between the Mountains, Waterbreak-its-Neck, a fine Waterfall.

Three Miles to the left of the Road from Penybank to Rayder, the Mineral Wells of Llandrindod.

At Nantmell. 6 Miles from Penybank, a handfome Church.

Four Miles thence, on the left (on the Hill) Llwynbarried, a good Houfe belonging to Mr. Evans.

Near the Town of Rayder, fine Scene on the River Wye.

From the P . over Mountains, near Rayder, leading, to Camyftwith, the View to the S. E. is very fine.

Two Miles from the Public Houfe at Pentre, near Camyftwith, to the left of the Road to Aberyft with, in the Vale of Ifhwen, is Havod, the elegant new built Houfe of Col. Johnes ; with fome fine Woods. romantic Scenes, and Waterfalls.

Four Miles to the right Hand from Camyftwith, is the celebrated De-

vil's Bridge, with fome fine Scenes on the river Rydall, near it.

Seven Miles from Camyftwith, to the right hand, in the Woods, near the Road, is Nantios, the Seat of Mr. Powell ; and thence the views from the Road to Aberyftwith, extenfive and beautiful, including the Vale of Rydall, Llanbadern, Chad, Aberyftwith, and the Sea.

HODDESDON to *Hitchin*.

To *Hertford*	—	$4\frac{1}{4}$
Waterford	$1\frac{3}{4}$	6
Stapleford	$1\frac{1}{2}$	$7\frac{1}{2}$
Watton	$1\frac{3}{4}$	$9\frac{1}{4}$
Broadwater	4	$13\frac{1}{4}$
Stevenage	$2\frac{1}{2}$	$15\frac{3}{4}$
Little Wymundley	$2\frac{1}{4}$	18
Hitchin	2	20

HULL to *Howden*.

Anlaby	—	4
Kirk Ella	1	5
Riplingham	4	9
North Cave	5	14
Gilberdike	5	19
Howden	4	23

HUNTINGDON to ELY.

To Hemingsford		—	$4\frac{1}{4}$
St. Ives		$2\frac{1}{4}$	$6\frac{1}{2}$
Needenworth		2	$8\frac{1}{2}$
Frith		$3\frac{1}{2}$	12
Sutton,	*Camb.*	$4\frac{3}{4}$	$16\frac{3}{4}$
Wentworth		$2\frac{1}{4}$	19
Witchford		$2\frac{1}{2}$	$21\frac{1}{2}$
ELY		2	$23\frac{1}{2}$

HUNTINGDON to CAMBRIDGE, and thence to *Ipswich.*

To Godmancheſter	—	1
l. to Fenny Stanton	5	6
CAMBRIDGE	10	16
Quy	5	21
Bottiſham	2	23
Newmarket	6	29
Kentford Bridge	4½	33½
Barrow Bridge	4½	38
Bury St. Edmund's	5½	43½
Beighton	5½	49
Woolpit	3	52
Hawleigh New-Street	2½	54½
Stow-Market	2½	57
Needham Market	3	60
Bayſham	3	63
Claydon	1¾	64¾
Ipſwich	4½	69¼

At 4, on the r. from Bury St. Edmund's, is Bougham Parſonage, Dr. Preſton.

At 7, on the l. Teſtoe, a white Houſe, Mr. Wray; and on the r. Drinkſton, a new built white Houſe, belonging to Joſhua Grigſby, Eſq.

At 10, on the r. Hawleigh Park, Mr. Sulyard's; and on the l. leaving Hawleigh on the r. is Hawleigh Place, Mr. Ray; near which are the Remains of Hawleigh Caſtle.

HUNTINGDON to *March.*

To Hartford	—	1½
Old Hurſt	4	5½
Pidley	2	7½
Somerſham	2	9½
March, p. 195.	14	23½

HUNTSPILL to *Somerton.*

To Paulet,	*Som.*	—	2½
Pertington		1	3½
Woolavington		1¾	5¼
Aſhton		7	12¼
Somerton		8	20¼

ILFRACOMB to *Torrington.*

To Stracum,	*Devon*	—	5
Ham		2	7
Waterton		6	23
Northam		2	15
Bideford		2	17
Torrington		6¼	23¼

IPSWICH to *Cromer.*

To Claydon,	*Suff.*	—	4½
Coddenham Bacon		2¾	7¼
Stonham Pye		4	11¼
Thwaite Street		5¼	16½
Stoke White-Horſe		1½	18
Yaxley Street		2¼	20¼
Oſmondſtone,	*Norf.*	3¾	24
Long Stratton		9	33
Stratton Bridge		1½	34½
Newton Bridge		2	36½
NORWICH		7½	44
St. Faith's		4	48
St. Faith's Newton		1	49
Maſham		4½	53½
Ayleſham		2½	56
Roughton		6½	62½
North Repps		1½	64
Cromer		2	66

At Coddenham, Shrubland-Hall, late the Seat of the Rev. John and Nicolas Bacon, now of William Middleton, Eſq. and near it is

Crowfield-Hall, another Seat of William Middleton, Esq.

Near the Stoke White-Horse, on the left, is Thornham-Hall, the Seat of the Duchess Dowager of Chandos.

Five Miles from Alysham is Gunton-Hall, Seat of Lord Suffield.

KENDAL to *Hawkshead*.

To Bonning Yate	—	3½
Winander Mee Ferry	5½	9
Briers	1	10
Sawray	1	11
Hawkshead	2	13

KENDAL to *Whitby*.

To *Kirby Stephen*, West.	—	23
Bowes, *Yorksh.*	15	38
Barnard Castle, Durh	4	42
Darlington	16	58
Yarum, *Yorksh.*	10	68
Stokesley	8½	76½
Scallingdam	16	92½
Whitby	11¾	104¼

KIDDERMINSTER to *Tenbury*.

To Spring Grove	—	2
Bewdley	1	3
Clough's Top	5	8
Newnham	5	13
Monk's Bridge	2	15
Tenbury	2	17

On the l. of Kidderminster, Sir Edward Winnington, Bart.

At 13, on the l. Newnham Court, late Francis Rock, Esq.

LEEDS to *Manchester*.

To Birstall, *Yorksh.*	—	7
Huddersfield	8½	15½
r. to Marsden	7	22½
Delph	5	27½
Austerlands, *Lanc.*	3	30½
Green-acres Moor	1	31½
Oldham	1	32½
Hollinwood	2	34½
Failesworth	1½	36
Newton Heath	1	37
Miles Platting	1¾	38¾
Manchester	1¼	40

At 16½ to r. Milnsbridge, William Radcliff, Esq.

At 37, Culcheth-Hall, Edward Graves, Esq.

Another Road, viz.

To Birstall	—	7
Gomersal	½	7½
Clifton	4	11½
Brigthouse	1	12½
Rastric	½	13
Elland	2	15
Greetland	1	16
Ripponden	3	19
Baitings	2½	21½
Littleborough, *Lanc.*	4¾	26¼
Rochdale	3¾	30
Smythyford	2¾	32¾
Middleton	2¾	35½
Henton	3	38½
Chetham Green	2	40½
Manchester	2½	43

At 7½, Oakwell-Hall, —— Barker, Esq.

To the l. of 11½, Kirklees, Sir George Armytage, Bart.

To the l. of 19½, Howroyde, Joshua Horton, Esq.
To the l. of 20, Rushworth School a good Endowment.

Leeds to *Halifax*.

To Kirkstal Bridge	—	3
Stanningley	3	6
Bradford	3½	9½
Great Horton	2	11½
Beggarington	3½	15
Halifax	3	18
Another Road, viz.		
To Birstall	—	7
r. to Gomersal	½	7½
Spen Hall	1	8½
Belly Bridge	3¾	12¼
Lightcliffe	½	12¾
Hipperholm	1	13¾
Halifax	2¼	16

Leeds to *Tadcaster*.

To Seacroft	—	4
Kidhall	3½	7½
Over Bramham Moor to *Tadcaster*	6½	14

To the left of 8, Bramham Park Lady Goodrick.
To the r. beyond 10, Haslewood-Hall, Sir Walter Vavasour, Bart.

Leeke to *Stockport*.

To Bosley, *Chester*	—	7
Macclesfield	5	12
Butley	3	15
Peynton Park	4	19
Stocport	5	24

At 14, on the l. Titherington-Hall, William Brooksbank, Esq.
At 15, on the l. Butley-Hall, Peter Downes, Esq.
At 17, on the l. Addington-Hall, John Legh, Esq.
At 13, on the r. Sir George Warren, K. B.

Leominster to *Hay*, a New Road.

To Monkland	—	2½
Delwin	3½	6
Sarnsfield	4	10
Kennersley	1¾	11¾
Willersley	3	14¾
Winfortun	¾	15½
Whitney Bridge	3	18½
Clifford	1¼	19¾
Hay	2	21¾

Four Miles from Leominster is Burton-Court, John Brewster, Esq.
Near Delwin is Henwood, Lacon Lambe, Esq.
At Sarnsfield-Court, Webb Weston, Esq.
At 11¾, Kennersley Castle, the Seat of Thomas Clutton, Esq.

Lewes to *East Bourne*.

To Middlenham	—	2
Laughton	4	6
Burghill	2	8
Nash Street	1	9
Horse Bridge	2	11
Willingdon	6	17
East Bourne	2	19

Lichfield to *Buxton*.

To Mavesyn Ridware	—	5
Abbots Bromley	6	11

Uttoxeter	7	18
Barrow Hill	5	23
Beacon and Weaver Hills	4	27
Caldon Lime Works	3	30
Onecote	3	33
Longnor	9	42
Buxton	4	46

At 7, on the l. Colton-Hall, Lady Raymond.
One Mile beyond Bromley, on the l. Blithfield-Hall, Lord Bagot.
At 16, on the l. Loxley-Hall, Clement Kynnersley, Esq.
At 23, on the l. Thomas Wilkinson, Esq.
At 25, on the r. Colwic-Hall, Rev. John Dewes.
At 26, on the r. Wooton-Hall, Davis Davenport, Esq.
A little farther, on the l. Wooton-Lodge, Mrs. Unwin.
At 29, on the l. Cotton-Hall, Thomas Gilbert, Esq.

LICHFIELD to *Shrewsbury*.

To Muckley Corner	—	2½
r. *to* Four Crosses	7½	10
Ivetsey Bank	7½	17½
Watling Street, *Shrop.*	11½	29
Hay Gate	1	30
Atcham	6½	36½
Shrewsbury	3½	40

At 6, on the r. Mr. Gildart.
At 14, on the r. is Stretton, Right Hon. Mr. Connolly.
At 19, on the l. is Weston, Sir Henry Bridgman, Bart.
At 30½, on the r. is Orton, Mr. Cludde.
At 31, on the l. the Wrekin-Hill.

At 36, on the r. is Ottingham, Tern-Hall, Lord Berwic.
At 37½, on the r. cross the Severn, is Longnor. Mr. Burton.

LICHFIELD to *Stourbridge*.

To Muckley Corner, *Staff.*	—	3
Bloxwich	6	9
Wolverhampton	5	14
Kinswinford	7	21
Stourbridge	3	24

At 5 Miles, on the l. of Wolverhampton, is Himley-Hall, Visc. Dudley and Ward.
At 21, on the r. Summer-Hill, Joseph Freeman, Esq.

LINCOLN to *Doncaster* by *Gainsborough*.

To Stretton	—	9½
Gainsborough	8½	18
Walkrith Ferry	3	21
Walkeringham, *Nott.*	1	22
Gringley	2½	24½
Everton	3	27½
Bawtry, Yorksh.	3	30½
Rossington Bridge	4	34½
Doncaster	4	38½

LINCOLN to *Horncastle*.

To *Wragby*, p. 187.	—	11
Langton	2	13
Baumbergh	4	17
Edlington Bar	2	19
Horncastle	2	21

At 13, on the l. Panton House, Edmund Turnor, Esq.

At 16, on the right, is Gouthy, R. Vyner, Efq.

At Edlington, John Short, Efq.

LIVERPOOL to *Halifax*.

To Redhaftle, *Lanc.*		6
Prefcot	2	8
Ravenhead	3	11
Afhton	6	17
Wigan	5	22
Weft Houghton	7	29
Bolton	4	33
Bury	6	39
Marland	6	45
Rochdale	2	47
Blackftone Edge	7	54
Halifax	9	63

At 4, on the r. Highfield-Hall, Thomas Park, Efq.
At 6, Knowefly-Hall, Earl of Derby.
At 10, on the l. Eccleston-Hall, Thomas Eccleston, Efq.
At 14, on the l. Blackbrook, James Orrell, Efq.
At 15, on the l. Garfwood-Hall, Sir Robert Gerrard, Bart.
At 20, on the r. Hawley-Hall, Bryan William Molyneux, Efq.
At 21, on the l. Winftanley-Hall, William Banks, Efq.
At 30, on the r. Hulton Park, William Hulton, Efq.
At 43, on the l. Bamford-Hall, William Bamford, Efq.
At 46, on the r. Caftleton-Hall, Thomas Smith, Efq.
Half a Mile farther, on the r. Caftlemere-Hall, John Walmfley, Efq.

LIVERPOOL to *Hull*.

To *Prefcot*, Lanc.		8
Warrington	10	18
Manchefter	19	37
Oldham	8	45
Huddersfield, Yorkfh.	17	62
Wakefield	17	79
Pontefract	9	88
Rawcliff	16	104
North Cave	16	120
Hull	15	135

LIVERPOOL to *Kirby Lonfdale*.

To Walton, *Lanc.*		3
Alton	8	11
Ormfkirk	2	13
Rufford	8	21
Longton	5	26
Prefton	6	32
Garftang	11	43
Golgate	7	50
Lancafter	4	54
Caton	4	58
Hornby	5	63
Turnftall	4	67
Kirby Lonfdale	3	70

At 7, on the r. Ince-Hall, Henry Blundell, Efq.
At 15, on the r. Latham-Hall, Richard Willbraham Bootle, Efq.
At 37, on the r. Barton-Lodge, Robert Shuttleworth, Efq.
At 39, on the l. Myerfcow-Hall, James Greenalgh, Efq.
A little farther, on the l. Myetfcrow Houfe, Robert Gibfon, Efq.
Farther, on the r. Cloughton-Hall, William Fitzherbert Brockholes, Efq.
At 42, on the l. Kirkland-Hall, Alexander Butler, Efq.
At 52, on the l. Afhton-Park, Lord Archibald Hamilton.
At 56, on the l. Halton-Hall, William Bradfhaw, Efq.

At 57, on the r. Quarmor-Park, late Hon. Edward Clifford.

At 65, on the r. Melling-Hall, Mifs Gillifon.

At 66, on the r. Winnington-Hall, John Marfden, Efq.

At 68, on the r. Burrow-Hall, Thomas Fenwick, Efq.

LIVERPOOL to Newcaftle upon Tyne.		
To Ormfkirk	—	13
Rufford	$5\frac{1}{2}$	$18\frac{1}{2}$
Tarleton Bridge	3	$21\frac{1}{2}$
Prefton	$9\frac{1}{2}$	31
Wirefdale	20	51
Wray	13	64
Bentham	4	68
Bainbridge, Torkfh.	23	91
Swaledale	7	98
Lartington	12	110
Benfieldfide, Durh.	28	138
Newcaftle, Northum.	18	156

On the l. 3 Miles from Liverpool to Ormfkirk, is Ince Blundell, the Seat of Henry Blundell, Efq.

On the r. about 2 Miles from Ormfkirk, is Moor-Hall, the Seat of William Stanley, Efq.

On the r. from Ormfkirk to Rufford, about 3 Miles, is Latham-Hall, the Seat of Richard Wilbraham Bootle, Efq. famous for the Defence made there by Lady Derby, againft the Protector's Forces, during the Civil Wars.

Near Rufford, on the l. is Rufford-Hall, the Seat of Sir Robert Hefketh.

Near Tarleton-Bridge, on the r. is Bank-Hall, the Seat of P. Legh, Efq.

LLANBEDER to Aberiftwith.		
To Llanleir, Card.	—	6
Velindra	$1\frac{1}{2}$	$7\frac{1}{2}$
Llanrufted	$8\frac{1}{2}$	16
Aberiftwith	$7\frac{1}{4}$	$23\frac{1}{4}$

LUDLOW to Derby.		
Rock's Green, Shrop.	—	$1\frac{1}{2}$
The Moor	$3\frac{1}{2}$	5
Botterel Afton	$5\frac{1}{2}$	$10\frac{1}{2}$
Wrickton	$\frac{1}{2}$	11
Down	$4\frac{1}{2}$	$15\frac{1}{2}$
Bridgeworth	$3\frac{1}{2}$	19
Wyken	$3\frac{1}{2}$	$22\frac{1}{2}$
Shipley	4	$26\frac{1}{2}$
Trefcot, Staff.	3	$29\frac{1}{2}$
Compton	3	$32\frac{1}{2}$
Wolverthampton	$1\frac{1}{2}$	34
Wednesfield	2	36
Bloxwich	$3\frac{1}{2}$	$39\frac{1}{2}$
Pelfal	$1\frac{1}{2}$	41
Muckley Corner	$4\frac{1}{2}$	$45\frac{1}{2}$
Pipe Hill	$1\frac{1}{4}$	$46\frac{3}{4}$
LICHFIELD	$1\frac{3}{4}$	$48\frac{1}{2}$
Street Hay	2	$50\frac{1}{2}$
Winchnor Bridge	$4\frac{1}{4}$	$54\frac{3}{4}$
Branfton	4	$58\frac{3}{4}$
Burton on Trent	2	$60\frac{3}{4}$
Monk's Bridge, Derb.	$3\frac{1}{4}$	64
Little Derby Houfe	3	67
Derby	5	72

To the l. of Wichnor Bridge is Wichnor Lodge, Mr. Levett.

On the r. Caton, Mr. Horton.

At 8 Miles from Lichfield, on the r. is Walton, Mr. Defbrowe.

At Burton, on the right, Earl of Uxbridge.

One Mile before it, on the r. Stapenhill, Mr. Henfhaw.

At 10½, on the r. from Lichfield, is Drakelow, Sir Nigel Gresley, Bart.
At 4 Miles from Burton, on the l. is Eggington, Sir Edward Every.

Ludlow to Worcester by *Bromyard*.

To Lempster	—	10
Bromyard	13	23
WORCESTER	14	37

Lynn to *Harwich*.

To Hardwic	—	1¾
Middleton	2¾	4½
Bilney	3	7½
Nerford	3¼	10¾
Swaffham	4¼	15
Stanford	9	24
Croxton	6	30
Thetford	1½	31½
Barnham, *Suff.*	2½	34
Ickworth Thorp	5	39
Ixworth	2	41
Wetherden	7½	48½
Hawleigh New-Street	1	49½
Stow Market	2½	52
Needham Market	3	55
Ipswich, p. 299.	9½	64½
Bourn Bridge	1½	66
Shotley Gate and Ferry	8½	74½
Harwich	1¾	76¼

Four Miles beyond Thetford is Euston-Hall, a Seat of the Duke of Grafton.

Lynn to *Yarmouth*.

To Gaywood, *Norf.*	—	1¾
Gayton	5¾	7½
Ruffham Lodge	6½	14
Lycham	3½	17½
Mileham	2½	20
Billingford	6½	26½
Leonard Bridge	5	31½
Attlebridge	3¾	35¼
Drayton	1¾	37
NORWICH*	5	42
Thurston	9	51
Hadsko	9	60
Yarmouth	9½	69½

* *Another Road from Norwich to Yarmouth*, p. 325.

Maidstone to Canterbury.

To Berstead, *Kent*	—	4
Hollingbourn	3	7
Doddingham	6	13
Newnham	2	15
Ospringe	4	19
Bockton Street	4	23
CANTERBURY	6	29

Maidstone to *Guildford*.

To Ditton, *Kent.*	—	4
Gallic Hill	5	9
Borough Green	1½	10½
Igtham	1	11½
Seal Charte	1½	13
Seal	1½	14½
Riverhead	3	17½
Sundridge	2	19½
Brasted	¾	20¼
Westerham	1¾	22
Limpsfield,	3	25
Oxted Street	1½	26½
Godstone Green	2¾	29¼
Bletchingley	1¾	31

Nutfield	1¼	32¼
Ryegate	4	36¼
Buckland	2¼	38½
East Betchworth	1	39½
Dorking	3	42½
Westcott	1½	44
Abinger Hammer	3½	47½
Gumshall	1	48½
Shere	1¼	49¾
Guildford	5	54¾

A little beyond Ditton, on the left, is Bradbourn-House, Seat of the late Sir Roger Twisden, Bart.

A little beyond Riverhead, on the l. is Montreal, the Seat of L. Amherst; and on r. is Chepstead Place, —— Polhill, Esq.

Near Sunbridge is Coombank, a Seat of the late Duke of Argyll.

To the r. of 19 is Chevening-Place, a Seat of Earl Stanhope.

At Brasted is another Seat of Lord Frederic Campbell; and ½ a Mile beyond it is Hill-Park, late E. of Hillsborough, now Mr. Cotton, famous for fine Cascades; also at Brasted, a new House of Dr. Turton.

At Westerham is Squirries, the Seat of John Ward, Esq.

Near Godstone, on the r. Rooks Nest, Mr. Becher, late Col. Clarke, now Mr. Strachey.

Adjoining to it is Flower, belonging to Sir Robert Clayton, now inhabited by Mr. Nevill.

On the r. of these is Morden, the Seat of Sir Robert Clayton.

At Ryegate, a Seat of the late Robert Scawen, Esq late of Mr. Nash, now Mr. Birkhead; and a House of Baron Masercs.

About 2 Miles beyond Ryegate, on l. Wonham House, Mrs. Stables.

At Buckland, on the left, T. Beaumont, Esq.

At East Betchworth, on the right, Mr. Petty, late Mr. Kilby, before Mr. Spooner.

On the left, beyond, Mrs. Bouverie.

At West Betchworth, Betchworth Castle, Sir Hen. St. John Mildmay, now inhabited by Mr. Peters.

At Dorking, on l. Dibden, late Duke of Norfolk, then the late Sir Wm. Burrell; at the Entrance of the Town, on l. Shrub Hill, Lord Leslie.

At 43, on the right, on the Hill, is Denbighs, built by Jonathan Tyers, Esq. late the Seat of Lord King, now Mr. Dennison; on the left, Berry-Hill, lord Grimston, inhabited by Mr. Shum.

About 45, on the left, the Rookery, Richard Fuller, Esq. Banker.

Beyond this, a Mile on the left, is Lonesome, Mrs. Haynes.

At 46½, on the left, Wooton-Place, Sir Frederic Evelyn, Bart.

A little beyond this, turn off on the left to Lord Macartney's, on Abinger Common; Mr. Perrin, and Mr. Thompson, at Leith Hill.

At 47, late Marquis of Donegal's, now new-built by Capt. Pitts.

At Gumshall is Towerhill, on the left, Rev. Mr. Bray.

At Shere, Mr. Wm. Bray.

Beyond Shere, on l. is Albury-Park, late E. of Aylesford, now Mrs. Finch; and Weston House, W. Man Godschall, Esq. formerly the Duncombes.

Beyond this, on a Hill, on the l. is Martha's Chapel, at the Foot of which, on the South, is an old Seat, formerly the Randylls, now Earl Spencer's.

Maidstone to *Tunbridge* and *Tunbridge Wells.*

To the Bower	—	⅓
Barming Cross	2	2½
Barming	½	3
Teston	.1	4
Wateringbury	1	5
Mereworth Cross	1½	6½
Rotling Hall	1	7½
Goose Green	1¼	8¾
Hadlow	1	9¾
Tunbridge	4	13¾
Quorry Hill	1½	15¼
Southborow	1¼	16½
Nonsuch Green	¾	17¼
Tunbridge Wells	1½	18¾

Near Teston, on r. is Baram's Place, the Seat of Sir Philip Boteler, Bart.

A little beyond Wateringbury is Wateringbury-Place, the Seat of Sir Thomas Stile.

To the left of Mereworth-Cross is Mereworth - Castle, the Seat of Lord Le Despencer.

Near Southbury, on the right, is Old Bounds, the Seat of Lord Darnley; and New Bounds, the Seat of John Anson, Esq.

Maldon *to Rochford.*

To Purley Wash	—	3
North Fambridge	3½	6½
Fambridge Ferry	½	7
South Fambridge	1	8
Rochford	3	11

Those who dislike a Ferry may go by Woodham, and cross the River when the Tide is out at a Place called Hull-Bridge, but where the Bridge has been down many Years At low Water it is very shallow;

but this Way is five Miles round; or they may go still higher, and cross the Water at Battlesbrige, and so to Rayleigh.

Manchester to *Black-pool*

To Claremont, *Lanc.*	—	3
Clifton	4	7
Bolton	5	12
Chorley	12	24
Bomberbridge	5	29
Frenchwood	4	33
Preston	1	34
Kirkham	10	44
Black-pool	10	54

Two Miles beyond Manchester, on the r. Pendleton-Hall, William Douglas, Esq.

At 3, on the r. Edgecroft-Hall, Rev. John Dauntsey.

At 4, on the r. Clifton-Hall, Thomas Gashill, Esq.

At 8, on the r. Carsley-Hall, Egerton Cross, Esq.

At 9, on the r. Darley-Hall, Rev. Christ. Whitehead.

At 10, on the r. Birch-House, Douring Rasbottom, Esq.

At 13, on the r. Halliwell-Hall, Capt. Roger Dewhurst.

At 19, on the r. Rivington-Hall, Robert Andrews, Esq.

At 22, on the l. Duxbury-Hall, Sir Frank Standish, Bart.

At 23, on the l. Gillibrand-Hall, Thomas Gillibrand, Esq.

At 25, on the l. Chorley-Hall, Abraham Cromptons, Esq.

At 26, on the l. New Crooke-Hall, Samuel Crooke, Esq.

At 33, on the l. Walton-Hall, Sir Henry Houghton, Bart.

A little farther, on the l. Nicolas Starkey, Esq.

At 35, on the r. Green Bank, E. J. Gerrard, Esq.
At 36, on the l. Tulketh-Hall, Roger Hesketh, Esq.
At 49, on the l. Lytham-Hall, John Clifton, Esq.

MANCHESTER to *Halifax*.

To Rochdale	—	12
Halifax	16	28

MANCHESTER to WORCESTER.

To *Stocport*, Chesh.	p. 132. and 223.	—	6½
Macclesfield		12	18½
Leek, Staff.		13	31½
Sandon		18½	50
Stafford		4½	54½
Dunston		3½	58
Penkridge		2½	60½
Spread Eagle		2½	63
Wolverhampton		7½	70½
Over Pen		2	72½
Himley		3½	76
Seven Stars		½	76½
King's Swinford		1	77½
Stourbridge, Worc.		3	80½
Old Swinford		1	81½
Padmoor		¾	82¼
Holy Cross, *Staff.*		2	84¼
Forefield Green		2	86¼
Broomsgrove		4¼	90½
Upton		3¼	93¾
Droitwich		3	96¾
Fennel Green		3½	100¼
WORCESTER		2¾	103

Another Road to Wolverhampton.

To Winslow	—	12
Congleton, *Chesh.*	12	24
Newcastle, *Staff.*	12	36
Stone	7	43
Stafford	9	52
Penkridge	6	58
Wolverhampton	10	68

Thence to Worcester, as above.

Two Miles beyond Wolverhampton, on l. Mr. Bradeney.
Four Miles on left, Woodhouses, Sir Sam. Hillier.
At Himley, Himley-Hall, Viscount Dudley and Ward.
A Mile beyond Padmoor, on the l. Hagley, late Lord Lyttelton.

MANCHESTER to *Warrington*.

Pendleton Green	—	2
Eccles	2½	4½
Erlow	4	8½
Erlow Green	1	9½
Caddished	1	10½
Hollin Green	1¼	11¾
Fistleton Green	2¼	14
Warrington	4½	18½

MANCHESTER to *Skipton*.

Rochdale, *Lanc*	—	11¾
Burnley	15½	27¼
Colne	6½	33¾
Skipton, Yorksh.	11¾	45½

MANSFIELD to *Matloc Bath*.

To Skegby, *Nott.*	—	3
Tibshelt, *Derb.*	3½	6½
Morton	2	8½
Stretton	1	9½
Butterlay	3½	13
Tansley	1½	14½

Matloc	$1\frac{1}{2}$	16
Crofs Derwent River to		
Matloc Bath	2	18

Before Tibfhelf, on r. Hardwick-Hall, a noble Houfe of the Duke of Devonfhire.

MANSFIELD to *Newark*.

To Shirewood Inn	—	$3\frac{1}{2}$
r. to Farsfield	4	$7\frac{1}{2}$
Eddingley	1	$8\frac{1}{2}$
Halam	$1\frac{1}{2}$	10
Southwell	$1\frac{1}{2}$	$11\frac{1}{2}$
Newark, p. 276.	7	$18\frac{1}{2}$

At $10\frac{1}{2}$, on the left, Norwood, Sir Richard Sutton.

Another Road, viz.

From *Mansfield* to Shirewood Inn	—	$3\frac{1}{2}$
l. to Kirklington	6	$9\frac{1}{2}$
Hockerton	$2\frac{1}{2}$	12
Averham	3	15
Kelham	1	16
Newark	2	18

At Kelham, Lord George Sutton.

From MARGATE to *Portfmouth* and *Southampton*, along the Coaft of *Kent* and *Suffex*.

To St. Peter's	—	3
Ramfgate	3	6
St. Lawrence	$\frac{3}{4}$	$6\frac{3}{4}$
Cliff's End	$1\frac{1}{2}$	$8\frac{1}{4}$
Ebbes Fleet	$1\frac{1}{4}$	$9\frac{1}{2}$
Sandwich	2	$11\frac{1}{2}$
Deal	5	$16\frac{1}{2}$
Walmer	$1\frac{1}{2}$	18
Ringwold	$1\frac{1}{2}$	$19\frac{1}{2}$
Dover	6	$25\frac{1}{2}$
Folkftone	$8\frac{1}{2}$	34
Sandgate Caftle	$2\frac{1}{2}$	$36\frac{1}{2}$
Hythe	2	38
New Romney	9	$47\frac{1}{2}$
Lydd	3	$50\frac{1}{2}$
Rye	12	$62\frac{1}{2}$
Winchelfea	3	$65\frac{1}{2}$
Geftling	4	$69\frac{1}{2}$
Haftings	4	$73\frac{1}{2}$
Bexhill	6	$79\frac{1}{2}$
Pevenfey	8	$87\frac{1}{2}$
Sea-houfes	4	$91\frac{1}{2}$
Eaft-Bourne	$1\frac{1}{2}$	93
Eaft-Dean	$2\frac{1}{2}$	$95\frac{1}{2}$
Seaford	$5\frac{1}{2}$	101
Blatchington Fort	$\frac{3}{4}$	$101\frac{3}{4}$
Bifhopftone	$\frac{3}{4}$	$102\frac{1}{2}$
Newhaven, a Bridge	2	$104\frac{1}{2}$
Rottendean	5	$109\frac{1}{2}$
Brighthelmftone	4	$113\frac{1}{2}$
Shoreham Bridge	$7\frac{3}{4}$	$121\frac{1}{4}$
The Pad	$\frac{1}{4}$	$121\frac{1}{2}$
Lanceing	1	$122\frac{1}{2}$
Sompting	1	$123\frac{1}{2}$
Patching Pond	5	$128\frac{1}{2}$
Angmering Park	1	$129\frac{1}{2}$
Arundel	4	$133\frac{1}{2}$
Almsford	3	$136\frac{1}{2}$
Mackerel's Bridge	$\frac{3}{4}$	$137\frac{1}{4}$
Croker Hill	$2\frac{1}{4}$	$139\frac{1}{2}$
Maudling	2	$141\frac{1}{2}$
Chichefter	2	$143\frac{1}{2}$
Fifhbourne	2	$145\frac{1}{2}$
Nutbourne	$3\frac{1}{2}$	149
Emfworth, *Hants*	$1\frac{1}{2}$	$150\frac{1}{2}$
Havant	2	$152\frac{1}{2}$
Bedhampton	1	$153\frac{1}{2}$
Corham	$3\frac{1}{2}$	157

Portsea Bridge and Works	½	157½
Hilsea Barracks	1	158½
Portsmouth	3	161½
Southwick	8	169½
Wickham	4	173½
1½ from the Town, on the Waltham Road		
l. to Botley	5	178½
West End	4	182½
Southampton	5	187½

At Winchelsea the Abbey Church, with Monuments for Knights Templers; Remains of the Friery; the Castle; Manufacture of Crape.

At Gestling, a Seat of Dr. Sir Wm. Ashburnham, Bart. (now Bishop of Chichester.)

At Hastings, the Castle.

At 4 Miles from Hastings is Bulver Hithe, where William the Conqueror landed.

Before Bexhill, on r. see General Murray's on the Hill. Under the Hill, Mr. Pelham's Park.

At Pevensey, great Remains of the Castle.

At Sea-houses, Lord George Cavendish, in Right of his Wife, Lady Betty Compton.

At 5½ on the r. from Brighthelmstone, is Beckingham, — Bridges, Esq.

At 9, on the r. entering Lanceing, Mr. Lloyd.

At 10, on the r. at Sompting, Mr. Barker.

At 11, on the l. Mr. Margeson.

At 15, at 2 Miles on the r. Michel Grove, Sir John Shelly, Bart.

At 16, on r. Angmering Park, Sir John Shelly's.

At 23, on the l. Capt. Montague; on the r. Deal Park, Sir George Thomas; and a little beyond is Slindon, Earl of Newburgh.

At 26, on the r. beyond, is Boxgrove Priory.

At 28, on the r. is Goodwood, Duke of Richmond.

At Chichester, see the Cathedral and the Cross in the High Street.

Between Chichester and Nutbourne, on the r. see Chichester Harbour.

At Bedhampton, on the r. is Belmont, Jervoise Clark Jervoise, Esq. and 1½ farther, on the l. see Langston Harbour and the Hulks.

At 8, on the r. from Portsmouth, is Southwic House, Robert Thistlethwaite, Esq.

At 9, on the r. is Ashland, Mrs. Eddowes.

At 12, on the r. is Wickham Place, George Grenier, Esq.

At 17, on the l. is Botley, John Clever and John Hall, Esqrs.

At 1½, from Botley, on the r. is Botley Grange, John Hare, Esq.

At 4, from Botley, on the l. is Town Hill, Nathaniel Middleton, Esq.

At 5, on the r. is Swadling, Wm Chamberlayne, Esq. late Lord Hawke; and a little beyond, on the l. is South Stoneham, Sir Hans Sloane.

At 2 Miles before Southampton, on the l. is Portswood House, Gen. Stibbert; and, opposite, Mrs. Mawhood.

At 1½ farther, on the l. is Belle Vūe, Sir Richard King.

From MATLOC to *Chatsworth*	—	11
Ditto to *Derby*, p. 155.	—	15

From MATLOC to *Bakewell*, p. 156.	—	10
Ditto to *Ashbourn*	—	11
Ditto to *Chesterfield*	—	11

Y

MERIDEN to *Warwic*.

To Kennelworth	—	8
Warwic	5	13

MIDHURST to WINCHESTER.

To Woolbeding Br.	—	1½
Trooton Bridge	2	3½
Turwic	1½	5
Rogate	1	6
Maiden Oak	1¾	7¾
Durford, *Hants*	¼	8
Sheet Bridge	1	9
Petersfield	1¾	10¾
Langridge	2½	13¼
Bordean	1	14¼
Bramdean	5¾	20
Cheriton	2½	22½
Maudlin	5	27½
WINCHESTER	1½	29

At Petersfield, Mr. Jolliffe.

MONMOUTH to GLOCESTER.

To Troy House, *Monm.*	—	1
High Meadow, *Glocest.*	3	4
Mitchel Dean	11	15
Huntley	4	19
Churcham	3	22
Highnam	2	24
GLOCESTER	2	26

At Troy House, Duke of Beaufort.

At 4, on the r. High Meadow, Viscount Gage.

At 23, on the l. Highnam Court, Sir John Guise, Bart.

NEWBURY to WINCHESTER.

To Newton, *Hants*	—	1¾
Whitway	2¼	4
Lichfield	4	8
Whitechurch	5	13
Bullington	5	18
Sutton, where, cross Stockbridge Road	1	19
WINCHESTER	7	26

At 1½, on l. Mrs. Montague.

At Newton, Admiral Darby.

Before Whitway, on the r. Earl of Carnarvon.

At Bullington, Mr. Sidney.

NEWCASTLE to CARLISLE, (*the New Military Road.*)

From the West Gate to Chapel Hill, *Northum*	—	4
Headon on the Wall	3	7
Harlow Hill	3½	10½
Port Gate	6½	17
Chollerford Bridge	4	21
Walwic	1¼	22¼
Carrawburgh	2½	24¾
Winshields	7¼	32
Glenwhelt	5½	37½
Ternon	4	41½
Brampton	5	46½
High Crosby	5	51½
Drawdikes	1	52½
Stanwix	2½	55
The Scotch Gate of CARLISLE	1	56

Two Miles before Brampton, on r. is Naward Castle, E. of Carlisle.

NEWCASTLE to CARLISLE, (*the Old Road.*)

To Denterburn	—	3
Walbottle	2	5
Hiddon on the Wall	3	8
Hurlowhill	3	11
Aydon	$4\frac{1}{2}$	$15\frac{1}{2}$
Corbridge	$1\frac{1}{2}$	17
Dilſton	$1\frac{1}{2}$	$18\frac{1}{2}$
Hexham	$2\frac{1}{2}$	21
Haydon	6	27
Lipwood	$1\frac{1}{2}$	$28\frac{1}{2}$
Millhouſe	$2\frac{1}{2}$	31
Stowhouſe	$1\frac{1}{4}$	$32\frac{1}{4}$
Milcriche	$1\frac{1}{2}$	$33\frac{3}{4}$
Haltwhiſtle	$2\frac{1}{4}$	36
Glenwhelt	4	40
Ternon	4	44
Brampton	5	49
CARLISLE	$9\frac{1}{4}$	$58\frac{1}{4}$

At Dilſton is a Ruin of the late Earl of Derwentwater's Seat, forfeited in the Rebellion, 1745.
One Mile from Hexham, on the r. is Beaufront, the Seat of John Errington, Eſq.

NEWCASTLE to *Mancheſter.*

To Lawton, *Cheſter*	—	6
Aſtbury	5	11
Congleton	1	12
Goſlin Green	4	16
Monk's Heath	3	19
Street Lane Ends	3	22
Wilmſlow	2	24
Cheadle	5	29
Mancheſter	7	36

At 8, on the l. Rode-Hall, Rich. Wilbraham Bootle, Eſq.

At 10, on the r. Moreton-Hall, Thomas Fowis, Eſq.
At 14, on the r. Eaton-Hall, Eaton Lee, Eſq.
At 15, on the r. Marton-Hall, late Sir Tho. Fleetwood, Bart.
At 17, on the r. Thornycroft-Hall, Edward Thornycroft, Eſq.
At 20, on the r. Alderley-Hall, Sir John Stanley, Bart.
At 23, on the r. Fulſhaw-Hall, Samuel Fynney, Eſq.
A little farther, on the l. Hawthorn-Hall, Thomas Page, Eſq.

NEWCASTLE to *Northwich.*

To Lawton	—	6
The Salt Works	2	8
Sandbach	4	12
Middlewich	5	17
Davenham	4	21
Northwich	2	23

At 6 is Lawton-Hall, John Lawton, Eſq.
Two Miles farther on the l. Lawton Salt Works.
At 13, on the r. Elworth-Hall, Rev. John Hulſe.
One Mile to the r. of Middlewich is Kinderton Lodge, late Lord Vernon.
At 20, on the r. Boſtoc-Hall, Edw. Tomkinſon, Eſq.

NEWHAVEN to *New Shoreham.*

To Moarſted, *Suſſex*	—	3
Saltden	1	4
Rottendean	1	5
Brighthelmſtone	4	9
Hove	$1\frac{1}{2}$	$10\frac{1}{2}$
Buckingham Houſe	$4\frac{1}{2}$	15
New Shoreham	4	19

NEW PASSAGE (over the *Severn*) to *Abergavenny*.

St. Peter's Park Wall	—	1
Caerwent	$2\frac{1}{2}$	$3\frac{1}{2}$
Lantriffent	$6\frac{1}{2}$	10
Uíke	$2\frac{1}{2}$	$12\frac{1}{2}$
Llanellan Bridge	2	$14\frac{1}{2}$
Abergavenny	$6\frac{1}{2}$	21

NEWPORT to *Leek* by *Stafford*.

To Ranton Abbey, *Staff.*	—	8
Stafford	6	14
Sandon Hall	4	18
Leek	20	38

At 8, Sir Charles Cope, Bart.
At 18, Lord Harrowby.

NEWPORT to *Cannoc* by *Wolverhampton*.

To Woodcote Hall, *Staff.*	—	3
Albrighton	8	11
Tetenhall	5	16
Welverhampton	2	18
Old Fallings	2	20
Hilton Hall	3	23
Cannoc	4	27

At 20, on l. John Gough, Esq.

NEWPORT to *Newcastle*.

To *Eccleshall*	—	9
Swinnerton Hall	4	13
Clayton	5	18
Newcastle	2	20

At 2 Miles, on the r. from Newport, Aqualate-Hall, Charles Baldwyn, Esq.

At 8, on the l. Johnson-Hall, Rev. Francis Mecke.
At 10, on the l. Eccleshall Palace, Bishop of Lichfield
At 13, on the r. Swinnerton-Hall, Basil Fitzherbert, Esq.

NORWICH to *Yarmouth*, (*the new Road*.)

To Blowfield	—	6
Accle	5	11
Yarmouth	11	22

Another Road, p. 312.

On this Road, and also from Bury *to* Osmondstone, *the Name of the Parish is cut on the Mile-stones; an useful Improvement.*

NORWICH to *Lynn*.

To Aylesham, *Norf.*	—	10
Holt	9	19
Clay	3	22
Wells	6	28
Burnham	4	32
Houghton	8	40
Lynn	10	50

NORWICH to *Worstead* and *North Walsham*.

To Sprowston	—	2
Rackheath	$1\frac{1}{2}$	$3\frac{1}{2}$
Wroxham	$3\frac{1}{2}$	7
Hoveton	2	9
Tunstead	1	10
Worstead	2	12
North Walsham	3	15

At Sprowston, on the r. Sir Lambert Blackwell's.
At Rackheath, on the r. — Stracey, Esq.

At Wroxham, on the l. a new-built House of Mr. Collyer.

Beyond Wroxham, on the r. —— Wace, Esq.

At Worstead, the new House of Mr. Boxgrave.

At North Walsham, —— Cooper, Esq.

Two Miles from North Walsham, is Witton House and Park, the magnificent Seat of the Heiress of the late J. Norris, Esq.

Another Road to North Walsham.

To Cotton Hill		1/4
r. *to* Beeston	2 3/4	3
Coltishall	3 3/4	6 3/4
Scottow Common	2 3/4	9 1/2
Westwic	2	11 1/2
North Walsham	2 1/2	14

At Beeston, on the r. is the Seat of J. Micklethwayte, Esq.

At Coltishall, on the right, Mr. Watts.

At Westwic, on the r. Westwic House, the beautiful Seat of B. Petre, Esq.

NORTHALLERTON to *Middleham.*

To Ainderby	——	2 1/2
Morton	1/2	3
Cross Leeming Road	3	6
Aiskew	1	7
Bedale	1	8
Middleham	10	18

NORTHAMPTON to *Warwic.*

To Daventry	——	11
Southam	11	22
Warwic	10	32

At 2, on left, Upton-Hall, T. S. Watson, Esq.

Two Miles from Southam, to the l. Offchurch Bury, J. W. Knightley, Esq.

NOTTINGHAM to *Manchester.*

To Bobber's Mill	——	1 1/2
Baysford	1	2 1/2
Cinder Hill	1	3 1/2
Nuttal	1	4 1/2
Watnal	1 1/4	5 3/4
Griesly Church	1 1/4	7
More Green	1/2	7 1/2
Selston	4 1/2	12
Pye Bridge, *Derb.*	1	13
Somercotes	1	14
Alfreton	2	16
Peacock Inn	2	18
Matloc	6 1/2	24 1/2

Or,

From *Nottingham* to

Ripley, *Derb.*	——	14
Matloc	11	25
Wensley	3 1/2	28 1/2
Winster	1 1/2	30
Pike-Hall (a public House)	3	33
Hurdlow House	6 1/2	39 1/2
Over Street	1	40 1/2
Buxton	5 1/4	45 3/4
Manchester, p. 146.	22 1/2	68 1/4

At Nuttal, Sir Charles Sedley.

At Watnal, Mr. Roufon.

At Pye Bridge you cross the River Erwash, navigable to Langley Bridge, four Miles below.

Two Miles from Matloc, down the River, on the opposite Side, is Matloc Bath.

Near Pike-Hall, Druidical Circle of Stones, and a Barrow.

NOTTINGHAM to *Doncaster.*

To Red Hill,	*Nott.*	—	4¼
The Hut		5¾	10
Ollerton		8½	18½
Palethorp		2½	21
Blythe		10½	31½
Harworth		3½	35
Roffington,	*Yorksh.*	4	39
Roffington Bridge		1	40
Doncaster		4	44

To the r. of the Hut, see Sir Richard Sutton.

Two Miles before Ollerton, on the right, Rufford, late Sir George Saville.

At Palethorp, on the left, Thoresby Park, late Duke of Kingston's.

From 23 to 25, on the left, Clumber Park, Duke of Newcastle.

At Blythe, C. Mellish, Esq.

Another Road, viz.

From Nottingham to Red Hill,	*Nott.*	—	4¼
Mansfield		9¾	14
Warsop		5	19
Norton		2¼	21¼
*Worksop**		4½	25¾
Carlton		3¼	29
Godthrop		3	32
Tickhill,	*Yorksh.*	3	35
Doncaster, p. 181.		7½	42½

At 9, on the left, Newstead Abbey, Lord Byron.

At 21, on the left, Welbec Abbey, Duke of Portland.

At 25, on the left, Worksop Manor, Duke of Norfolk.

* *Another Road to Worksop.*

To Ollerton, *above.*	—	18½
Worksop	9	27½

NOTTINGHAM to *Bakewell.*

To *Peacock Inn*, p. 330	—	18
Matloc	6¼	24½
Darley	3½	28
Rowsley	2	30
Bakewell	3	33

A Mile before Bakewell is Haddon-Hall, Duke of Rutland.

At Bakewell, Mr. Twigg, and a Mill for Spinning Cotton.

NOTTINGHAM to *Grantham.*

To Radcliff,	*Nott.*	—	5½
Saxondale		2½	8
Bingham		1	9
Whatton		2½	11½
Elton		2	13½
Bottesford,	*Leic.*	2½	16
Grantham	Linc.	7	23

To the r. of Bottesford is Belvoir Castle, a Seat of the Duke of Rutland.

NOTTINGHAM to *Leeds,*
(*a new Road.*)

To *Mansfield*	—	14
Chesterfield	12	26
Sheffield	12	38
Rotherham	6	44
Barnsley	14	58
Wakefield	10	68
Leeds	9	77

Another new Road.

To *Mansfield*	—	14
Purbly-Lane	12	26
Rotherham (Ferry)	10	36

Barnsley	14	50
Wakefield	10	60
Leeds	9	69

OKEHAMPTON to *Bideford.*

To Five Oaks	—	2
Hatherleigh	5	7
Petrocstow	4	11
Little Torrington	5½	16½
Torrington	1	17½
Bideford	6¼	23¾

OLDHAM to *Rochdale.*

Oldham to Royton	—	2
Lower Place	3	5
Rochdale	1	6

On the r. of 2. Royton-Hall, Joseph Pickford, Esq.

Another Road.

Oldham to Ashton-under-line	—	4

OLDHAM to *Bury.*

Oldham to Chadderton	—	2
Middleton	2	4
Bury	5	9

On the r. of Chadderton, Chadderton-Hall, Sir Watts Norton, Bart.

ONGAR to *Hatfield Broad-Oak.*

To Fifield	—	3
Abbots Roding	3	6
White Roding	2	8
Hatfield Broad-Oak	3	11

OXFORD to BRISTOL.

To Botley, Berks	—	1½
l. to Tubney Warren	3½	5
Fifield	1½	6½
Kingston Inn	3½	10
Farringdon	6	18
Coleshill	4	22
Highworth, Wilts	2	24
River Ray	5½	29½
Purton	2½	32
Guersden Green	6	38
Guersden	1½	39½
Milbourn Green	1½	41
Malmesbury	1	42
Foxley	3	45
Luckington	4½	49½
Tormanton, Gloc	2½	52
Hinton	6	58
Pucklechurch	2	60
Mangerfield	2¼	62¼
BRISTOL	5¾	68

Quarter of a Mile from Oxford, Grandport-house, W. E. Taunton, Esq.

At 8, Kingston Bagpuze, —— Walker, Esq.

Beyond Kingston Inn, new House, Mr. Hayward.

At 14, on r. Buckland, Sir J. Throckmorton, Bart.

At 15, on r. Carswell, the ancient House of the Southbys, Henry Southby, Esq.

At Coleshill is the Seat of Sir Mark Stuart Pleydell, Bart. built in 1654, by Inigo Jones, which, having since undergone no Alteration or Addition, is remarkable for being the most (if not the only) complete Work now remaining of that great Architect, now Hon. Mr. Bouverie's.

3

Oxford to Cambridge,
(the new Road.)

To *Thame*,	Oxf.	—	13
Aylesbury,	Bucks	9	22
Tring,	Herts	7	29
Dunstable,	Bedfordsh.	10	39
Hitchin,	Herts	15	54
Baldock		5	59
Royston		8	67
CAMBRIDGE		13	80

Oxford to Cambridge,
(the old Road.)

To Gosford Bridge		—	5
Wendlebury		5	10
Bicester		3	13
Stretton Audley		3	16
Gaynat,	*Bucks*	6¾	22¾
Buckingham		2	24¾
River Ouse		6	30¾
Stanton Bridge		4¼	35
Newport Pagnel		3½	38½
Astwood		6	44½
Stagsden,	*Bedf.*	2½	47
Bedford		5	52
Cardington Cross		2	54
Moggerhanger		4½	58½
Girtford Bridge		1½	60
Sandy		¾	60¾
Potton		3¼	64
Cockain Hatley		2	66
CAMBRIDGE		14	80

From Newport Pagnel to Bedford is a very bad Road.

At Astwood, Mr. Lowndes.

Oxford to Chichester.

Bagley Wood,	*Berks*	—	3
Abingdon		3½	6½
Milton		3½	10
East Ilsley		7	17
Biddon		2½	19½
Donnington Castle		6	25½
Newbury		1	26½
Knightsbridge,	*Hants*	3½	30
Kingsclear		3½	33½
Basingstoke		9¼	42¾
Hackwood Hall		1¾	44½
Weston		3½	48
Alton		5	53
Chawton		1½	54½
Farringdon Street		1½	56
East Tysted		2	58
Petersfield		8	66
Stainbridge,	*Sussex*	1½	67½
Harting Hills		3½	71
Cowshall House		6	77
CHICHESTER		4	81

Another Road, viz.

To Dorchester,	*Oxf.*	—	8½
Shillingford		1½	10
r. to Shillingford Br.		½	10½
Wallingford		2	12½
Reading, p. 350.		15	27½
Harford Bridge,	*Hants*	12½	40
Farnham,	*Surry*	10	50
Rood Lane		7	57
Midhurst,	*Sussex*	12½	69½
CHICHESTER, p. 28.		11¼	80¾

About 2 Miles before Abingdon is Radley, Lord Rivers, but inhabited by Admiral Bowyer.

On l. 3 Miles beyond E. Holey, Langley-Hall, Sir Walter James.

On l. of Donnington is Shaw, Sir Joseph Andrews.

On the right, is the Castle behind Mr. Basket's House.

A little more to the right is the Grove, late Mr. Andrews, now Mr.

Brummell, late Secretary to Lord North; pleasant Walks, by fine Water.

In Donnington, Mr. Cowslip.

At Hackwood, Duke of Bolton.

At Chawton, Mr. Knight.

Near Reading is Caversham, late Lord Cadogan, now Mr. Marsac.

At Farnham Castle, Bishop of Winchester.

Near Farnham, Waverley Abbey, Rev. Sir Charles (Bostock) Rich, Bart, L. L. D.; and Moor Park, formerly Sir W. Temple.

At Midhurst, Cowdry House, late Lord Montague, now Mr. Poyntz, who married his Sister and Heir.

OXFORD to *Basingstoke.*
(*the new Road.*)

To *Wallingford*, p. 336	—	12½
Pangbourn, p. 346.	9	21½
At Bostoc Lane End enter the Bath Road		
Aldermaston	9	30½
Tadley, *Hants*	2½	33
Pamber	1½	34½
E. Sherborne	2	36½
Basingstoke	3	39½

At Aldermaston, on the l. is a House and Park, formerly belonging to the ancient Family of the Forresters, since to Wm. Lord Stawell; by a marriage with whose Daughter it became the Property of the late Ralph Congreave, Esq.

At East Sherborne, on the l. is the Vine, the Seat of John Chute, Esq. heretofore belonging to the Family of the Sands, who were Lord Sands of the Vine.

OXFORD to *Derby.*

To Kedlington Green, *Oxfordsh*	—	4½
Cross London Road	3	7½
Hopcroft's Holt	4½	12
Deddington	4	16
Adderbury	3	19
Banbury	3½	22½
Mollington	4¼	26¾
Farnboro', *Warw.*	1	27¾
Cross the Oxford Canal	2¼	30
Ladbrook	3½	33½
Southam	1¾	35¼
Long Itchington	2¼	37½
Marton	2	39½
Princethorp	1¼	40¾
Ryton Bridge	4	44¾
Wynald	2¼	47
COVENTRY	2½	49½
Nuneaton, p. 233.	8¼	57¾
Manchester	3¼	61
Atherston	1	62
Sheepy, *Leic.*	3	65
Twycross	2	67
Snareston	4	71
Ashby de la Zouch	5	76
Pistern Hill, *Derb.*	2½	78½
Bridge over Trent	5	83½
Swarkston	½	84
Derby	5	89

At 6, on the right, Shipton, Lady Hind, a White House and Tower.

At 11½, on r. Rousham, Sir Clement Cotterell Dormer, Knt. and, on left, Barton Church.

At 22, on the r. Heaford and Steeple Aston Churches.

At 14, on r. Somerton, in Bottom, North Aston, Mr. Bowles.

At Adderbury, on r. a Seat of the Duke of Buccleugh; and on l. an old House, some time Sir George Cobb.
A little beyond Adderbury, on r. is Astrop, Mr. Willes, and the Wells.
At Manchester, Oldbury, Mr. Okeover, and a Roman Station.

OXFORD to *Leeds*, through *Warwic*, COVENTRY, and *Derby*, the best and most usual Road.

To *Skipston*, p. 110.	—	28
Hartford Br. *Warw.*	3	31
Wellesburn	7	38
Burford	4	42
Warwic	2	44
COVENTRY	10	54
Nuncaton, p. 233.	8¼	62¼
Snareston *, p. 338.	13¼	75½
Over Seal, *Derb.*	1¼	76¾
Castle Griesley	2¼	79
Stanton	2	81
Stapenhill	1	82
Burton on Trent	1	83
Monks Bridge	3	86
Little Over	6	92
Derby	2	94
Duffield Bridge	4½	98½
Huston Hall	9¼	107¾
Wingerworth	7¼	115
Chesterfield	2½	117½
Leeds, p. 153.	43	160½
* Or from Snareston to *Derby* by		75½
Ashby de la Zouch	5	80½
Cavendish Bridge	10	90½
Derby	7	97½

At Drakelow, near Castle Griesley, Sir Nigel Bowyer Griesley.
At Wingerworth, Sir Henry Hunloke.

OXFORD to LICHFIELD.

To *Birmingham*, p. 109	—	62
Aston	1½	63½
Berington	2½	66
Sutton Colefield	3	69
Hill	2	71
Shenstone	3	74
LICHFIELD	4	78

At Aston Park, Lady Holt.
At Shenstone, on the r. Mr. Hector; and on the left, Mr. Dolphin.

OXFORD to *Oakingham*.

To Dorchester, *Oxf.*	—	8½
Shillingford	1½	10
r. Shillingford Bridge	½	10½
Wallingford, Berks	2	12½
Reading, p. 349.	15	27½
Lodden Bridge	2½	30
King Street	1¼	31¼
Oakingham	3	34¼

OXFORD to PETERBOROUGH.

Gosford Bridge	—	5
Middleton Stoney	8	13
Ardley	3	16
Barley Mow, *N. amp.*	5	21
Brackley	2	23
Syresham	4	27
Over Whittlebury Forest to		
Silverston	3	30
Towcester	4	34

Blisworth	4	38
Northampton	5	43
Weston Favel	2½	45½
Great Billing	2	47½
Ecton	1½	49
Wilby	3	52
Wellingborough	2	54
Thingdon	3	57
Thrapston	8	65
Thorp Watervill	2½	67½
Barnwell	2¾	70¼
Oundle	2	72¼
Warmington	3¼	75½
Elton	1½	77
Chesterton	2½	79½
Allwalton	½	80
Overton Watervill	1½	81½
Overton Longvill	1	82½
Woodstone	1½	84
PETERBOROUGH	1	85

To the l. of 8 is Blechingdon, A. Annesley, Esq. and a Mile farther, also on l. Kirtlington Park, Sir Henry Dashwood.

At Middleton Stoney, the Earl of Jersey.

Beyond Towcester, on right, Easton Neston, Earl of Pomfret.

At 45½, the Place where the celebrated Mr. Hervey wrote his Meditations.

At Great Billing, Lord John Cavendish.

To the r. of Ecton, Mr. Isted.

At Thingdon, Sir W. Dolben, Bart.

Two Miles before Thrapston, and about a Mile to the left of the Road, is Drayton House, Viscount Sackville.

At Elton, on left, Elton-Hall, the Earl of Carysfort.

At Chesterton the Seat of Mr. Waller.

OXFORD to SALISBURY and *Poole*.

To *Abingdon*, Berks	—	6½
Wantage	9	15½
Hungerford	12½	28
Marton, *Wilts*	6½	34½
North Tudworth	8	42½
South Tudworth	1	43½
Shipton	1½	45
Ford	9¼	54¼
SALISBURY	2¾	57

This is a bad Road, and will not do for a Chaise; you must go to

Newbury, p. 336.	—	26½
Highclear	5	31½
Up. Hursborne	6	37½
Inham	2½	40
Andover	2½	42½
Or,		
Abingdon	—	6
Ilsley	11	17
Newbury	9	26
Andover	16½	42½
Salisbury	17½	60
Thence to		
Poole	28	88

OXFORD to *Stamford*.

To *Oundle*, p. 341.	—	72¼
Tansor	1¾	74
Fotheringhay	1½	75½
Massington	2	77½
Yadwell	1	78½
Wansford	1	79½
Stamford, Linc.	5½	85

At 75½, the Ruins of Fotheringhay Castle, where Mary Queen of Scots was beheaded.

A Mile before Stamford, on r. Burleigh House, Earl of Exeter.

Oxford to Winchester.

Aldermaston, p. 337.	—	30½
Baughurst	2½	33
Ramsdale	2	35
Over Rocks Down, Worting, and Basingstoke Down to		
Popham Lane	9½	44½
WINCHESTER, p. 45.	12	56½

On the r. of Ramsdale is Ewhurst, Sir Robert Mackbeth, Knt.

Oxford to Worcester.

To *Enstone*, p. 100. Thence to	—	15¼
WORCESTER, p. 101.	41¾	57

Paddington to the Eagle at *Snaresbrook* on *Epping Forest*.

To Islington	—	2¼
Dalston	2½	4¾
Clapton	1	5¾
Lea Bridge	1	6¾
Loy Layton	1	7¾
Nott's Green	½	8¼
Snaresbrook	¾	9

Padstow to *St. Michael*.

To Treviblin, *Corn.*	—	3¾
St. Columb	4¾	8½
St. Michael	7	15½

Peterborough to *Leicester*.

To Thorpe		—	2
Castor		2½	4½
Ailsework		½	5
Wansford		3	8
Duddington		6	14
Uppingham,	Rutl.	8	22
E. Norton,	*Leic.*	8	30
Tugby		1	31
Skeffington		2	33
Billesdon		1½	34½
Houghton		2½	37
Thurnby		2	39
Leicester		4	42

Before Thorpe, on l. late Sir Robert Bernard.

At 3, on right, Milton, Earl Fitzwilliam.

At 35 is Skeffington-Hall, Sir W. C. Farrell-Skeffington, Bart.

Penrith to *Cockermouth*.

To Hutton	—	5½
Hesketh	7¾	13¼
Thorney Stone	4¾	18
Uldale	1½	19½
Ouse Bridge	4½	24
Cockermouth	5¼	29¼

At Hutton, Hutton-Hall, —— Fletcher, Esq.

Another Road, viz.

To Stainton	—	2½
Penruddoc	3½	6
Threlkeld	7½	13½
Keswic	4	17½
Braithwaite	2¾	20¼

Lawton	4	25¼
Cockermouth	5	29¼

To the right of Penruddoc, 2 Miles of the Road, is Graystoc Castle and Park, the Duke of Norfolk's.

PLYMOUTH to *Bodmin*.

To *Saltash*, Corn.	—	4½
Notter Bridge	3	7½
Landrech	1	8½
Tidiford	1½	10
Catchfrench	2½	12½
Coldrinnic	2	14½
Catuther	2½	17
Leskard	1½	18½
Refsrun	12	30½
Bodmin	2	32½

PLYMOUTH to *Dartmouth*.

To *Modbury*, p. 38.	—	14½
Gary Bridge	5	19½
Holwell	3½	23
Dartmouth	7	30

POOL to *Lymington*.

To Ifford, Hants	—	8¾
Christ Church	1¾	10½
Somerford Bridge	4¼	14¾
Milton	½	15¼
Evilton	4¾	20
Lymington	2	22

On the right, beyond Christ Church, on a Cliff, Earl of Bute.

On the left, beyond Milton, Major Rooke.

PORTSMOUTH to CHICHESTER.

To Cosham, Hants	—	4½
r. to Havant	4½	9
Nutbourn, Sussex	3½	12½
Fishbourn	3½	16
CHICHESTER	2	18

PORTSMOUTH to OXFORD.

To Southwic, Hants	—	8
Wickham	4	12
Waltham	5	17
Stephen's Castle Down	4½	21½
Salt Lane	1½	23
Tichbourn	2½	25½
Alresford	2¼	27¾
Dummer	9	36¾
Worting	4	40¾
Aldermaston, Berks	9	49¾
Pangbourn	6	55¾
Wallingford	10½	66¼
OXFORD, p. 350.	12¼	78½

PORTSMOUTH to SALISBURY.

To Southwic	—	7¾
Wickham	4	11¾
Botley, Men's Bridge, Stoneham, *Rumsey*	16½	28¼
Heath Post	2¼	30½
Cowfield	6	36½
White Parish	1	37½
Whaddon	3½	41
Alderbury	¾	41¾
SALISBURY	3¾	45½

On the r. beyond Alderbury, see Clarendon Park, Gen. Bathurst.

PRESCOT to *Ashton-under-line*.

To Sankey Chapel, Lanc.	—	7

Warrington	3	10
Hollins Green	6	16
Eccles	8	24
Manchester	4	28
Ashton-under-line	8	36

At 5, on the l. Bold-Hall, Miss Bold.

At 9, on the l. the Bank, Thomas Patten, Esq.

At 10, on the l. Fairfield-Hall, Miss Blackburne.

At 16, on the r. Mill Bank, Walter Keerfoot, Esq.

At 25, on the l. Thomas Butterworth Bayley, Esq.

A little farther, on the l. Charles Ford, Esq.

At 26, on the l. Pendleton-Hall, William Douglass, Esq.

At 29, on the l. Ancoats-Hall, Sir John Parker Mosely, Bart.

PRESCOT to *Coln.*

To Blackbrook, *Lanc.*	—	6
Wigan	8	14
Chorley	9	23
Blackburn	12	35
Padiham	7	42
Burnley	5	47
Coln	6	53

Two Miles from Prescot, on the l. Eccleston-Hall, Tho. Eccleston, Esq.

At 7, on the l. Garswood-Hall, Sir Robert Gerrard, Bart.

At 39, on the l. Read-Hall, James Hilton, Esq.

At 42, on the l. Ountread-Hall, —— Starkey, Esq.

At 45, on the r. Palace House, Robert Holden, Esq.

A little farther, on the l. Royle Hall, Edward Townley, Esq.

At 50, on the l. Carr-Hall, John Cleyton, Esq.

PRESTEIGN to *Caermarthen.*

Beggars Bush, *Radn.*	—	2
Knierton	1½	3½
New Radnor	2	5½
Matts	7	12½
Builth, Brec.	3½	16
Cavenabeth	1½	17½
Laver	2½	20
Pont Ridgley	1	21
Ludlow Vaugh	6¾	27¾
Llanymadovry, Caerm.	7¼	35
Caermarthen, p. 83.	26	61

PRESTON to *Bridlington.*

To Crashawbooth	—	24
Rushworth, *Yorksh.*	22	46
Brighouse	8	54
Gildersome	8	62
Leeds	5	67
Selby	24	91
Skipton	19	110
Cranwic	12	122
Bridlington	15	137

PRESTON to *Skipton.*

Blackburn, *Lanc.*	—	11¾
Burnley	11¾	23
Coln	6½	29½
Skipton, Yorksh.	11¼	41¼

READING to *Aylesbury.*

To Purley, *Berks*	—	5
Pangbourn	1	6
Basclden	1½	7
Streatley	1½	9
Moulsford	2¼	11¼

Wallingford	3¾	15
Shillingford Bridge	2	17
Shillingford, *Oxf.*	½	17½
Warborough	½	18
Newington	2½	20½
Stadhampton	1½	22
Little Milton	1¾	23¾
Cross the Oxford Road at the 3 Pigeons	3	26¾
Three Elms	3	29¾
Thame	¾	30½
Hadenham, *Bucks*	3	33½
Dinton	2¼	35¾
Stone	1	36¾
Hartwell	1¼	38
Aylesbury	2	40

At 3¾, on r. Purley Church.
Beyond Purley Church, on r. under the Hill, in Oxfordshire, is Mapledurham, Mr. Blount; a little beyond this, also in Oxfordshire, is Hardwic, Mr. Powys.
At Purley is Purley-Hall, the Rev. Dr. Wilder's.
Near Baselden, on the l. is Baselden Park, Sir Francis Sykes, Bart.
At Dinton, Sir John Vanhattam, Bart.
At 1½ Mile from Stone are the Earl of Chesterfield's Grounds and Park.
At Hartwell, Sir Wm. Lee, Bart.
Two or three Miles from Thame is Netley Abbey.

Reading to *Abingdon*.

To Shillingford, *above.*	—	17½
l. to Dorchester	1½	19
l. to Burcot	1½	20½
Clifton	1¼	21¾
Cullum Bridge	2¾	24½
Abingdon, Berks	1	25½

To the right of Clifton, about a Mile, is Newnham Courtney, Earl Harcourt.

Reading to *Buxton*.

To *Wallingford*, p. 349	—	15
Oxford, p. 337.	12½	27½
Birmingham, p. 110.	61½	89
Lichfield*, *Staff.*	16	105
Bromley	5	110
Yoxall Bridge over the Trent	1	111
Sudbury, Derb.	10	121
Cobely	2	123
Clifton	6	129
Ashbourn	1	130
Buxton, p. 145.	20	150

* *Another Road from Lichfield to Buxton*, p. 304.

Three Miles and a half beyond Lichfield, you cross the navigable Canal on Bromley Common.
At Cobely, to the right, is a pretty romantic Church.
About 3 Miles beyond Ashbourn is Ham, the Seat of Mr. Porte.

Reading to *Hatfield*.

To *Henley*, Oxf.	—	8
Great Marlow, *Bucks*	7	15
High Wycomb	5	20
Amersham	7	27
Cheyness	5	32
Chorley Wood	1	33
Rickmansworth, *Herts*	2	35
Watford	3	38
St. Alban's	8	46
Hatfield	5	51

On the right, before Wycomb, is a Seat of the Marq. of Lansdown.
At Rickmansworth, on r. Moor Park, late Sir Thomas Dundas; on the left, Bury Park, Wm. Field, Esq.
On left, before Watford, is Cashiobury Park, Earl of Essex.
At St. Alban's, Holloway House, Earl Spencer.
At Hatfield, Hatfield House, Marquis of Salisbury.

READING to *Basingstoke* and WINCHESTER.

To Whitley	—	2
Three-Mile Cross	1	3
Swallowfield, *Wilts*	3	6
Heckfield Heath, *Hants*	1	7
Stratfield Say	2	9
Stratfield Turges	1	10
Sherfield	1	11
Sherfield Church	1¼	12¼
Basing Turnpike	¾	13
Chinham Chalk-Pits	2	15
Basingstoke	1	16
WINCHESTER, p. 45.	17½	33½

At Stratfield Say, Lord Rivers.
At Swallowfield, late Mr. Dodd, now Mr. Beavan.

READING to *Andover*.

To Aldermaston	—	10
Kingscleare, *Hants*	7	17
Whitchurch	7	24
Andover	7	31

RICHMOND to *Kendal*.

To Redmire	—	10¾
Carperby	3	13¾
Askrig	4¼	18
Bainbridge	1½	19½
Ingleton	18½	38
Kendal, p. 159.	19	57

Another Road, viz.

To *Askrig*, above	—	18
Hardrow	5½	23½
Thwaite Bridge	3½	27
Little Town	5	32
Sedberg	8	40
Lincoln's Inn Bridge	2½	42½
Kendal	8½	51

At Askrig, two Water-falls, and another at Hardrow.

RICHMOND to *Hartlepool*.

To Scorton	—	5½
Ailey Hill	3	8½
North Cowton	1	9½
Enter Low Common	4	13½
Piersburgh	6	19½
Yarm	3	22½
Stocton	4	26½
Hartlepool	10	36½

RICHMOND to *Askrig*.

To Maske	—	5
Fremington	4	9
Reeth	½	9½
Helah	1½	11
Feetum	2	13
Askrig	6	19

Another Road, above.

RICHMOND to *Lancaster*.

To Ingleton, *above*.	—	38
Hornby	8	46
Lancaster	8	54

At Hornby, fee the Remains of the Caftle, the ancient Seat of the Lords Mounteagle. See alfo the Seat of Sir Edward Stanley.

From Hornby to Lancafter, a moft beautiful and picturefque ride.

RICHMOND to *Stainthorp.*

To Gilling	—	3
Forcett	5	8
Caldwell	1½	9½
Winfton Br. *Durh.*	2½	12
Stainthorp	3	15

At Two Miles, on the left, Afke, Lord Dundas.

At Forcett, on the left, Forcett-Hall, Robert Shuttleworth, Efq.

RICHMOND to *Pierce Bridge.*

To Skeeby	—	2
Pierce Bridge	9	11

Ross to *Burford.*

To Lee, *Glocefter.*	—	5
Churcham	7	12
Glocefter	4	16
Haydon	6	22
Cheltenham	4	26
Dowdefwell	4	30
Frog Mill	2	32
Northleach	5	37
Sherborne Park	4	41
Burford	5	46

At 13, on the l. Highnam Court, Sir John Guife, Bart.

Nearly oppofite on the r. High Grove, Sir Charles Barrow, Bart.

At 24, on the l. Swindon, William Beale, Efq.

At 25, on the r. Arle Court, Philip York Efq.

At 26, on the l. the Cottage, Richard Cox, Efq.

A little farther, on the r. Sanford Houfe, Richard Wood, Efq.

At 31, on the l. Sandywell Park, Mrs. Tracey.

At 4 Miles on the l. of Northleach, is Sherborne Houfe, Lord Sherborne.

Ross to *Monmouth.*

Crofs the River Wye to

Wilton	—	¾
Weare End	¾	1½
Pencraig	1¾	3¼
Crofs Keys	1	4¼
Old Forge	¾	5
Whitchurch	1	6
Croker's Afh	¾	6¾
Dickfon	2¼	9
Monmouth	1	10

At the Weare End, on the right, the Rev. Mr. Jones's.

At 2½ Miles to the left, over Wye, the Hill-Houfe, Mifs Clerk.

Juft before you enter Pencraig, on an eminence to the right, Germany, a neat little Cottage, remarkable for commanding one of the moft beautiful and picturefque Profpects between London and Caermarthen.

To the left of Pencraig, Giddis, Mr. Ware.

At 7 Miles, to the right, the Fort, Henry Barnes, Efq. directly oppofite to which, and adjoining the high Road, is Little Doward, famous for a fine Roman Encampment, defcribed by Camden; as likewife for fome romantic Views, on the Wye, to be seen from its summit.

At 8 Miles, to the left, over Wye, Hadnee, Rev. Mr. Griffin.

At Dickson, on the right, Dr. Powell.

From *Rowsley Bridge*, *Derbyshire*, to *Wardlow Turnpike*.

To Beeley	—	1¼
Edensor (or Ensor)	1¾	3
Baslow Bridge	1½	4½
Calver Bridge	1½	6
Stony Middleton	1½	7½
Wardlow Turnpike	3¼	10¾

At Edensor, Chatsworth, Duke of Devonshire.

St. Alban's to *Ware*.

To *Hatfield*	—	5¾
Cole Green	3¾	9½
Hartingfordbury	2¼	11¾
Hertford	1¼	13
Ware	3	16

At Cole Green, Earl Cowper.

St. David's to *Holywell*.

Cardigan, p. 92.	—	33½
Blanyport, *Card*	5½	39
The Four Boroughs	7½	46½
Llanarth	5	51½
Aberavan Bridge	4	55½
Aberath	1½	57
Molinamore	3	60
Llanrusted	3	63
Lambeden Vaur	8½	71½
Ruddy Pene	4	75½
Tallyport	2¾	78¼
Trethol	1¾	80
Llanihangle	3	83
Garick	1½	84½
Maclynleth, Mont.	4½	89
Dunlas	1½	90½
Llanvoring	3	93½
Mathavern	1½	95
Abertwydo	3	98
Aberangel	1½	99½
Dinasmouthy, Merion.	3½	103
Llanumouthy	4	107
Bullagrois	2	109
Pont Raven Vaughan	5½	114½
Llanavor	3¼	117¾
Sala	3	120¾
Llavar	1¼	122
Pont Maithree	7	129
Bettus	1¾	130¾
Ruthyn, Denb.	10¼	141
Llanguiven	6	147
Holywell, Flintsh.	9	156

Near Trethol is a Seat and Park, formerly belonging to Sir Rich. Price.

Salisbury to *Campden*.

To Old Sarum, *Wilts*	—	1¾
Everley	14¼	16
Birbich	5	21
Savernac Forest	3	24
Marlborough	3	27
Ogbourn Massey	2¾	29¾
Ogbourn St. George	2¾	32
Marsham	8	40
Highworth	3½	43½
Inglesham	2½	46
Lechlade, Gloc.	3	49
Little Farringdon, *Berks*	1½	50½
Filkins, *Oxfordsh.*	2	52½
Burford	5	58

The Beacon, *Gloc*	6½	64½
Stow	3	67½
Longborough Mill	3	70½
Campden	6¼	76¾

At Boughton (separated from Filkins only by a small Stream of Water) is the Seat of Sir William Chaloner Burnaby, Bart.

SALISBURY to *Devizes* and GLOCESTER.

At the Gallows, *r. to* Woodford Hut	—	6
Long Barrow Cross	1½	7½
At 12¾ *r. to* the Red Horn Turnpike	9	16½
Lide	2½	19
Nursteed	2	21
Devizes	1	22
Rowde	2	24
Sandy Lane	4	28
Red Hill	1¾	29¾
Derry Hill	½	30¼
Chippenham	2¼	32½
GLOCESTER, p. 77.	34	66½

Beyond Rowde, on the r. Earlstoke late Mr. Delmé, now Mr. Joshua Smith.

At Sandy Lane, on the l. Spy Park Sir Edward Bayntun, Bart. and beyond it, on the right, Beau wood, Marquis of Lansdown.

SHEFFIELD to *Buxton*.

To Little Sheffield	—	1
At 5, *l. to* Grindleford Br. *Derb.*	9	10
Great Hucklow	4¼	14¼
Tideswell	2¾	17
Fairfield	6	23
Buxton	1	24
Or,		
From Sheffield to Castleton	—	15
Buxton	10	25
Or,		
From Sheffield to Stony Middleton	—	12
Tideswell	5	17
Buxton	7	24

SHEFFIELD to *Manchester*.

To Little Sheffield.	—	1
At 5, *r. to* Hathersage, *Derb*	8	9
Hope	4½	13½
Castleton	1½	15
Sparrow Pitt	4	19
Chapel to Frith	2	21
Whaley Bridge, *Chesh.*	3½	24½
Manchester, p. 146.	16¼	40¾

Near Castleton, is Mam Tor, and the Devil's Arse in the Peake.

SHEFFIELD to *Worksop*.

Masborough	—	6
Eckington	2	8
Renishaw	1	9
Balbrough	3	12
Whitwell	3	15
Worksop	3	18

Near Masborough, on the left, is Masborough-Hall, Mr. Staniforth.

On the right, of Renishaw is Renishaw-Hall, the Seat of Francis Sitwell, Esq.

A Balbrough, on the left, is Balbrough-Hall C. Rhoades, Esq.

Between Whitwell and Workfop, on the r. is a Seat of the Duke of Norfolk.

Shepton-Mallet to *Briftol.*

To Little London, *Som.*	—	3
Old Down	2	5
Clutton	5	10
Pensford	4	14
Whitchurch	3	17
Briftol	3	20

This Road is continued to Sherborne from Shepton-Mallet, which Roads meet here from Bath and Briftol.

Shrewsbury to *Buxton.*

To Shawfbury, *Shrop.*	—	7
Hodnet	6	13
Tern Hill	3	16
Drayton	3	19
Balding Gate, *Staff.*	8½	27½
Whitmore	1½	29½
Acton	1	30
Newcaftle under Line	3½	33½
Burflem	3	36½
Norton	2	38½
Endon	3	41½
Leek	4¼	45¾
Holme	3½	49¼
Flath	4½	53¾
Dove Head	1	54¾
Buxton	5¼	60

Shrewsbury to *Drayton.*

To Tern Hill	—	18
Drayton	3	21

Shrewsbury to *Aberyftwith,* by the Devil's Bridge.

To Welch Pool	—	18
Newtown	14	32
Llanydlor	13	45
Sputty	20	65
Devil's Bridge	1	66
Aberyftwith	12	78

Skipton to *Richmond.*

To Rilfton	—	5
Graffington	4½	9½
Conifton	2½	12
Kettlewell	3	15
Woodale	5	20
Bradley	1	21
Horfehoufe Chapel	1	22
Gammerfgill	1	23
Carleton	1	24
Coverham	3	27
Middleham	2	29
Leyburn	2½	31½
Bellerby	1½	33
Richmond	6½	39½

Middleham and Leyburn are in Weufley Dale, near which is Ayfgarth Force, a moft remarkable Water-fall.

Southampton to *Winchefter.*

To Otterborne	—	8
Compton	2	10
St. Croix	1	11
Winchefter	1	12

At 1, on the r. is Padwell, Edw. Horne, Efq.

At 3½, on the r. fee the Summer Houfe and Park of John Fleming,

Efq. the Manfion - Houfe not feen.

At 9¼, on the r. in the Hollow, a white Houfe, Mr. Shakefpeare.

On the r. of St. Croix is St. Catharine's Hill, on which is a Clufter of Trees, and an Intrenchment, from which Oliver Cromwell bombarded the City of Winchefter, and afterwards took it.

Entering Winchefter, on the l. fee the Palace built by King Charles II. but never finifhed. It is ufed in War-Time as a place of Confinement for Prifoners, and contained laft War near 6000.

SPALDING to *Lynn Regis*.

To Wefton	—	4
Whaplode	2¾	6¾
Holbeach	1½	8¼
Fleet	1¾	10
Lynn Regis, p. 245.	13¼	23¼

SPALDING to *Leicefter*.

Through Littleworth to St. James's Deeping	—	10
Market Deeping	2	12
Tallington	4	16
Uffington	2	18
Tarnford	2	20
Tinwell, *Rutland.*	2	22
Ketton	2	24
South Luffenham	3	27
Morcot	1	28
Glafton	2	30
Uppingham	2	32
Leicefter, p. 344.	20	52

R. of Tallington is Gretford, where refides the celebrated Dr. Willis.

R. of Uffington, Cafewic Lodge, Sir John Trollope, Bart.

At Uffington, a charming Manfion belonging to the Bertie family, now inhabited by Sir Samuel Fludyer, Bart.

At Ketton, Lady Jane Edwards.

R. of South Luffenham, John Heathcote, Efq.

At Morcot, Thomas Tryon, Efq.

At Glafton, the Seat of Lord Sherrard.

STAFFORD to *Shrewfbury*.

To Dunfton	—	3½
Penkridge	2½	6
Iverfey Bank	6	12
Oaken Yates	8	20
Watling Street	3	23
Shrewfbury	11	34

Another Road, viz.

From Stafford to Gr. Bridgeford, *Staff.*	—	3¼
l. to Lawn Head	3¾	7
Knightley	1½	8½
Sutton	4	12½
Forton	¾	13¼
Newport	1¾	15
Watling-Street, *Shrop.*	8	23
Hay Gate	1	24
Atcham	6½	30½
Shrewfbury	3½	34

STAMFORD to *Northampton*.

To Worthop	—	1
Eafton on the Hill	1	2
Colley Wefton	2	4
Duddington	2	6
Finefhade	2	8

Bulwic	2	10
Weldon	4	14
Stanion	3	17
Geddington	1	18
Weckley	2	20
Kettering	2	22
Wellingborough, p. 163.	7	29
Northampton, p. 260.	11	40

Worthorp is a Dowager Seat of the Earl of Exeter, in Ruins.

Eafton, famous for Slates for Buildings.

At Finefhade, the Seat of the Hon. John Monckton.

On the right of Finefhade is Laxton, a Seat of Lord Carbery's; on the l. Blatherwic, Mr. Obrien's.

Bulwic is the Seat of John Clarke, Efq.

On the right, between Bulwic and Weldon, is Deane, the Seat of the Earl of Cardigan.

At Geddington is the Seat of Mr. Lockwood; and near it is Boughton, the ancient Seat of the Duke of Montagu's family, a very fine Park, and Ridings quite through to Deane.

At Geddington is, likewife, a very fine Crofs in high Prefervation, erected in Memory of Queen Eleanor, and under it a remarkable large fine Spring.

STOCKPORT to *Buxton*.

To Bullock Smithy, Chefter		3
Lyne Park	3	6
Difley, a noted Inn	1	7
Whalley Bridge	3	10
Buxton	6	16

At 4, on the right, Poynton Hall, Sir George Warren, K. B.

At 6, on the right, Lyme-Hall, Peter Leigh, Efq.

STOCKPORT to *Clithero*.

To *Manchefter*, Lanc.	—	7
Heaton Houfe	4	11
Middleton	2	13
Rochdale	6	19
Whitwor	6	25
Burnley	10	35
Clithero	11	46

At 8, on the right, the Stocks, John Ridings, Efq.

At 10, on the left, Broughton-Hall, Samuel Clowes, Efq. Heaton-Houfe, Lord Grey de Wilton.

At 12, on the right, Accrington-Hall, Sir Afhton Lever, Bart.

At 13, on the right, Chaderton-Hall, Sir Watts Horton, Bart.

At 16, on the left, Hopwood-Hall, Edward Gregge Hopwood, Efq.

At 23, on the left, Healey-Hall, John Chadwick, Efq.

At 35, on the right, Townley-Hall, Charles Townley, Efq.

At 41, on the left, Wharley-Abbey, Afheton Curzon, Efq.

A little beyond, on the left, Clerk-Hill, James Whalley, Efq.

At 44, on the left, Standen-Hall, Henry Afpenwall, Efq.

STONE to *Chefter*.

To Darlefton Hall	—	1
Swinnerton-Hall	2	3
Woore, Chefhire	10	13
Chefter	28	41

At 1, on the left, Sir John Jervis, K. B.

At 3, Bazil Fitzherbert, Efq.

Near Stableford-bridge, on left, is Maer-Hall, James Bulkeley, Esq.

STONE to MANCHESTER.

To Hobbergate, *Staff.*	—	2
Rough Close	2	4
Leek	12	16
Manchester	31	47

STOURBRIDGE to LICHFIELD.

At 1 m. r. thro' Brettel Lane to Dudley		5
Cock Heath	4	9
Darlaston	1/2	9 1/2
Walsal	2 1/2	12
Rushall	1 1/2	13 1/2
Walsal Wood	1 1/2	15
Muckley Corner	3	18
Pipe Hill	1 1/4	19 1/4
LICHFIELD	1 3/4	21

STOCPORT to *Huddersfield.*

Hyde Chapel	—	4 1/4
Mottram	3 1/4	7 1/2
Tintwistle	2	9 1/2
Near Woodhead	4 3/4	14 1/4
l. to Holme, *Yorksh.*	4 3/4	19
Holmfirth	3	22
Thong Bridge	1	23
Honley	1 1/2	24 1/2
Lookwood	2	26 1/2
Huddersfield	1 1/2	28

STOURBRIDGE to *Tutbury.*

To *Dudley,* Staff.	—	5
Wednesbury	4	9
Walsal	3	12
Lichfield	9	21
Wichnor Lodge	6	27

Barton Hall	2	29
Burton	4	33
Rolleston Hall	3	36
Tutbury	2	38

At 10, on the left, Bescott-Hall, Jonas Slaney, Esq.

At 12, on the right, Reynard-Hall, Edward Walhouse Okeover.

At 13, on the right, Rushall-Hall, George Anson, Esq.

At 19, on the left, Edgehill-Hall, Mr. Fern.

At 27, on the l. Wicnor-Lodge, John Levett, Esq.

At 29, on the left, Barton-Hall, John Wightwick, Esq.

At 32, on the right, Drakelow-Hall, Sir N. B. Gresley, Bart.

Opposite is Sinai Park, Earl of Uxbridge.

At 36, on the right, Ofwald Mofeley, Esq.

TAMWORTH to *Burton.*

To Fisherwic Hall, *Stafford.*	—	4
Catton Hall	3	7
Burton	8	15

At 4, on the l. Marquis of Donegall.

At 14, on the r. Drakelow-Hall, Sir Nigel Boyer Gresley, Bart.

TAMWORTH to *Chester.*

To Packington Hall	—	4
Lichfield	3	7
Rugeley	7	14
Weeping Cross	7	21
Stafford	2	23
Creswell Hall	2	25
Eccleshall	5	30
Charnes	4	34
Chester	37	71

At 4, on the r. John Levett, Efq.
At 17, on the l. Oakedge-Hall, Hon. Mrs. Anfon.
At 20, on the r. over the River, Tixall-Hall, Hon. Tho. Clifford.
A little beyond 30, on the right, Eccleshall Palace, Bifhop of Lichfield and Coventry.
A little beyond 34, on the right, Broughton-Hall, Rev. Sir Thomas Broughton, Bart.

TAMWORTH to LICHFIELD.

To Hoppas Bridge	—	2
Packington	1½	3½
Over Whittington Heath to		
LICHFIELD	3½	7

At Packington, E. of Aylesford.
A Mile from Whittington Heath to the r. is Fifherwic Park, a noble Seat of the Marquis of Donegall, and a Mile beyond is Elford, the Seat of Lady Andover.

TAMWORTH to *Afhby de la Zouch.*

To Four County Gate	—	4
Meafam	6	10
Afhby de la Zouch	3	13

TAUNTON to *Dulverton.*

To Langford Bridge, Somerfet.	—	2
Heathfield	4	6
Wivelfcombe	6	12
Chipftable	4	16
Skilgate	4	20
Dulverton	4	24

At 10, on the right, is Barren Down, the Seat of Stukeley Lucas, Efq

TAUNTON to *Minehead.*

To Langford Bridge, Somerfet.	—	2
Combflory	5	7
Hartrow	4	11
Nettlecombe	5	16
Dunfter	5	21
Minehead	2	23

One Mile beyond Taunton is Staplegrove, the Seat of James Coles, Efq.
On the l. of Nettlecombe, Sir John Trevalyon, Bart.
At 1½, on the l. from Dunfter, is Hellicombe, Rev. Robert Leigh.

TAUNTON to *Oakhampton.*

To *Wellington*, p. 57.	—	7
Tiverton, p. 57.	14	21
Bickley Bridge	3¼	24¼
Stokelay Pomeroy	5¼	29½
Crediton	3½	33
Coleford	4	37
Bow	3½	40½
Newnal Mill	4	44½
Oakhampton	6	50½

TAUNTON to *Sherburne.*

To Hatch Court, Somerfet.	—	6
Ilminfter	6	12
Hinton St. George	4	16
Crewkherne	4	20
Eaft Chinnoc	4	24
Yeovil	5	29
Sherburne.	6	35

At Hinton St. George, Earl Poulett.
On the r. beyond Yeovil is Newton, the Seat of Wyndham Harbin, Efq.

At 32. on the left, Compton Houfe, Robert Goodden, Efq.

TAVISTOC to *Bodmin.*

To Kellington, *Corn.*	—	11
St. Neot's	8½	19½
Bodmin	7¾	27¾

TENBURY to *Evefham.*

To Monk's Bridge, *Worcef.*	—	2
Lyndridge	4	6
Stocton	3	9
Ridmarley	4	13
Newton	5	18
Thorngrove	2	20
Worcefter	3	23
Stoughton	2	25
Perfhore	7	32
Evefham	7	39

At 6, on the l. Hon. and Rev. Andrew St. John.
At 9, on the r. Edward Whitcombe, Efq.
At 10, on the l. the Elms, Mrs. Berry.
At 11, on the l. Abberley Lodge, Robert Bromley, Efq.
At 14, on the r. Whitley Court, Lord Foley.
At 18, on r. Rev. Tho. Harry Foley.
Oppofite the above, Holt Caftle, Lord Foley.
At 20, on the left, Grimley-Hall, Charles Hinde, Efq.

TETBURY to *Glocefter.*

To Upton Grove, *Glocef.*	—	2
Minchinhampton	4	6
Rodborough Fort	5	11

Stroud	1	12
Painfwic	4	16
Upton	3	19
Hermitage	2	21
Glocefter	1	22

One Mile from Tetbury, on the l. Chavenage Houfe, Henry Stephens, Efq.
At 2, on the r. Thomas Saunders, Efq.
At 9, on the left, Hill Houfe, Sir George Onef. Paul, Bart.
At 11, on the left, Rev. James Dallaway.
At 13, on the l. Stratford Houfe, Nathaniel Winfcombe, Efq.
At 16, on the left, Painfwic Houfe, Benjamin Hyett, Efq.
At 19, on the right, Creed Place, Capt. Kemble.
At 20, on the l. Matron Houfe, late George Aug. Selwyn, Efq.

TEWKESBURY to *Birmingham.*

To Twining, *Worcef.*	—	2
Ham Court	3	5
Severn Stoke	3	8
Kempfey	4	12
Worcefter	3	15
Claines	2	17
Droitwich	5	22
Bromfgrove	6	28
Northfield	7	35
Birmingham	8	43

On the r. of Severn Stoke, Croome Park, Earl of Coventry.
At 9, on the l. Capt. Rodney.
At 2 Mile from 15, on the left, Barbourn Houfe, George Cookes, Efq.
At 16, on the r. Blanketts, J. Newnham, Efq.

At 17, on the r. Perdifwell Houſe, Henry Wakeman, Eſq. and on the l. of 17, Richard Yeomans, Gent.

At 23, on the r. Hanbury-Hall, Henry Cecil, Eſq.

At 39, on the r. Moſeley-Hall, —— Greaves, Eſq.

THIRSK to *Scarborough.*

To Sutton	—	4
Scawton	5	9
Helmſley	5	14
Bewdlam	2½	16½
Kirby Moorſide	1	17½
Sinnington	3½	21
Middleton	3	24
Pickering	1	25
Thornton	2	27
Witton	1½	28½
Allerſton	1	29½
Ebberſton	1	30½
Snainton	1½	32
Scarborough, p. 185.	9½	41½

TUNBRIDGE WELLS to *Hurſt Green,* in the main Road from *London* to *Haſtings.*

(*A new Road.*)

To Frant	—	2
l. to Wanhurſt	4	6
Ticehurſt	3½	9½
Hurſt Green	5	14½

At 11, on r. Paſhley, Rich. Holliſt, Eſq.

Between 11 and 12, on the r. Boorſil, —— Roberts, Eſq.

TUNBRIDGE WELLS to *Brighthelmſton.*

Groombridge	—	3½
Maresfield	11½	15
Lewes	9	24
Brighthelmſton	8	32

Or, from

Tunbridge Wells to

Boarſhead Street	—	5½
Steel Croſs	½	6
Wellers Croſs	1	7
Crowboro' Beacon	¼	7¼
Uckfield	6¾	14
Lewes	8	22
Brighthelmſton	8	30

At 2, on the l. from Tunbridge Wells, is Eridge Place, the Earl of Abergavenny.

At 3 Miles, ſee before you the Spire of Crowboro' Chapel, which you paſs at 6½ on the leſt.

At 7 Miles is Crowboro' Common for two Miles, commanding a moſt extenſive Proſpect.

At 13, on the l. is Buxted Place, a fine Seat of George Medley, Eſq.

At 2, before Lewes, ſee on the r. Conningſbury, William Kemp, Eſq.

At 1½, on the r. from Lewes, is Aſh Coomb, Mr. Boyce; and 2½ farther on r. is Stanmer, Lord Pelham's.

TUNBRIDGE to *Eaſt Bourn.*

To Frant	—	2
Mark Croſs	3	5
Mayfield	3	8
Butcher's Croſs	2	10
l. to Croſs-in-Hand	3	13

r. to Horeham	3	16
Horfebridge	3½	19½
Hailfham	1½	21
r. to Eaft Boorn Sea Houfes	7	28
Eaft Bourn Town	2	30

There is now a new Turnpike Road making from Hailfham to Eaft Bourn, through Willingdon, by which it is

From Hailfham to ·Willingdon	—	5
Eaft Bourn	2	7

At Frant, on the r. Eridge Park, Earl of Abergavenny.

At Mayfield are the Ruins of a Palace, the former Refidence of Dunftan, Archbifhop of Canterbury.

At 12, on the l. the Gatehoufe, Mrs. Dalrymple.

Beyond Crofs-in-Hand, Heathfield Park, the Seat of Francis Newbery, Efq. with the Tower built in honor of the late Lord Heathfield.

Horeham, the Seat of Sir John Dixon Dyke, Bart.

Near Horfebridge, —— Caverly, Efq.

TUNBRIDGE WELLS to *Eaft Grinftead.*

Groombridge	—	3½
Hambridge	2	5½
Hartfield	2½	8
Foreft Row	4	12
Eaft Grinftead	3	15
Or,		
To Afhurft	—	5½
Eaft Grinftead	8	13½

To the right of Afhurft is Chafford Park.

To the left of 6, Stoneland Park, Vifcount Sackville.

UTTOXETER to *Drayton.*

To Upper Tean, *Staff.*	—	7
Draycot	2	9
Meer	2	11
Stoke	5	16
Newcaftle	2	18
Madely Park	5	23
Loggerheads	5	28
Drayton	4	32

At 11, on the r. Caverfwall Caftle, Vifcount Vane.

UTTOXETER to *Afhbourn* and *Leek.*

To Rocefter	—	4
Colwich-Hall	4	8
Afhbourn	3	11
Okeover-Hall	3	14
Ilam-Hall	4	18
Leek	7	25

At Okeover-Hall, a celebrated Painting.

At Ilam, fome remarkable natural Curiofities.

UTTOXETER to *Manchefter.*

To Checkley, *Staff.*	—	5
Cheadle	5	10
Booth-Hall	2	12
Rownall Hall	4	16
Leek	5	21
Manchefter	32	53

Three Miles beyond Checkley is Huntley-Hall, Philip Bulkeley, Efq.

Two Miles beyond Cheadle, on the r. Booth-Hall, John Granville, Esq.

At 16, on the l. Rownall-Hall, Edward Phillips, Esq.

WAKEFIELD to *Halifax*, continued to *Burnley*.

To Dewsbury	—	5
Heckmondwyke	2	7
Mill Bridge	1½	8½
Belly Bridge	3½	12
Lightcliffe	¾	12¾
Hipperholm	1	13¾
Halifax	2¼	16
Hebden Bridge	8	24
Todmorden, *Lanc.*	5	29
Burnley	3½	32½

WALTHAM to *Odiham*

To Stephen's Castle Down	—	4½
Salt Lane	1½	6
Tichbourn	2½	8½
New Alresford	2¼	10¾
Old Alresford	1½	12¼
Bradley Lane	4¼	16½
Herriand Common	4½	21
Odiham	5	26

WARRINGTON to *Burslem*.

To Stretton	—	4
Great Budworth	4	8
Lostoc Green	4	12
Carnage	5	17
Lawton	11	28
Burslem	5	33

On the r. of 8, Marbury-Hall, Hon. Rich. Barry.

At 9, on the r. Wincham-Hall, Hon. Booth Grey.

WARRINGTON to *Buxton*.

High Legh	—	6
Hough Green	2	8
Knutsford	3	11
Chelford	5	16
Monk's Heath	2	18
Macclesfield	5	23
Walker's Barn	3	26
Buxton	8	34

At 18, on the l. Sir John Stanley Bart.

Nearly opposite, on the r. Capesthorn-Hall, Davis Davenport, Esq.

At 19, on the r. Henbury-Hall, Bowyer Jodrell, Esq.

WARRINGTON to *Hawkshead*.

To Winwic	—	3
Newton	2	5
Wigan	7	12
Bomberbridge	13	25
Preston	4	29
Garstang	11	40
Lancaster	11	51
Castle Head	10	61
Conishead Priory	10	71
Ulverstone	2	73
Nibthwaite	8	81
Hawkshead	9	90

One Mile from Warrington, on the r. Oxford-Hall, late John Blackburne, Esq.

At 3, on the l. Winwick-Hall, Rev. Geoffry Hornby.

At 5, on the l. Golbourn Park, Capt. Thomas Legh.

At 6, on the r. Haddock-Hall, Peter Legh, Esq.

At 10, on the r. Hawley-Hall, Bryan Will. Molyneux, Esq.

At 11, on the l. Winstanley-Hall, William Banks, Esq.

At 13, on the r. Haigh-Hall, Earl of Balcarras.

At 15, on the l. Standish-Hall, Edward Standish, Esq.

At 22, on the l. Euxton-Hall, William Anderton, Esq.

At 24, on the l. Farrington-Hall, Sir Will. Farrington, Bart.

At 25, on the r. Cuerden-Hall, Bannister Parker, Esq.

At 28, on the l. Walton-Hall, Sir Henry Philip Hoghton, Bart.

At 24, on the r. Barton Lodge, Robert Shuttleworth, Esq.

At 66, on the r. Holken-Hall, Lord George Cavendish.

At 71, the Priory, Wilson Braddyll, Esq.

WARRINGTON to *Malpas.*

To Stretton	—	4
Afton Bridge	4	8
Colebrook	7	15
Tarporley	2	17
Bulkley	5	22
Malpas	5	27

At 6, on the l. Whitley-Hall, Sir John Chetwode, Bart.

At 10, on the r. Grange-Hall, Thomas Tarleton, Esq.

At 23, on the l. Cholmondeley-Hall, Earl Cholmondeley.

WARRINGTON to *Woodhead Chapel.*

To Statham	—	3
Dunham Park	4	7
Altringham	2	9
Sharston	3	12
Stockport	4	16
Hyde Chapel	4	20
Motteram-in-Long-dendale	3	23
Woodhead Chapel	7	30

At 7, on the r. Dunham-Hall, Earl of Stamford.

At 11, on the l. Withinshaw-Hall, Will. Egerton, Esq.

WARWIC to *Stone Bridge.*

To Guy's Cliff	—	1
Leek Wotton	2	3
Kenilworth	2	5
Redfin Lane Turnpike	$2\frac{1}{4}$	$7\frac{1}{4}$
George in the Tree	$1\frac{3}{4}$	$9\frac{1}{2}$
Stone Bridge	$3\frac{3}{4}$	$13\frac{3}{4}$

N. B. *This Road joins the great Chester Road, 9 Miles on this Side Birmingham.*

Guy's Cliff, a Seat of Mr. Greathsed.

At Kenilworth, the noble Remains of its Castle, belonging to the Earl of Clarendon.

Two Miles from the George, on the left, is Tempal Balsam, famous for its elegant Church and Hospital; and, a Mile to the right, is Berkswell-Hall, the Seat of Mr. Knightley.

WEATHERBY to *Ripley.*

To Spofforth	—	3
Knaresborough	$4\frac{1}{2}$	$7\frac{1}{2}$
Ripley	$4\frac{1}{2}$	12

At 5½, on the right, Plumpton-Hall, Daniel Lascelles, Esq.
At Knaresborough, the Dropping Well.

Welsh Pool to *Newtown*.

A good Turnpike Road, leaving Montgomery on the left	—	13½

Whitby to Durham.

To Lyth, *Yorksh.*	—	3¾
Scalingdam	6¼	10
An Alum Mine	8	18
Guisborough	2	20
Ormsby	4¾	24¾
Marton	2¼	27
Stocton, Durh.	5¾	32¾
Norton	2¼	35
Grindon	3	38
Layton Chapel	1½	39½
Layton	1½	41
Sedgefield	2½	43½
Shinkley	9	52½
Durham	2½	55

Whitchurch to *Leek*.

To *Woore*, Staff.	—	14
Newcastle	8	22
Heakley-Hall	5	27
Endon	3	30
Leek	4	34

At 20, on the right, Keel-Hall, Ralph Sneyd, Esq.

Whitchurch to *Stocport*.

To Pilsley Green, *Cheshire*	—	4
Namptwich	5	9
Crewe Green	5	14
Sandbach	4	18
Swettenham	5	23
Chilford	5	28
Parsonage Green	4	32
Wilmslow	1	33
School Hill	4	37
Cheadle	1	38
Stocport	3	41

At 5, on the left, Wrenbury-Hall, Tho. Starkey, Esq.
At 14, Crewe-Hall, John Crewe, Esq.
At 21, on the l. Brereton-Hall, —— Legge, Esq.
At 22, on the l. Davenport-Hall, Eusebius Horton, Esq.
At 23, on the r. Swettenham-Hall, Thomas Willis, Esq.
At 26, on the r. Withington-Hall, John Glegg, Esq.
At 32, on the l. Hawthorn-Hall, Thomas Page, Esq.

Winchester to Salisbury.

To Pitt	—	2¼
Hursley	3	5¼
Armfield	2¼	7½
Rumsey	3	10½
Heath Post	3¼	13¾
Cowsfield Gr. *Wilts.*	6	19¾
White Parish	1	20¾
Whaddon	3½	24¼
Alderbury	¾	25
Salisbury	3¾	28¾
Another Road, viz.		
To *Stockbridge*	—	9½
Salisbury, p. 32.	16	25½

At 5½, on the r. is Hursley Lodge, Sir William Heathcote.
At 6½, on the l. is Glandfield, Mr. White.

Going over Rumfey Bridge, on the l. is Broad Land, a fine Seat of Vifcount Palmerfton.

At 5½, on the left, from Kumfey, is Melchet Park. Major Ofborne.

At 9, on the r. is Brickworth, Henry Ayres, Efq.

At 3½, on the r. before Sarum, is Clarendon Park, Gen. Bathurft.

At 2¼, on the left, before Sarum, in a Hollow, is Longford, a Seat of the Earl of Radnor.

WITNEY to *Woodfloc*.

To Eynfham Heath	—	3
Long Hanborough	2	5
Bladen	1½	6½
Woodfloc	1½	8

On the right of Eynfham Heath is Eynfham-Hall, the Seat of Mrs. Duberly.

WOLVERHAMPTON to *Shrewfbury*, by the Iron Bridge.

To Shiffnal	—	10
Iron Bridge	8	18
Shrewfbury	12	30

WORCESTER, by *Wolverhampton*, to *Stafford*.

To Ayford	—	2½
Omberfley	2½	5
Broadwater	10	15
Whittington	4	19
Stew Poney	1½	20½
Preftwood	¾	21¼
Seven Stars	2¾	24
Himley	½	24½
Wolverhampton	5½	30
Penkridge	10	40

Stafford	6	46

Or, From WORCESTER, by *Broomfgrove* to *Wolverhampton*, p. 317. — 26¼

Or, From WORCESTER to — 15

Stourbridge	6	21
Wolverhampton, p. 317.	10	31

WORCESTER to *Glocefter*, by *Hereford*.

To *Bromyard*	—	14
Hereford	14	28
Rofs	15	43
Glocefter	15	68

WOLVERHAMPON to *Newport*.

To Tettenhall, Staff.	—	1½
The Werg	1½	3
r. to Kingfwood	3	6
Albrighton, Shrop.	1½	7½
Woodcote	8	15½
Afton	2	17½
Newport	1	18½

WOORE to *Eafham Ferry*.

To Audlem, Chef.	—	6
Combermere Abbey	4	10
Whitchurch	4	14
Cholmondeley	6	20
Barnhill	4	24
Chefter	10	34
Büchford	4	38
Great Sutton	3	41
Eafham Ferry	3	44

At 10, on the r. Sir Robert Salusbury Cotton, Bart.

On the r. of 20, Earl Cholmondeley.

York to *Hornsea.*

To Grimston	—	$2\frac{1}{2}$
Wilberfosse	$4\frac{1}{4}$	$7\frac{3}{4}$
Barnby	$3\frac{1}{4}$	$10\frac{1}{2}$
Hayton	$3\frac{1}{2}$	14
Shipton	$2\frac{1}{2}$	$16\frac{1}{2}$
Market Weighton	$1\frac{3}{4}$	$18\frac{1}{4}$
Bishop Burton	$7\frac{1}{4}$	$25\frac{1}{2}$
Beverley	$2\frac{1}{2}$	28
Hull Bridge	2	30
Routh	$1\frac{1}{2}$	$31\frac{1}{2}$
Leayen	$3\frac{1}{2}$	35
Catwic	1	36
Seaton	$2\frac{1}{2}$	$38\frac{1}{2}$
Hornsea	$2\frac{1}{2}$	41

York to *Pocklington.*

To Barnby, above	—	$10\frac{1}{2}$
l. to Pocklington	$1\frac{1}{2}$	12

York to *Kendal.*

To Street Houses	—	6
Tadcaster	3	9
Collingham	$6\frac{1}{4}$	$15\frac{1}{4}$
Harewood	$4\frac{3}{4}$	20
Arthington	3	23
Pool	2	25
Otley	3	28
Skipton, p. 163.	15	43
Settle, p. 159.	16	59
Kendal, p. 159.	30	89

York to *Ripley* and *Graffington*, continued to *Gisburn.*

To Skip Bridge	—	$8\frac{1}{2}$
At $9\frac{3}{4}$ *l. to*		
Allerton Mauliverer	$4\frac{1}{2}$	13
Flasby	$1\frac{1}{2}$	$14\frac{1}{2}$
Knaresborough	3	$17\frac{1}{2}$
Ripley	$4\frac{1}{2}$	22
Pateley Bridge	$9\frac{1}{2}$	$31\frac{1}{2}$
Greenhow Hill	3	$34\frac{1}{2}$
Hebden	6	$40\frac{1}{2}$
Grassington	2	$42\frac{1}{2}$
Rilston	$4\frac{1}{2}$	47
Flasby	$1\frac{1}{2}$	$48\frac{1}{2}$
Gargrave	1	$49\frac{1}{2}$
Gisburn	$1\frac{1}{2}$	58

At Allerton is Thornville Royal, late Duke of York's, now Col. Thornton's, who purchased it of his Royal Highness for 110,000l.

At Knaresborough, the Dropping Well, Castle, and Sir Robert's Cave.

At Ripley, Sir John Ingilby, Bart.

York to *Rippon*, continued to *Pateley Bridge.*

To Skip Bridge	—	$8\frac{1}{2}$
Green Hammerton	$1\frac{1}{2}$	10
Little Ouseburn	$2\frac{1}{4}$	$12\frac{1}{4}$
Boroughbridge	$4\frac{3}{4}$	17
Kirby Hill	1	18
Rippon	5	23
Rispleth	$5\frac{1}{2}$	$28\frac{1}{2}$
Pateley Bridge	$6\frac{1}{2}$	35

Two Miles beyond Rippon, on the left, Studley Royal, late Mrs. Allanson; and two Miles farther, on the right, Grantley-Hall, Lord Grantley; and near it is Hackfall, a romantic Place of the late Mr. Aislabie's.

York to *Glamborough Head.*

To Gate Helmesley	—	6
Stamford Bridge	1½	7½
Garraby Street	5	12½
Fridaythorpe	6	18½
Kilham	13	31½
Bridlington	8	39½
Sewerby	1½	41
Flamborough	2	43
Flamborough Head	2	45

York to *Hull.*

To Grimston Smithy	—	2½
Kexby Bridge	3¼	5¾
Wilberfosse	1½	7¼
Barnby Moor	3¼	10½
Pocklington New Inn	2¾	13¼
Hayton	¾	14
Shipton	2½	16½
Market Weighton	1¾	18¼
Bishop Burton	7¼	25½
Beverley	2½	28
Hull Bank	5½	33½
Newland	1½	35
Sculcoates	1¼	36¼
Hull	¾	37

Near Market Weighton, on the r. Londsborough Park, the Duke of Devonshire.

Market Weighton, the ancient Delgovitia of the Romans.

At Bishops Burton, the Seats of Richard Watts and William Bethell, Esqrs.

At Beverley, the Minster, and the Seat of Sir James Pennyman, Bart.

At Hull Bank, on the l. the Seat of Colonel Burton.

York to *South Cave* and *Brough Ferry.*

To Market Weighton	—	18¼
Sancton	2½	20¾
Newbald	1¾	22½
South Cave	3¾	26¼
Brough Ferry	3¼	29½

Cross the Humber from Brough to Wintringham, Lincolnshire, 3 Miles, and thence along the old Roman Road to Lincoln, Newark, Peterborough, London, &c.

At Newbald, the Seat of Walter Fawkes, Esq.

At South Cave, the Seat and extensive Plantations of Henry B. Barnard, Esq.

York to *Hull*, by *South Cave.*

To *South Cave*	—	26¼
Welton	5	31¼
Melton	½	31¾
Ferriby	¾	32½
Swanland	1	33½
Anlaby	2¼	35¾
Hull	4	39¾

This Road by Welton, &c. very pleasant, being on the Banks of the Humber, with fine Views of that River, the Lincolnshire Coast, &c. &c.

CIRCUITS OF THE JUDGES.

N.B. The Aſſize Towns are marked as follows:

c. Towns where the Aſſizes are holden conſtantly every Circuit.
l. Where they are holden in the Lent Circuit only.
s. Where they are holden in the Summer Circuit only.
a. Where they are holden alternately with another Town.

HOME CIRCUIT.

	From LONDON to		
	Hoddeſdon, p. 193	—	17
c.	Hertford	4	21
	Epping	13	34
	Ongar	7½	41½
c.	Chelmsford	11½	53
	Graveſend, p. 266	22½	75½
a.	ROCHESTER	9	84½
a.	Maidſtone, p. 8.	8½	93
	Tunbridge, p. 315	14	107
l.	Grinſtead	15	122
a.	Croydon	19	141
c.	Kingſton	10	151
	LONDON, p. 25.	11½	162½

The Summer Aſſizes are holden alternately, at Guildford and Croydon for Surry; and at Lewes and Horſham for Suſſex.

MIDLAND CIRCUIT.

	From LONDON to			
c.	Northampton, p. 145.		—	66
	Wellingborough		11	77
	Kettering		7	84
c.	Oakham, p. 158.		21	105
	Stamford		11½	116½
	Bourn		11	127½
c.	LINCOLN, p. 186.		36	163½
	Newark	p. 279.	17½	181
	Southwell	p. 279.	7	188
c.	Nottingham	p. 279.	14	202
c.	Derby, p. 278.		15½	217½
	Loughbro'	p. 145	17	234½
c.	Leiceſter	p. 145	11	245½
	Hinkley	p. 232	14	259½
c.	COVENTRY	p. 232	13¼	272¾
c.	Warwic	p. 232	10	282¾

The Aſſizes in the Midland Circuit, ſometimes begin at Oakham, and end at Warwic; at other Times they begin at Warwic, ending ſometimes at Northampton, and ſometimes at Lincoln.

NORFOLK CIRCUIT.

	From LONDON to			
l.	Ayleſbury	p. 107	—	40½
	Winſlow	p. 107	10	50½
s.	Buckingham	p. 107	6¾	57¼
	Newport Pagnel		14	71¼
c.	Bedford		13¼	84½
	Eaton		11½	96
	Bugden		6	102
c.	Huntingdon		4	106
c.	CAMBRIDGE	p. 299	15	121
	Newmarket	p. 299	12	133
c.	BurySt.Edm.	p. 299	14½	147½
s.	Thetford	p. 204	12	159½
l.	NORWICH	p. 204	29	188½
	LONDON	p. 204	199	297½

OXFORD CIRCUIT.

	From LONDON to		
l.	Reading, p. 63.	—	39
c.	OXFORD, p. 340.	27½	66½

Or,
From LONDON to

	Place	Page	Miles	Total
s.	Abingdon, p. 76.		—	56
c.	OXFORD		7	63
c.	WORCESTER, p. 99		57	120
	Broomſgrove	p. 317	12½	132½
	Stourbridge	p. 317	10	142½
	Wolver-hampton	p. 317	10	152½
c.	Stafford	p. 317	16	168½
c.	Shrewſbury, p. 360		34	202½
	Ludlow	p. 248	29	231½
	Leominſter	p. 248	11	242½
c.	HEREFORD	p. 248	14¼	256¾
c.	Monmouth	p. 248	18	274¾
	Colford	p. 82	5	279¾
	Michael Dean	p. 82	11	290¾
c.	GLOCESTER	p. 82	12	302¾
	LONDON	p. 82	100	402¾

N. B. The above is the moſt uſual Circuit; though ſometimes it goes from Worceſter to Gloceſter, Monmouth, Hereford, Shrewſbury, and Stafford; and at other Times, from Oxford to Gloceſter, Monmouth, Hereford, Shrewſbury, Stafford, and Worceſter.

WESTERN CIRCUIT.

From LONDON to

	Place	Page	Miles	Total
c.	WINCHESTER, p. 43.		—	63½
	Stocbridge		8½	72
c.	SALISBURY		16	88
	Blandford	p. 33	22	110
c.	Dorcheſter	p. 33	16	126
	Bridport	p. 33	15	141
	Axminſter	p. 33	12	153
c.	EXETER	p. 33	26	179
	Oakhampton	p. 33	22	201
l.	Launceſton	p. 33	19	220
s.	Bodmin	p. 33	20	240

Return by the ſame Road to

	Place	Page	Miles	Total
	EXETER		61	301
	Collumpton		12	313
	Wellington		12	325
l.	Taunton, p. 58		7	332
	Glaſtonbury	p. 228	23	355
a.	WELLS	p. 228	5½	360½
c.	BRISTOL, p. 251.		19	379½
	Or,			
	From Taunton to		—	332
a.	Bridgewater		11	343
	Croſs		16½	359½
c.	BRISTOL		16½	376
	LONDON, p. 71.		114	490

N. B. The Aſſizes for Cornwall are held ſometimes at Truro.

NORTHERN CIRCUIT.

From London to

	Place	Page	Miles	Total
c.	YORK	p. 174	—	197½
	Eaſingwold	p. 174	13	210½
	Thirſk	p. 174	9½	220
	Northallerton	p. 174	12	232
	Darlington	p. 167	16	248
s.	DURHAM	p. 167	18	266
s.	Newcaſtle	p. 167	15	281
s.	CARLISLE, p. 325		56	337
	Penrith	p. 172.	18	355
s.	Appleby	p. 172.	14	369
	Orton	p. 142.	9½	378½
	Kendal	p. 142.	14	392½
c.	Lancaſter	p. 136	24	416½
	LONDON	p. 136	235	651½

N. B. In holding the Lent Aſſizes, the Northern Circuit extends only to York and Lancaſter: the Aſſize at Durham, Newcaſtle, Carliſle, and Appleby, being holden in the Summer Circuit only, which, on that Account, is diſtinguiſhed by the Appellation of *the Long Circuit*.

INDEX to the COUNTRY SEATS.

, Where the Seats bear no ancient Name, the Name of the present or late Possessor is given.

D d

E e

5

F I N I S.